BLACK AMERICA SERIES

DURHAM'S LINCOLN HOSPITAL

Black America Series

Durham's Lincoln Hospital

P. Preston Reynolds, M.D., Ph.D.

Arcadia Publishing

ISBN 978-0-7385-1366-9

Published by Arcadia Publishing
Charleston, South Carolina

Printed in the United States of America

Library of Congress Catalog Card Number: 2001090332

For all general information contact Arcadia Publishing at:
Telephone 843-853-2070
Fax 843-853-0044
E-mail sales@arcadiapublishing.com
For customer service and orders:
Toll-Free 1-888-313-2665

Visit us on the Internet at www.arcadiapublishing.com

About the Author

Dr. Preston Reynolds is an honors graduate of Duke University where she studied history as an undergraduate and Ph.D. student, and then medicine. After graduating from medical school, she completed her internal medicine residency at The Johns Hopkins Hospital before moving to the University of Pennsylvania for advanced fellowship training in general internal medicine and in the history of medicine. For more than 20 years, Dr. Reynolds has been studying efforts to racially integrate hospitals, both nationally and in communities throughout the country, and has published her research as books and in professional journals. She currently is a full-time professor at Johns Hopkins School of Medicine in the Departments of Medicine and History of Medicine, Science, and Technology. Dr. Reynolds is a diplomat of the National Board of Medical Examiners and American Board of Internal Medicine, as well as a fellow of the American College of Physicians and American Osler Society. She is an active member of national and international scientific and professional societies including Physicians for Human Rights, in which she has served as a member of the board of directors for 14 years. Physicians for Human Rights was co-recipient of the 1997 Nobel Peace Prize as a founding member of the International Campaign to Ban Landmines.

CONTENTS

ACKNOWLEDGMENTS

This book began as a historical account of a Southern hospital built for the care of African-American patients. Fortunately in the course of my research, I discovered a wealth of photographs that brought to life the inner workings of Lincoln Hospital and captured its vital contributions to the community and state. Accordingly, I would like first to acknowledge the individuals who contributed photographs, many of which have never been published. The individuals are most significantly Margaret Kennedy Goodwin, Carolyn Henderson, and members of the Lincoln Nurses Alumni Association, along with Robert F. Baker, Dr. William Cleland, Dr. Ralph Coonrad, Dr. Robert Dawson, Dr. Evelyn Schmidt, Dr. Charles Watts, and Selena Wheeler. In addition, photographs were obtained from Atlanta University Archives, Duke University Archives, Duke University Medical Center Archives, Duke University Special Collections, Shaw University Archives, and Durham Regional Hospital.

The text accompanying the photographs emerged from research in manuscript collections and public records as well as from oral histories conducted with individuals and family members, many of whom worked for over 25 years at Lincoln Hospital. Interviews with these individuals confirmed previous historical accounts and also provided new information and insights about the significance of Lincoln Hospital locally, regionally, and nationally. I want to generously and graciously thank these individuals: Dr. Lenox Baker Jr., Robert F. Baker, Dr. William Cleland, Dr. Ralph Coonrad, Dr. Robert Dawson, Margaret Kennedy Goodwin, Carolyn Henderson, Tom Howerton, Dr. Charles Johnson, Dr. Edward Miller, Dr. Max Schiebel, Mrs. Mary B.D.T. Semans, Dr. Eugene Stead, Dr. Charles Watts, Constance Watts, and Selena Wheeler. Without your support, encouragement, and gift of time this book would not have been possible.

The manuscript collections and public records used to document the details of the history of Lincoln Hospital are located in archives throughout the South. I would like to thank specially the archivists at Atlanta University Archives, Shaw University Archives, Duke University Archives, Duke University Special Collections, Duke University Medical Center Archives, North Carolina State Archives, the University of North Carolina–Chapel Hill, the Duke Endowment, and the Library of Congress.

I would like to express my tremendous gratitude to the people who carefully reviewed chapters and who assisted in moving this project effectively toward publication. These include Dr. William Cleland, Dr. Robert Dawson, James F. Gifford Jr., Margaret Kennedy Goodwin, Carolyn Henderson, Mary Kritsch, Jim Russell, Dr. Max Schiebel, and Dr. Charles Watts. Lastly, publication of the book was made possible by contributions from the North Carolina Mutual Life Insurance Company, Mechanics and Farmers Bank, Mutual Community Savings Bank, Lincoln Nurses Alumni Association, and Lincoln Community Health Center. The research was supported by grants from the National Library of Medicine/National Institutes of Health, Robert Wood Johnson Foundation, Fox Family Foundation, Mary Duke Biddle Foundation, and Durham Regional Hospital.

—P. Preston Reynolds

INTRODUCTION

Lincoln Hospital was founded in 1901 by Dr. Aaron Moore, Dr. Stanford Warren, and Mr. John Merrick to meet the medical needs of the African-American population in Durham, North Carolina. Its construction costs were met by Washington Duke who also gave $5,000 for an endowment. Lincoln Hospital's doors opened in August 1901, to all patients regardless of their ability to pay, a mission that lasted until the hospital closed in 1976. From the beginning it primarily served the African-American community in Durham; however, with few hospitals for African Americans available in the South, patients came from as far away as Virginia and South Carolina.

Lincoln Hospital served first as a place for patient care with modern facilities for major and minor surgery, care of infants and children, and the delivery of babies. In addition, it operated outpatient clinics, such as clinics dedicated to tuberculosis, venereal disease, cancer, well-baby care, and routine adult medicine. An emergency room staffed by interns, residents, and physicians was open 24 hours a day to patients. As Durham's population grew, so did Lincoln Hospital, both in terms of the number of beds but also in the size of its nursing staff, medical staff, administrative and support staff, and operating budget. Furthermore, collaboration among Lincoln Hospital and other Durham hospitals and Duke University School of Medicine strengthened over time. One of the most important partners of Lincoln Hospital was the Durham County Health Department because it helped conduct outpatient clinics and public education campaigns designed to lower the disease burden in the African-American community.

Beginning in 1903, Lincoln Hospital operated a nursing school that was incorporated officially in 1905 as a two-year program. Miss Julia Latta, a graduate of St. Agnes School of Nursing in Raleigh, North Carolina, was the first director of nursing. During her tenure from 1903 to 1910, she graduated 14 nurses into the community. Miss Patty Carter succeeded Miss Latta and remained a leader of Lincoln Hospital until her retirement in 1948. Beginning in 1911 under Miss Carter's direction of the Lincoln Hospital School of Nursing, the curriculum expanded to three years. The nursing program was fully accredited by the North Carolina State Board of Nursing until the mid-1960s. The pride and professionalism of these students is evident in their attire, their efforts to master clinical nursing skills, and finally, in their celebrations and graduation exercises.

In addition to its nursing school, Lincoln Hospital provided opportunities for internship and residency training in general surgery and internal medicine and, for a few residents, specialty training in obstetrics and orthopedics. With very few post-graduate positions available in the country, Lincoln Hospital served a vital national need in strengthening the professional qualifications of African-American physicians. Many of the physicians on staff at Watts and Duke Hospitals were involved actively along with their African-American colleagues in training the residents at Lincoln Hospital. These physicians also assisted Mrs. Margaret Kennedy Goodwin in her efforts to establish and direct one of the few medical technician training programs available to African Americans in the country. With expansion of knowledge and skills in laboratory and radiology sciences, this program was separated into two tracks with students choosing to pursue either a career as a radiology technician or laboratory technician. These allied health professional training programs complimented those for physicians and nurses, making Lincoln Hospital a place of education as well as patient care.

This book on Lincoln Hospital captures several themes significant to the history of health care for African Americans in the new South. These themes include, first, the role of bi-racial cooperation in establishing and then expanding the institution to ensure its position as a model African-American hospital. Through scenes of clinical operations, teaching conferences, trustee meetings, and professional associations, this bi-racial cooperation comes alive. Unknown to many, there was substantial involvement of the white medical and education professions in the clinical and teaching programs of Lincoln Hospital. Additionally, Mr. William Rich, superintendent of Lincoln Hospital from 1934 to 1959, worked closely with hospital administrators at Watts and Duke Hospitals as well as officials of the Duke Endowment to keep Lincoln Hospital competitive with hospitals throughout the Carolinas by delivering quality patient care. Accordingly, he was honored with membership on state commissions and in national organizations. Lincoln Hospital is a story about the leadership of Durham and their commitment to work across racial lines to provide medical care to all its citizens.

Second, the involvement of the community in the financial survival of the hospital is illustrated through photographs of linen donations, gifts of equipment by the Women's Auxiliary, renovations of a patient room by IOTA Phi Lambda Sorority, and even purchase of a food warmer by Alpha Kappa Alpha. Over the years, these activities—often coordinated closely with the local churches—cemented the value of the hospital in the hearts of the African-American citizens. Caring for "our hospital," African-American residents of Durham responded additionally with contributions to scholarship programs and fund-raising drives. In return, the hospital continued to serve as a trusted source of information through its public education campaigns, clinics, and health outreach programs.

Third, the Civil Rights Movement impacted Lincoln Hospital by forcing other institutions to open their doors to African-American patients and professionals, and thereby draining the hospital of some of its patient census and physician and nursing staff. Under the masterful leadership of John Wheeler and Tom Howerton, Lincoln Hospital merged into the Durham County Hospital Corporation with the knowledge that one day the hospital would cease to exist as an inpatient facility. Seeking to guarantee a point of medical care in the heart of Hayti, African-American leaders established the Lincoln Community Health Center in an aging institution. After closure of Lincoln Hospital in 1976, the health center was free to build a modern facility with adequate space to accommodate primary and specialty clinics and support services. The Lincoln Community Health Center under the leadership of Dr. Evelyn Schmidt remains a vibrant centerpiece of health care delivery in Durham today.

The collection of photographs of Lincoln Hospital and its successor, the Lincoln Community Health Center, capture the richness of the people whose lives are devoted to the healing professions. In the words of the master clinician-teacher Sir William Osler, "Distinctions of race, nationality, colour, and creed are unknown within the portals of the temple of Aesculapius. Dare we dream that this harmony and cohesion so rapidly developing in medicine, obliterating the strongest line of division, knowing no tie of loyalty, but loyalty to truth—dare we hope, I say, that in the wide range of human affairs a similar solidarity may ultimately be reached?" It is my hope that this book may serve as a catalyst for the healing of racial discord moving us further along the path toward a society that sees no distinction among people based on race, gender, creed, or nationality.

One

Origins

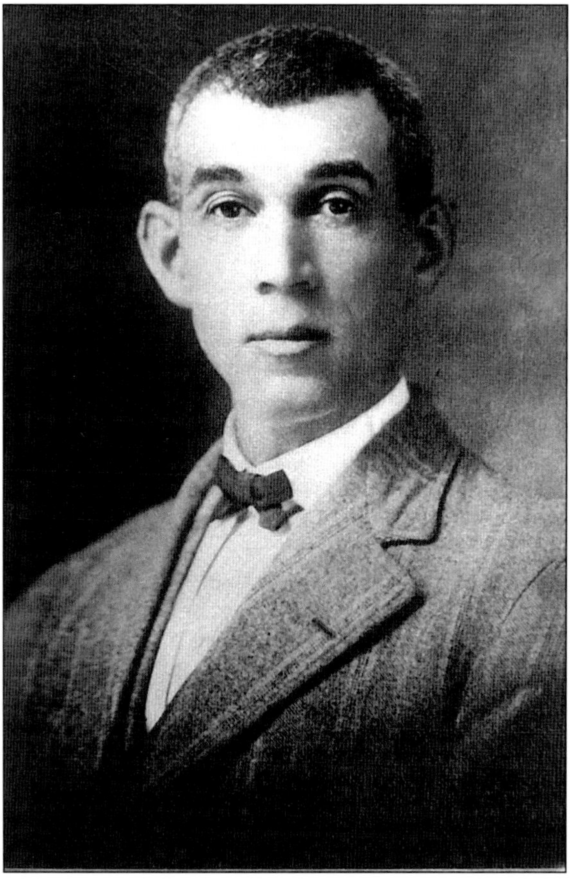

Aaron McDuffie Moore, the principal founder of Lincoln Hospital, was born in 1863 in Elkton, North Carolina, as one of ten children of Anna Eliza Spaulding and Israel Moore. He graduated from Leonard Medical School of Shaw University in 1888. Dr. Moore placed second in his group of examinees for medical license and opened an office for general practice in Durham that year. His intellectual ability combined with depth of character drew great admiration from white and African-American citizens. (Courtesy of Charles D. Watts.)

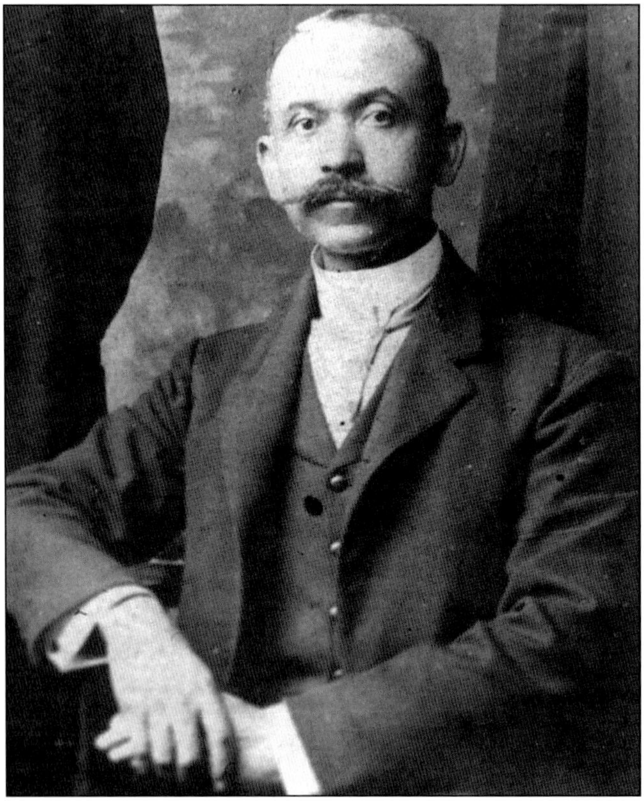

Stanford Lee Warren, a founder of Lincoln Hospital, was born in 1863 in Caswell County, North Carolina. He was the son of Anne Warren and, reportedly, Washington Duke. He grew up in Durham, worked in the Duke Tobacco Company, and attended Kittrell College and Leonard Medical School of Shaw University, from which he graduated in 1895. Dr. Warren was highly respected as a general practitioner-obstetrician. His quiet, reserved demeanor, impeccable attire, and devoted service to the poor among the African-American community drew tremendous gratitude and respect from all. (Courtesy of Selena Warren Wheeler.)

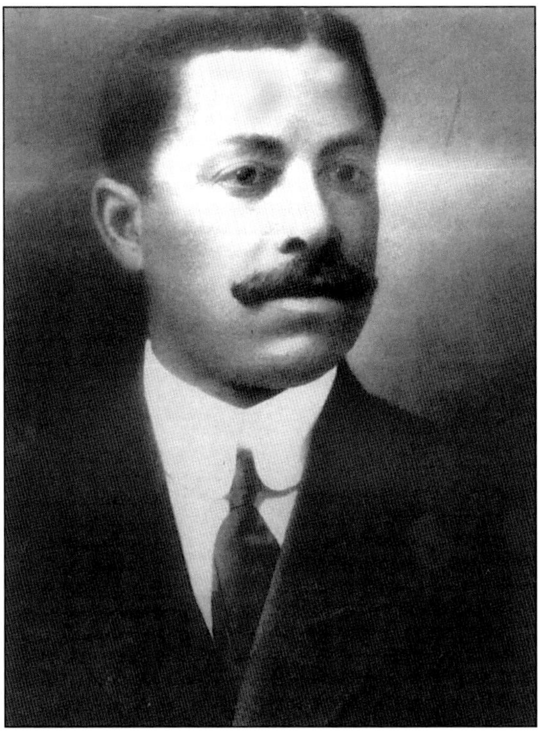

Another founder of Lincoln Hospital was John Merrick, born in 1859 in Clinton, North Carolina, to a slave woman, Margaret Merrick, and a white father. After the Civil War, he moved to Chapel Hill with his mother and brother. He later lived in Raleigh where he worked as a brick mason to help build Shaw University. In 1880 he moved to Durham, and over the years, he rose to become the wealthiest African-American businessman in the area. Merrick was instrumental in establishing numerous businesses, including the North Carolina Mutual and Provident Association that he founded in 1898. At the time of his death in 1919, the North Carolina Mutual Life Insurance Company had insurance in force worth $26 million and assets of nearly $1 million. (Courtesy of Charles D. Watts.)

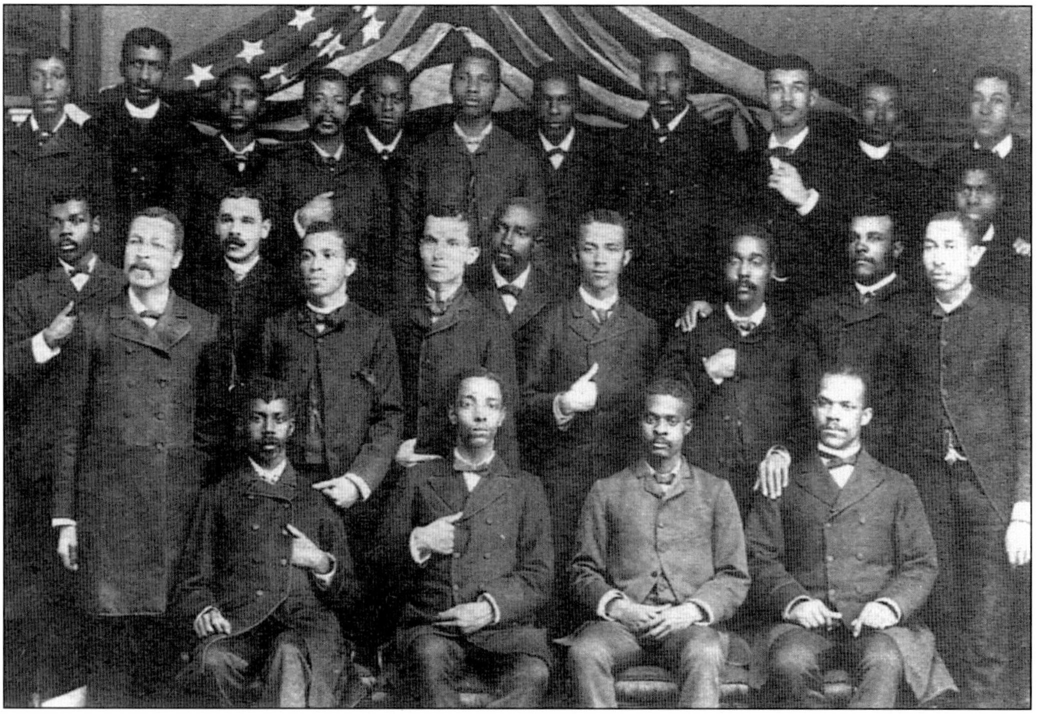

Leonard Medical School of Shaw University, founded in 1882 as the first four-year medical school in the country, was the training ground for seven of the eight early African-American physicians at Lincoln Hospital. They included Drs. Aaron M. Moore, Stanford L. Warren, Charles H. Shepard, Joseph N. Mills, Frank T. Page, Mathew D. Christmas, and William C. Strudwick. Aaron McDuffie Moore, a second-year medical student, is third from the right in the top row. (Courtesy of Shaw University Archives.)

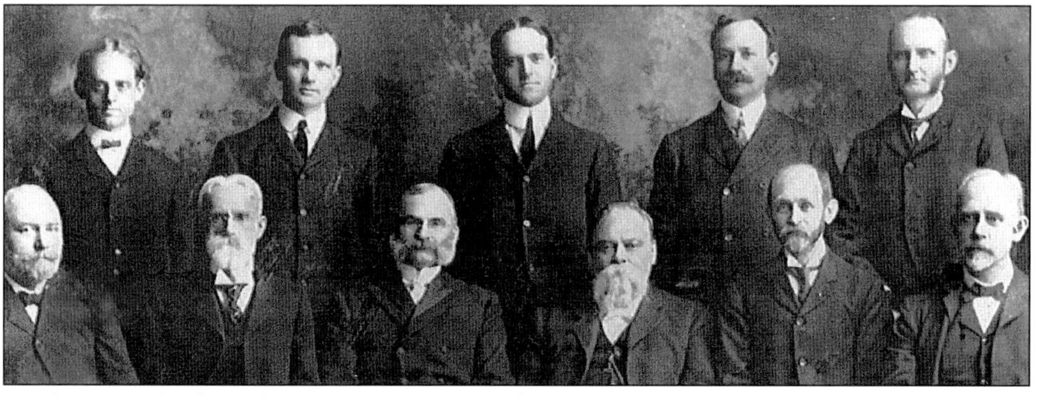

By the time the first class graduated in 1886, the faculty of Leonard Medical School had expanded to six with the addition of Drs. W.I. Royster, A.W. Knox, C.S. Pratt, K.P. Battle Jr., and R.H. Lewis, all leading white physicians practicing in the Raleigh community and most having graduated from Northern medical schools. The first faculty consisted of the following professors: James McKee, M.D., former superintendent of health for Wake County, who later became dean and served for 29 years; and I.A. Stafford, M.D., professor of anatomy and chemistry, who later became resident physician to the hospital. (Courtesy of Shaw University Archives.)

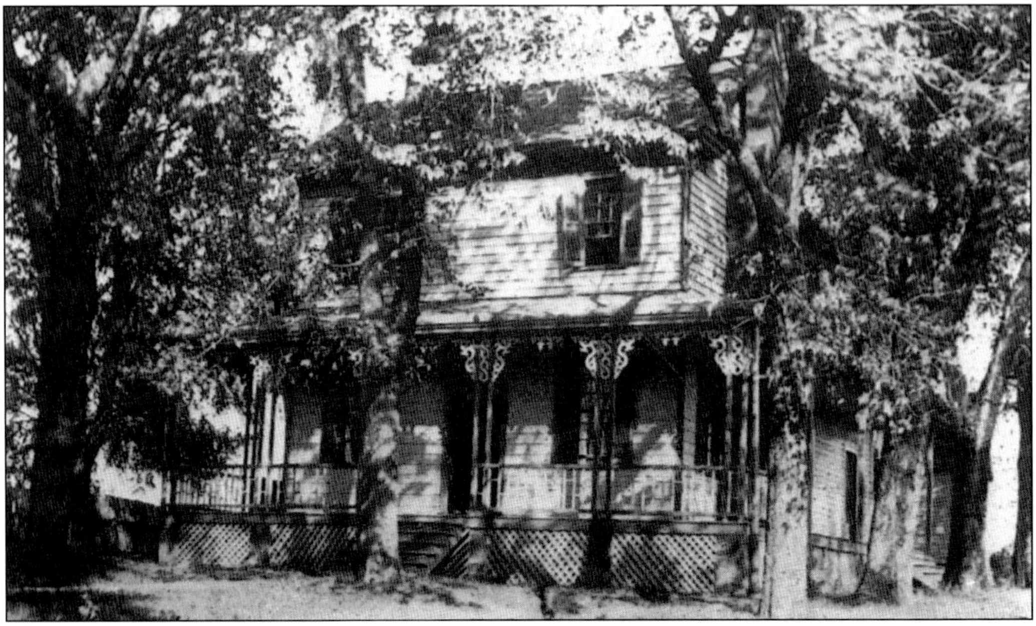

The Leonard Medical School Hospital had 25 beds with 3 patient wards. It opened for patients on January 10, 1885, thus enhancing the Leonard Medical School curriculum with clinical instruction. During the same year, an outpatient clinic and an ear and eye ward were added to the hospital. The hospital admitted 30 patients, mostly surgical cases, during its first year of operation. (Courtesy of Shaw University Archives.)

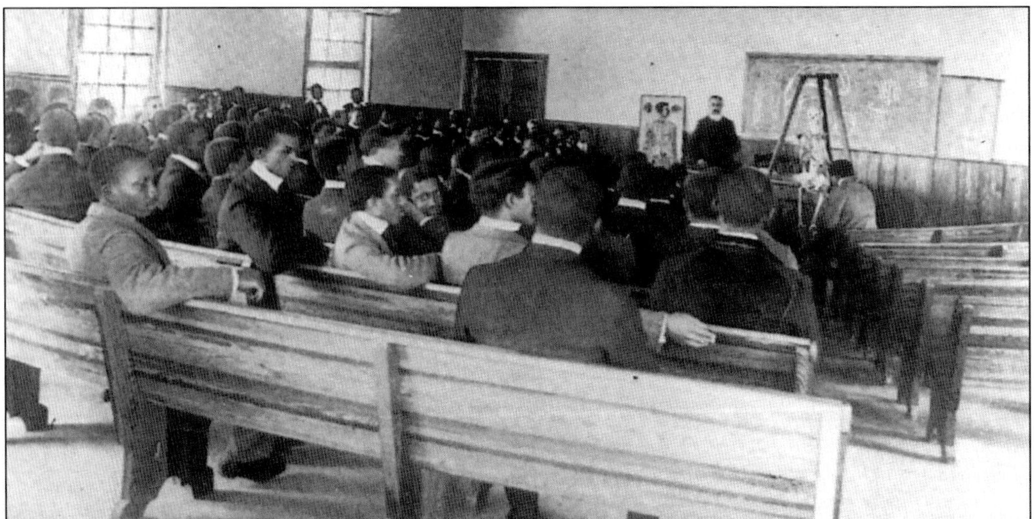

The first year of Leonard Medical School included courses in anatomy, physiology, and general chemistry. The second year focused on practical anatomy, medical chemistry, materia medica, pathological anatomy, and the practice of medicine and surgery. The third year placed students into clinical rotations in medicine, obstetrics, theory and practice, and surgery. The fourth year completed the curriculum with rotations in ophthalmology, otology, dermatology, syphilis, laryngology, neurology, diseases of women, pediatrics, and forensic medicine. (Courtesy of Shaw University Archives.)

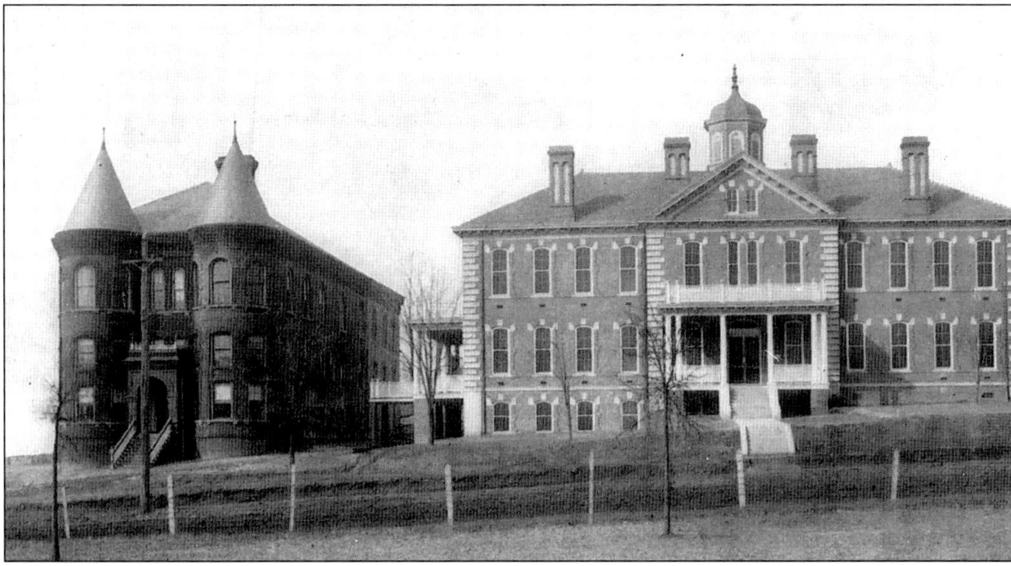

In 1914, Leonard Medical School opened a modern hospital with funds provided by the Rockefeller Foundation; however, it was unable to meet rising standards of medical education imposed by the Flexner Report in 1910. During its tenure, 480 medical students received their degrees from Leonard Medical School. In addition, the hospital provided a few positions for internship training. After 1918, when the medical school and hospital closed, these limited opportunities that existed locally disappeared. (Courtesy of Shaw University Archives.)

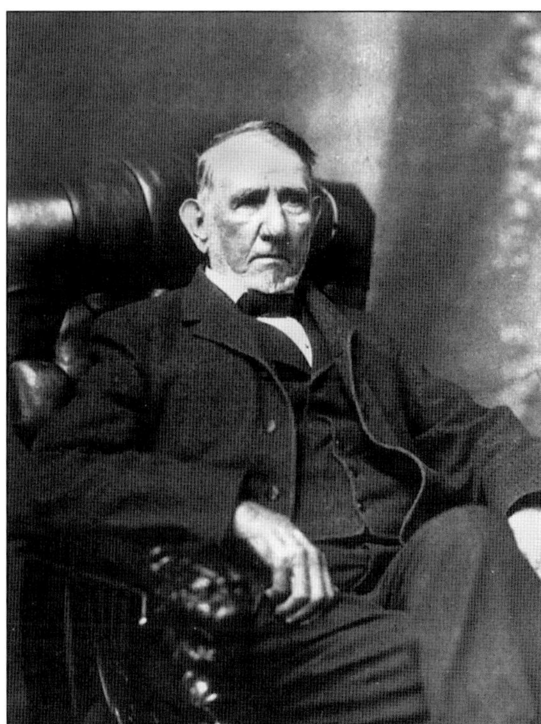

Washington Duke, founder of the Duke Tobacco Company, was approached by Dr. Aaron Moore, Dr. Stanford Warren, and John Merrick with the request to build a hospital for African Americans. While George Watts, partner of Washington Duke in the Duke Tobacco Company, offered to build a wing onto Watts Hospital for African-American patients, Dr. Moore thought a separate hospital would better meet the needs of these citizens and their physicians. (Courtesy of Duke University Archives.)

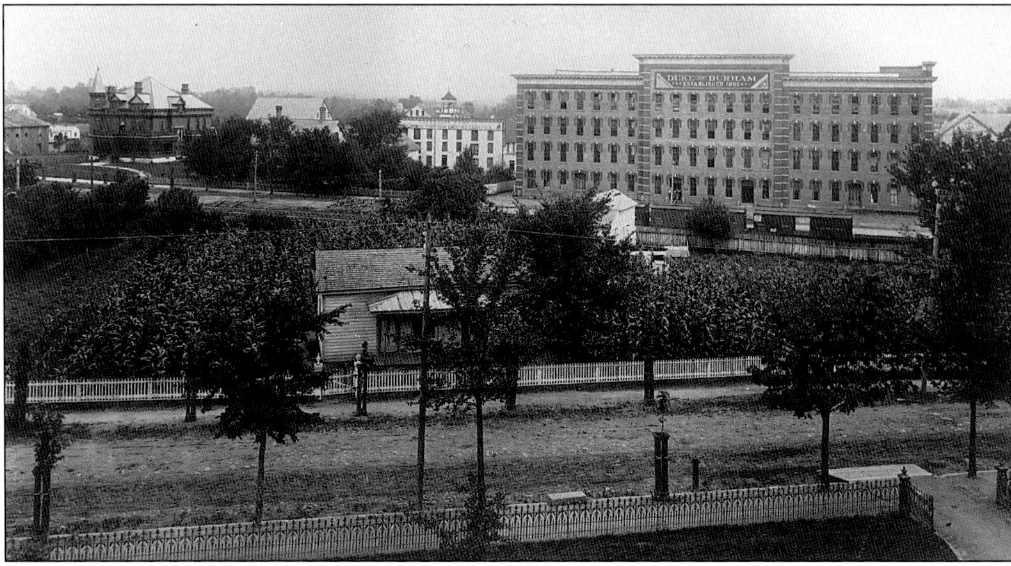

Assets generated by the Duke Tobacco Company were instrumental in laying the foundation for health care in Durham. George Washington Watts remained the principal philanthropist of Watts Hospital until his death in 1921. Washington Duke and his two sons, Benjamin Newton and James Buchanan, served as the principal philanthropists of Lincoln Hospital. Their legacy continued through generations of family members. (Courtesy of Duke University Special Collections.)

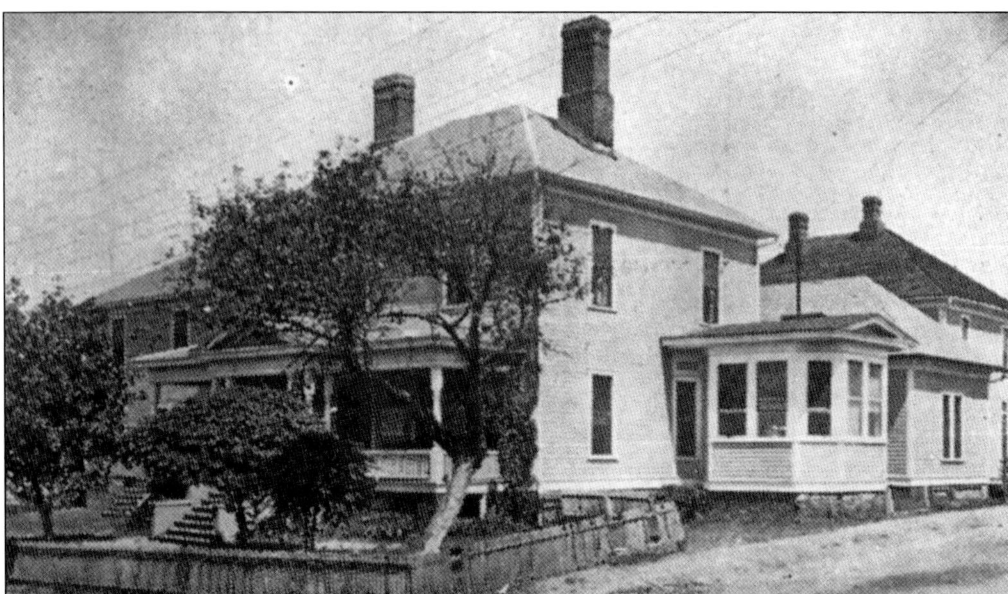

Lincoln Hospital was established through the generosity of Washington Duke and his sons. The cornerstone was laid on July 4, 1901, on land at the corner of Cozart and Proctor Streets. Built at a cost of $8,550, the hospital opened for patients the following month with beds for 50 patients. Patronage grew slowly, but by 1907 another ward was added at a cost of $20,000. (Courtesy of Duke University Medical Center Archives.)

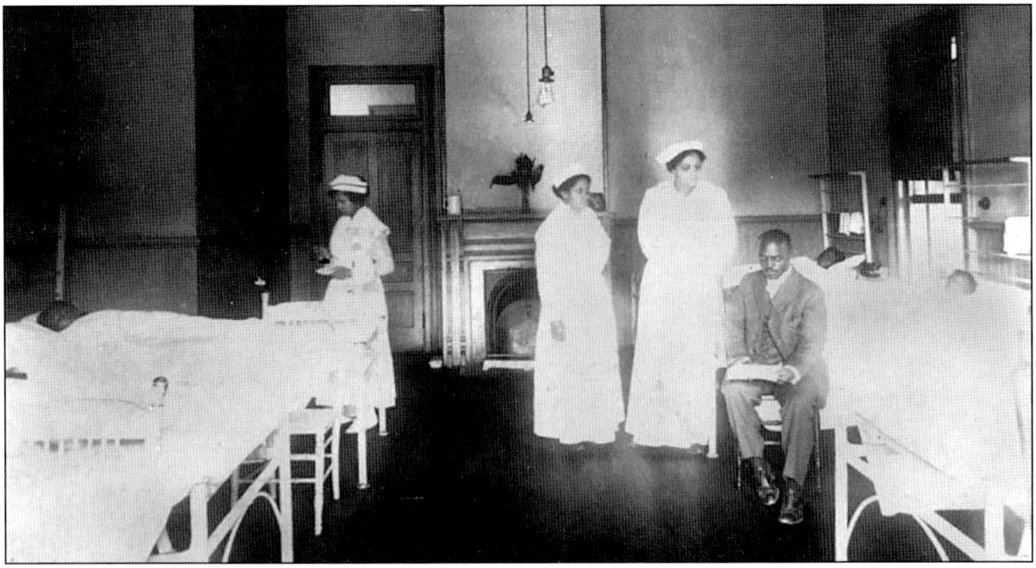

Lincoln Hospital was the fourth hospital for African Americans established in North Carolina, and it was the first with no religious affiliation. It was organized as a non-profit, general hospital available to all patients regardless of their ability to pay. Dr. Aaron Moore, as the first superintendent, established the rules. Every patient would be treated with respect and dignity and provided with the best medical care as if that patient were a family member. (Courtesy of Carolyn Henderson.)

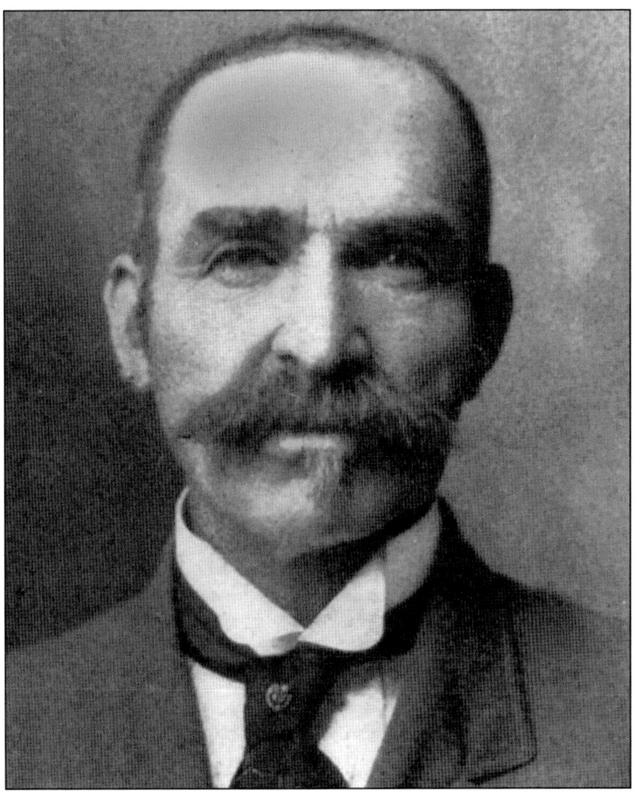

The Lincoln Hospital trustees represented the elite of Durham's African-American community. Richard B. Fitzgerald, a founding trustee of Lincoln Hospital, moved from Delaware to Durham to join his brother. In 1879, they purchased land with a vein of clay where Richard launched a brick-making business. His company grew into one of the largest operations in the area. In 1912 he produced 30,000 bricks a day, many of them finding their way into businesses, churches, and homes.

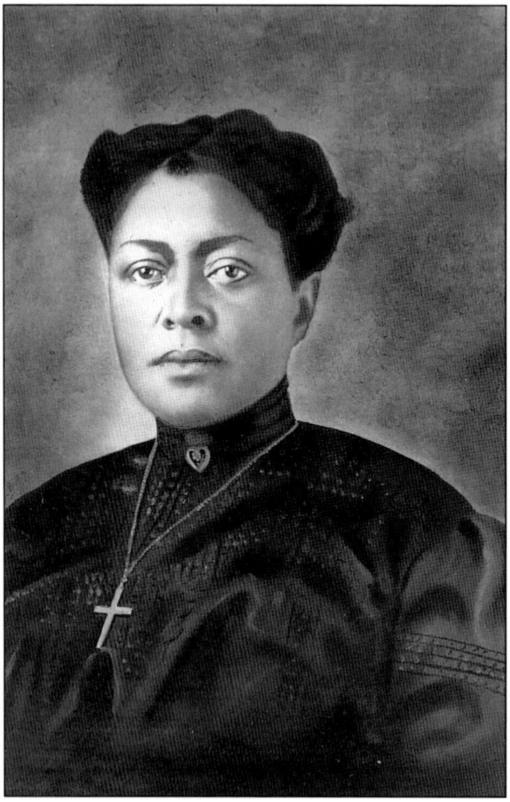

Miss Julia Latta, a graduate of St. Agnes School of Nursing in Raleigh, North Carolina, joined the Lincoln Hospital staff as director of nursing in 1903. The Lincoln Hospital School of Nursing was incorporated officially in 1905. The two-year curriculum continued from 1903 until 1910, when it was expanded to three years. During her tenure from 1903 to 1910, Miss Latta graduated 14 nurses into the community. (Courtesy of Evelyn Schmidt.)

Hospitals rarely had the resources to run a nursing school, but when they did the students provided essential patient care while learning on the job. Miss Patty Carter (middle, top row) joined the Lincoln Hospital staff as director of nursing in 1911. Physicians contributed to training the student nurses by teaching classes in the clinical sciences. All celebrated the students in their successful completion of the nursing curriculum on graduation day. (Courtesy of Carolyn Henderson.)

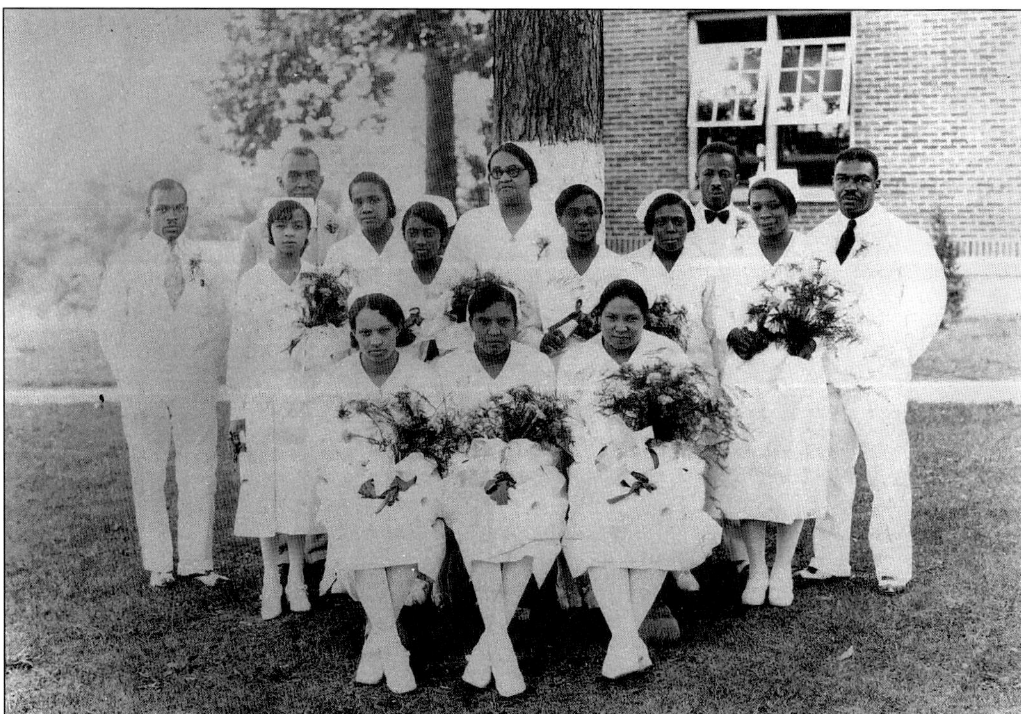

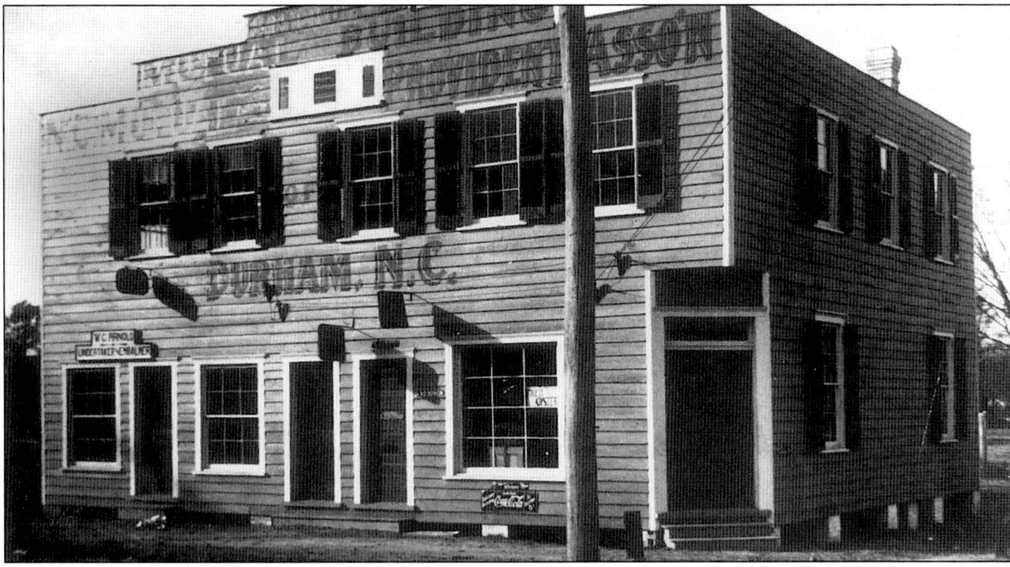

The North Carolina Mutual and Provident Association grew out of The Royal Knights of King David. After struggling for three years, Merrick and Moore reinvested $300 each and employed C.C. Spaulding as insurance agent and general manager. They opened their business in a corner of Dr. Moore's medical office located at 121½ East Main Street. There was a standing member of the Lincoln Hospital Board of Trustees appointed by the Mutual. (Courtesy of Charles D. Watts.)

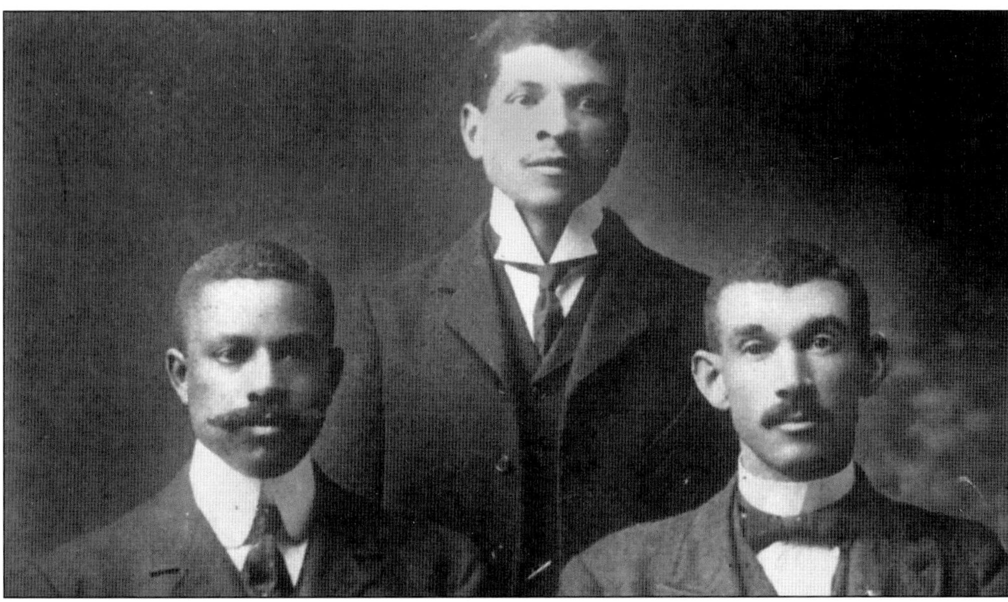

The "triumvirate," John Merrick (left), Charles Clinton Spaulding (center), and Dr. Aaron Moore (right) built the North Carolina Mutual Life Insurance Company into the largest insurance company in the world owned by African Americans. John Merrick served as president of the Lincoln Hospital Board of Trustees from 1901 to 1919; Dr. Aaron Moore as superintendent of the hospital from 1901 to 1923; and C.C. Spaulding as president of the board of trustees from 1940 until his death in 1952. (Courtesy of Charles D. Watts.)

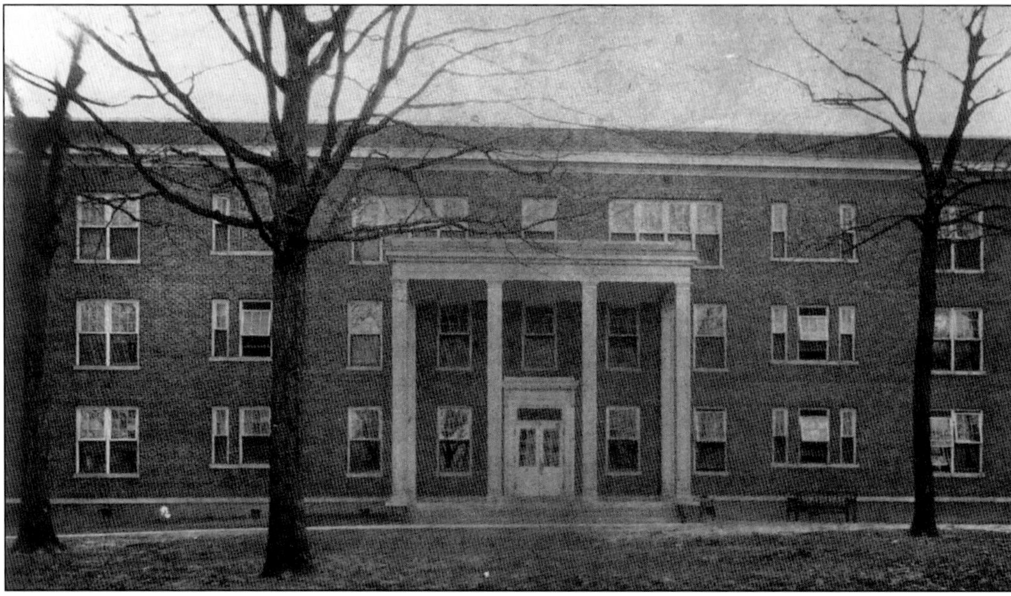

Plans were underway for a new facility when fire swept through the hospital in early 1922. The second Lincoln Hospital was constructed of all brick and opened January 15, 1925. It was the most modern hospital built for use by African Americans south of Washington, D.C. with 86 beds. From 1901 to 1925, Lincoln Hospital admitted over 7,000 patients, most of whom were charity cases. (Courtesy of *Modern Hospital*.)

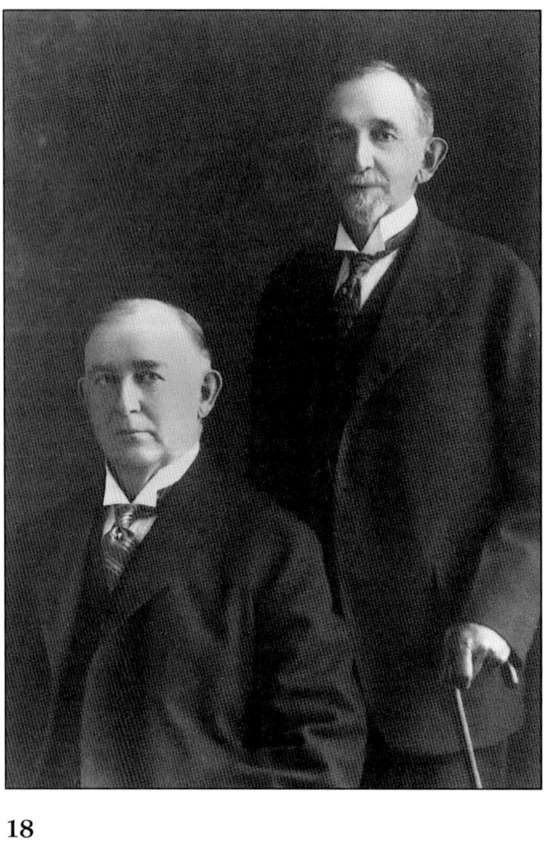

With the second hospital costing $150,000, the Duke brothers, James B. Duke (left) and Benjamin N. Duke (right), gave $75,000 to be matched equally by the Durham community. Ben Duke later provided $35,000 for a student nurses home. The Duke Endowment, established at the death of James B. Duke in 1925, distributed funds annually to hospitals in the Carolinas to cover part of their charity care. Lincoln Hospital received these monies as well as grants to purchase equipment and make renovations. (Courtesy of Duke University Archives.)

Charles H. Shepard was born in 1875 to the Reverend Augustus and Hattie Shepard and grew up in Raleigh, North Carolina. He graduated from Leonard Medical School in 1901 and established one of the largest medical practices concentrating on general surgery. Dr. Shepard was the first African-American physician in the state to perform successfully an abdominal operation. As superintendent of Lincoln Hospital from 1923 until 1934, he transformed it into a modern institution recognized by national authorities. (Courtesy of Margaret Kennedy Goodwin.)

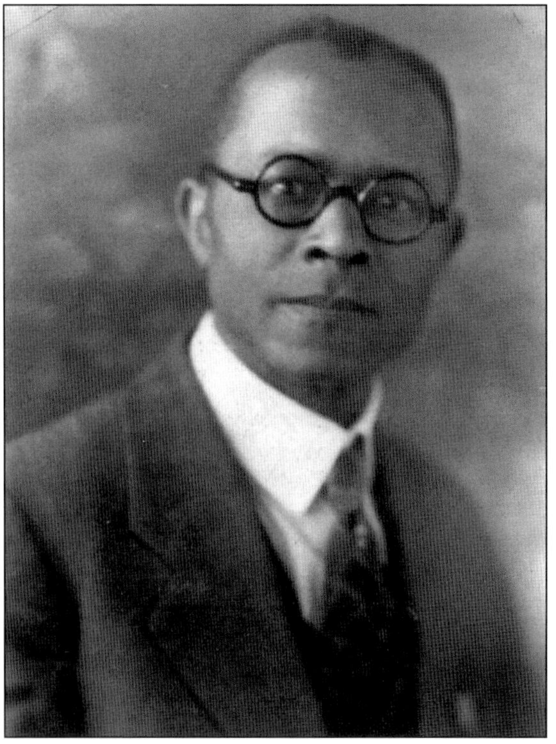

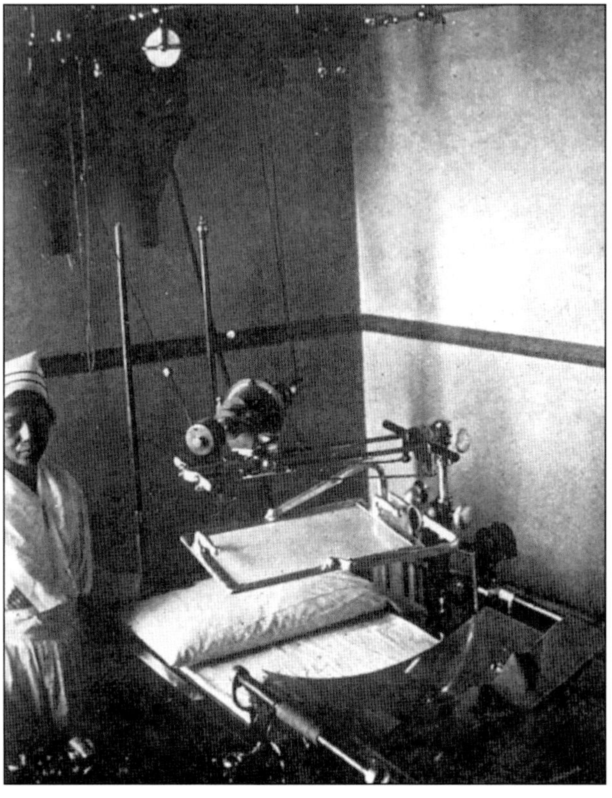

The laboratory and x-ray departments opened with the new hospital in 1925. Dr. Shepard was determined to make the x-ray department self-supporting. The hospital had a good machine that he planned to expand the usage of to treat cancer and other illnesses. Accordingly, the number of x-rays taken at Lincoln Hospital increased 400 percent from 147 x-rays in 1925 to 598 x-rays in 1930. (Courtesy of *Modern Hospital*.)

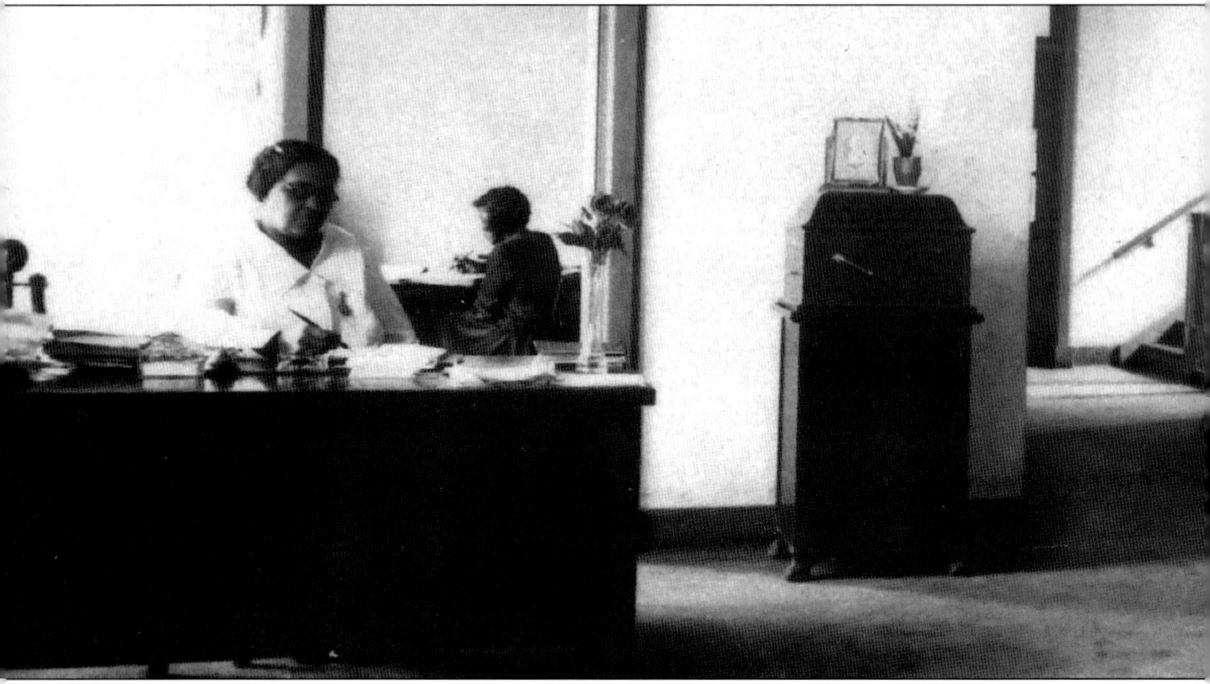

When the new hospital opened in 1925, Dr. Charles Shepard implemented changes to meet national standards for hospital quality. A patient chart system was put in place that required documentation of a history and physical on all patients. The first laboratory and x-ray

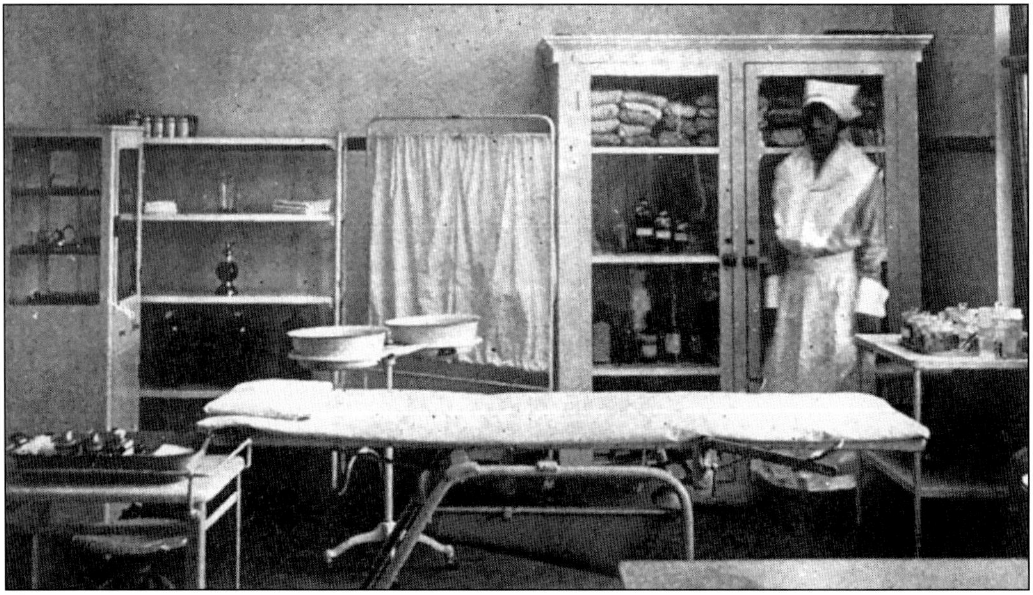

The number of minor surgeries performed at Lincoln Hospital increased annually. Between 1925 and 1930 the number of minor procedures rose 470 percent from a total of 140 to 656. These procedures generally included any operation not requiring general anesthesia, such as setting a broken bone or sewing up a laceration. With sterile conditions and good surgical technique, the mortality rate was essentially zero. (Courtesy of *Modern Hospital*.)

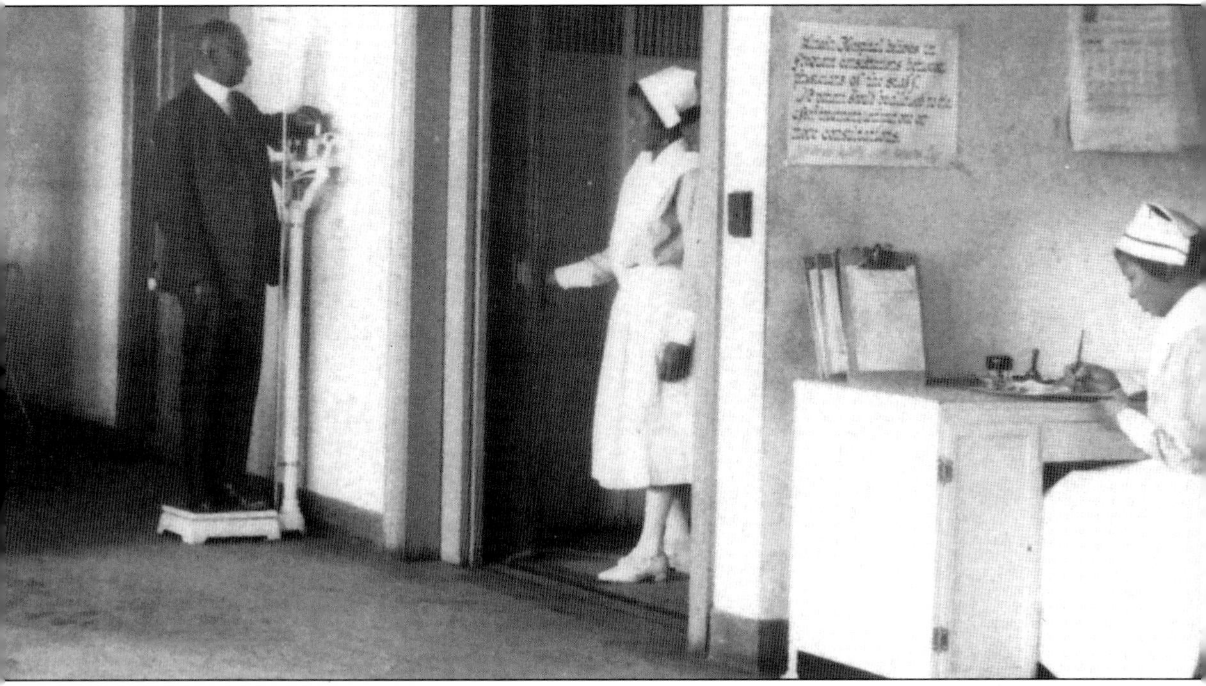

equipment were installed. In cooperation with the Durham County Health Department, the hospital operated two clinics, one for well-babies and one for patients with tuberculosis. (Courtesy of Margaret Kennedy Goodwin.)

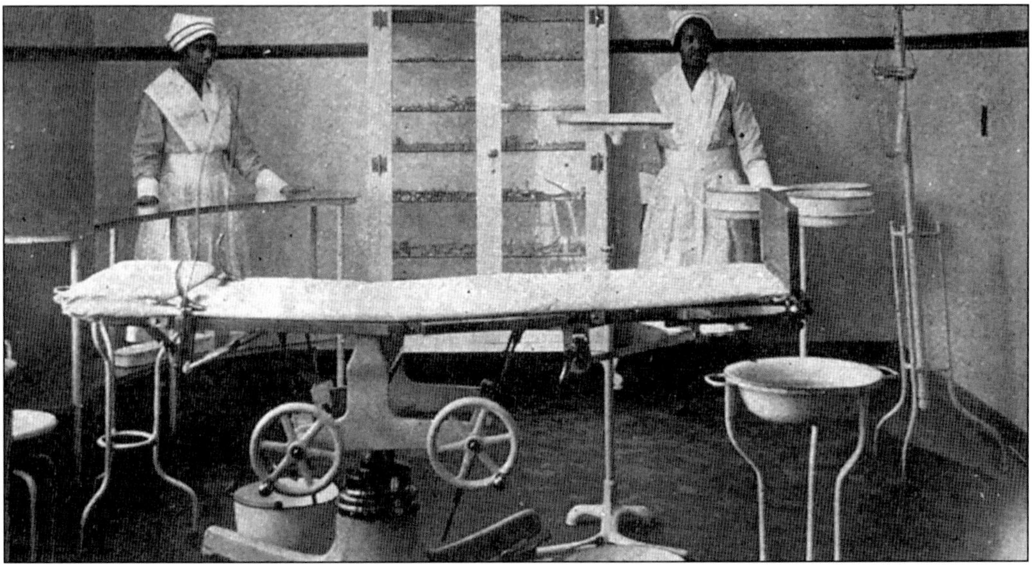

In 1925 most of the doctors on staff at Lincoln Hospital were still general practitioners, but many had started to concentrate their practice either in surgery, pediatrics, obstetrics, or urology. Those doctors who performed major operations primarily did only general surgery. From 1925 to 1930 the number of major operations conducted at Lincoln Hospital increased only slightly. The mortality rate remained at 8 percent, reflecting an indigent and sick patient population. (Courtesy of *Modern Hospital*.)

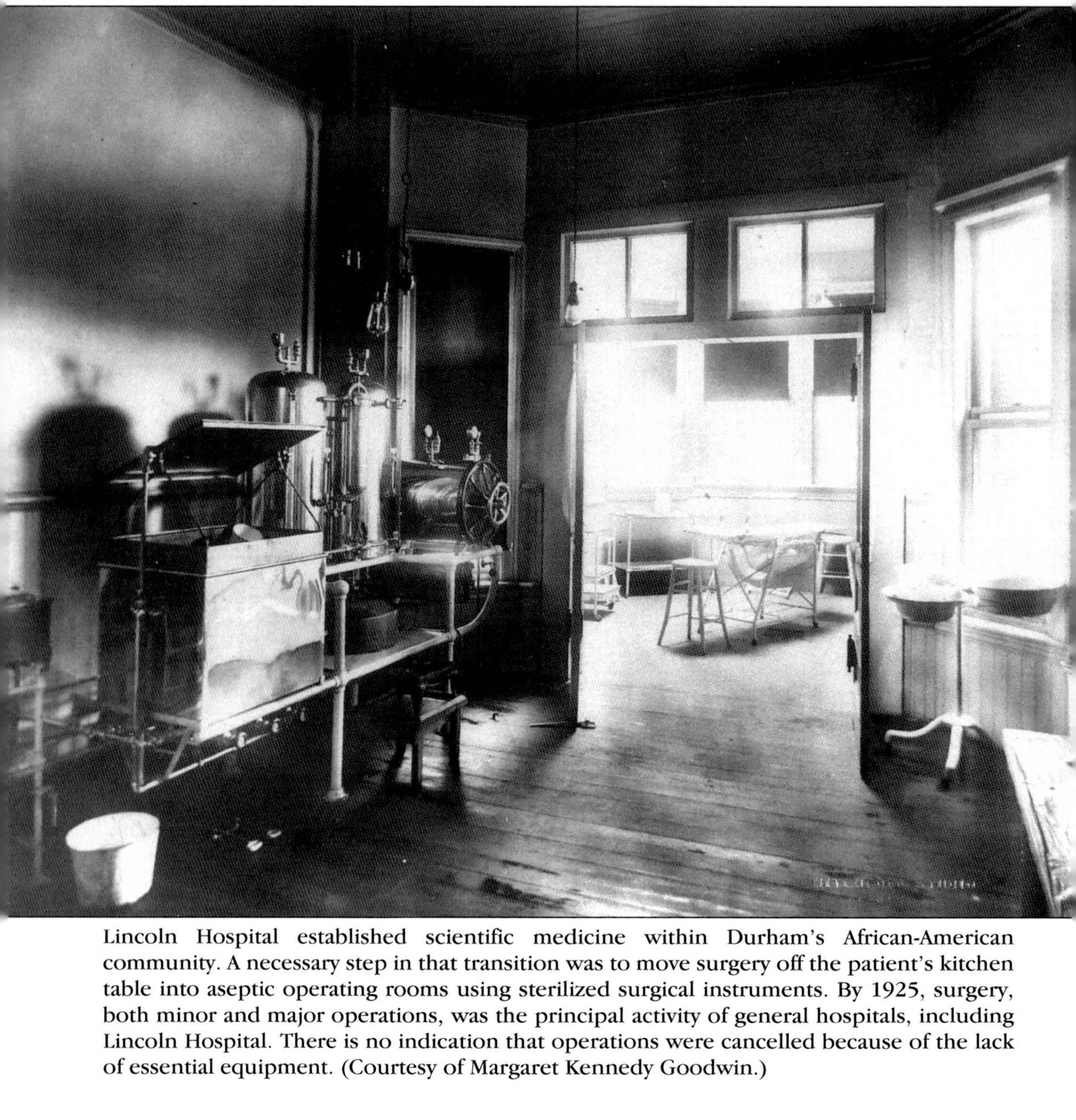

Lincoln Hospital established scientific medicine within Durham's African-American community. A necessary step in that transition was to move surgery off the patient's kitchen table into aseptic operating rooms using sterilized surgical instruments. By 1925, surgery, both minor and major operations, was the principal activity of general hospitals, including Lincoln Hospital. There is no indication that operations were cancelled because of the lack of essential equipment. (Courtesy of Margaret Kennedy Goodwin.)

Two

Hospital Leadership

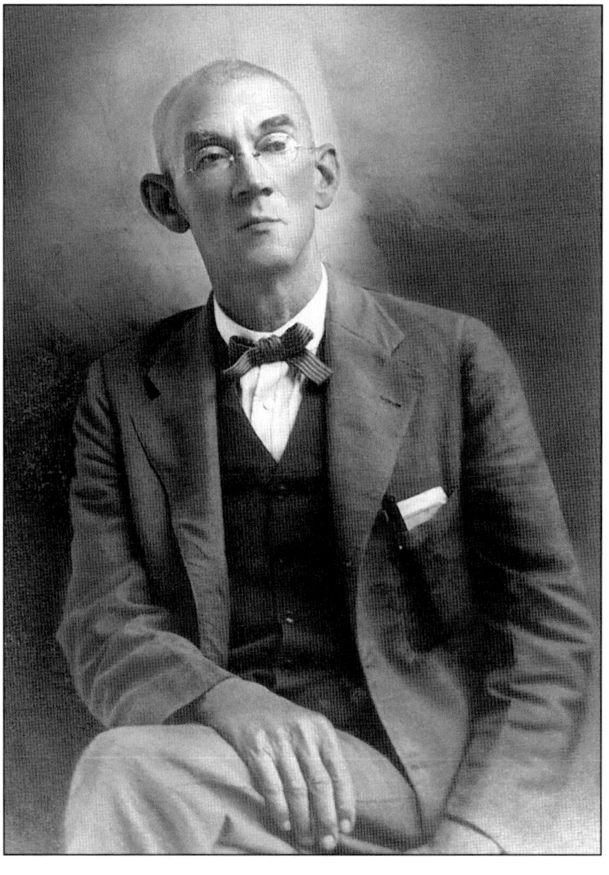

Dr. Aaron McDuffie Moore was the philosopher-physician and humanitarian-philanthropist whose intellect dominated emotions, but whose heart remained close to those he chose to serve. He is best known as a founder of Lincoln Hospital and, along with John Merrick, the North Carolina Mutual Life Insurance Company. Other institutions he started included the public library for African Americans, Mechanics and Farmers Bank, the Merrick-Moore-Spaulding Real Estate Company, Durham Drug Company, and Durham Textile Mill. His leadership of Lincoln Hospital in the earliest days was critical in laying the foundation of Christian service and scientific medicine as principles of patient care. (Courtesy of Evelyn Schmidt.)

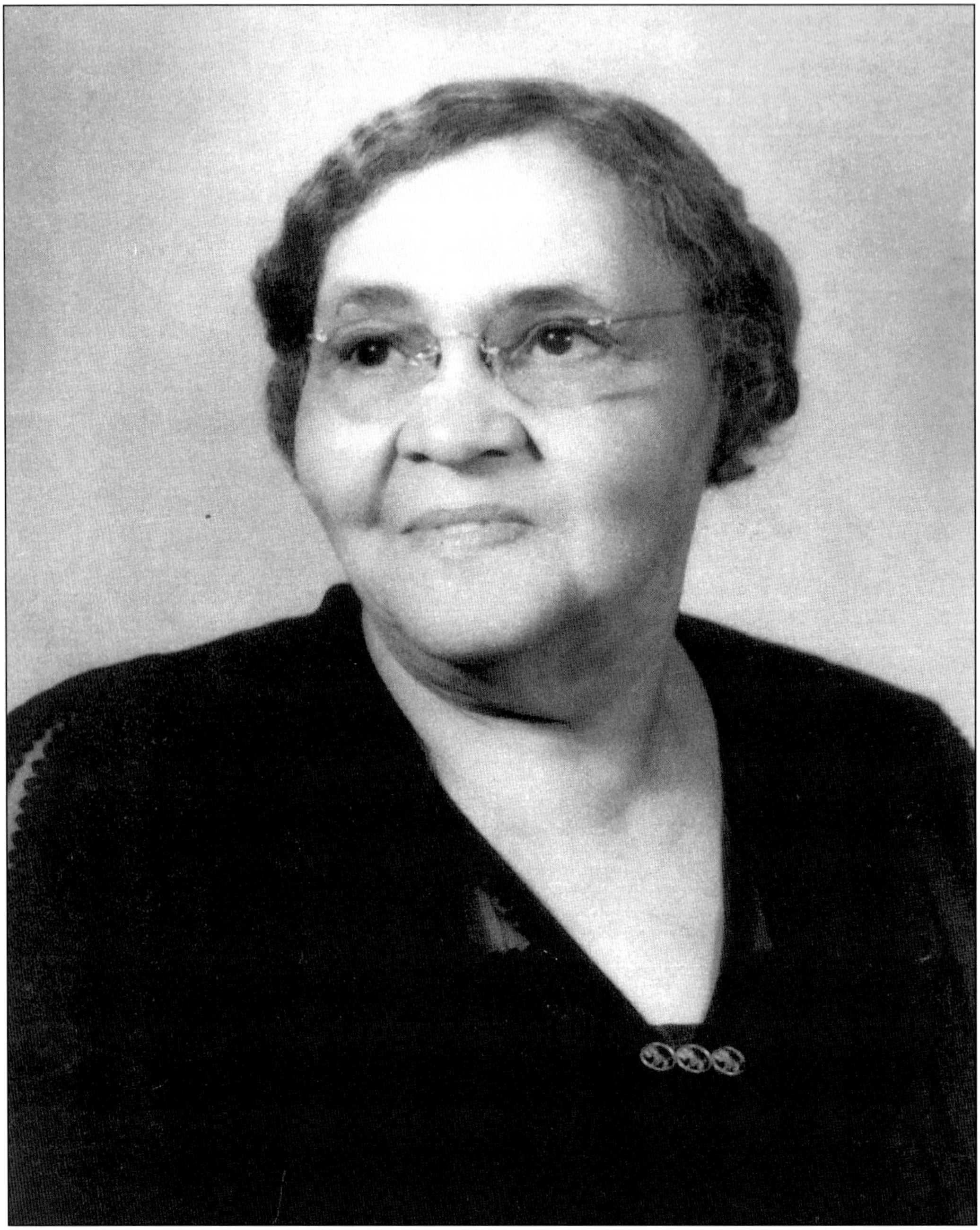

Miss Patricia Hawkins Carter, R.N., joined the administrative staff in 1911 as director of nursing. During her 37-year tenure with Lincoln Hospital, she served in nearly every leadership capacity, working closely with Dr. Aaron Moore, then Dr. Charles Shepard, and finally Mr. William Rich. Beginning in 1935, Miss Carter served officially as assistant superintendent of the hospital, a position she held until her retirement in 1948. She was known to prepare meals in the kitchen, dispense medicines from the pharmacy, mop floors, and help out wherever needed. In 1927 historian William K. Boyd attributed the success of the institution to her dedication and countless hours of work. (Courtesy of *The Scalpel*, 1946.)

Robert L. Flowers, Ph.D., was a member of the Lincoln Hospital Board of Trustees from 1924 to 1948 as a designated representative of the Benjamin Duke family. For many years, he served simultaneously as trustee of the Duke Endowment, vice president for finance, and later as president of Duke University and chair of the Board of Directors of North Carolina College, now North Carolina Central University. Dr. Flowers was instrumental in obtaining financial resources from various sources, including the Duke Endowment, to enable Lincoln Hospital to purchase modern equipment and expand its nursing quarters and patient wards. (Courtesy of Robert F. Baker.)

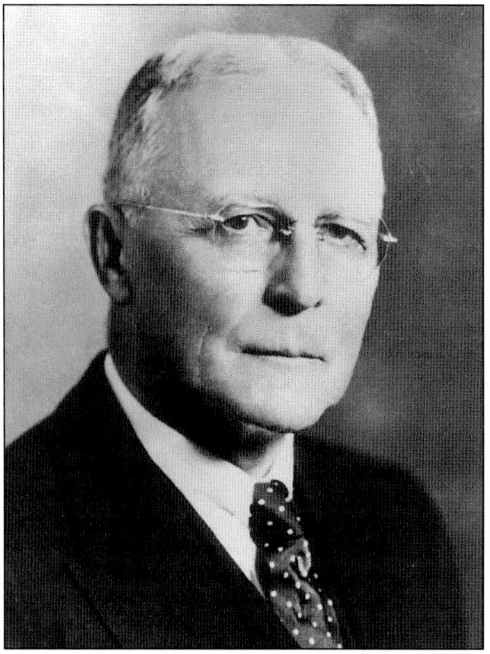

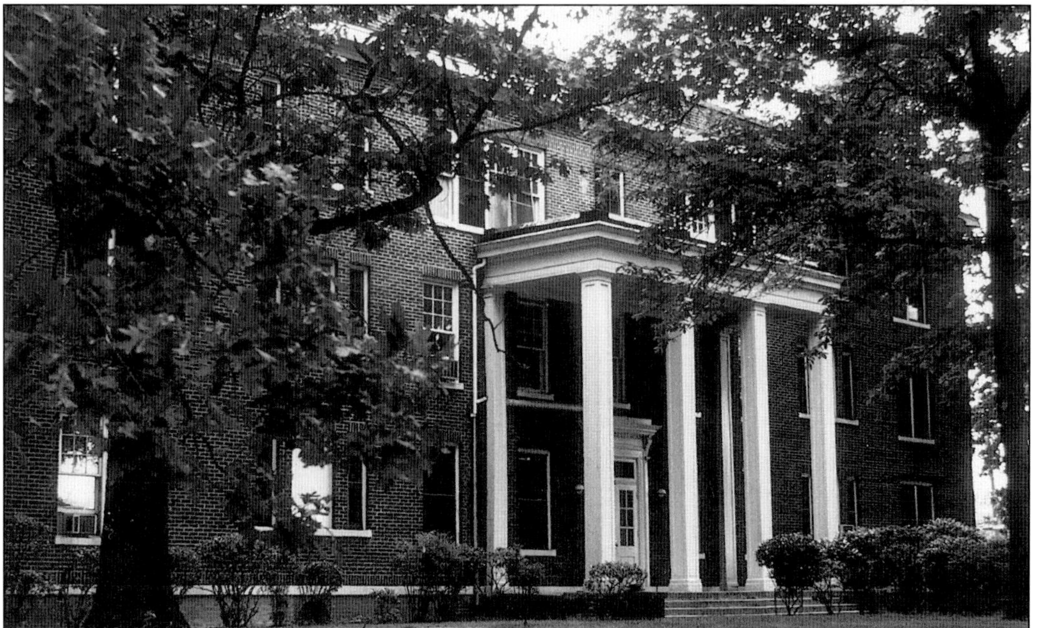

Lincoln Hospital emerged from the Depression as one of the leading African-American hospitals in the Carolinas as measured by statistics collected by the Duke Endowment and national hospital accreditation authorities. Its patient census grew steadily along with its administrative and nursing staff. In 1940 the hospital and medical staff saw 5,636 patients in the outpatient clinic; provided 20,858 days of care to inpatients; conducted 21,502 laboratory tests and 1,796 x-ray examinations; and performed 236 major and 1,399 minor operations. (Courtesy of Charles D. Watts.)

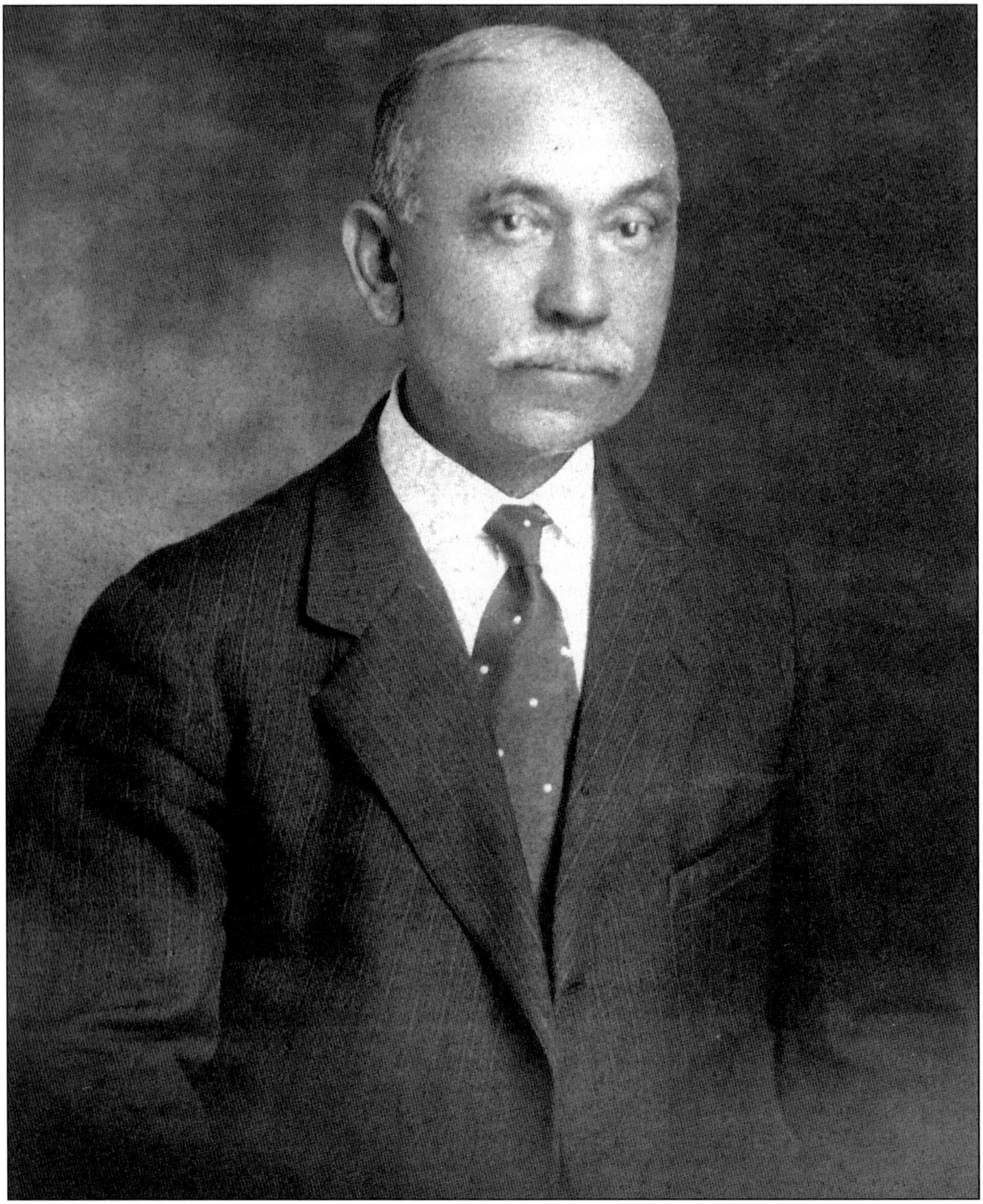

Dr. Stanford Warren served as president of the Lincoln Hospital Board of Trustees from 1919 until his death in 1940. During his era, Lincoln Hospital expanded into a modern, fully equipped hospital, constructed a new student nurses home, and established physician training programs recognized by national authorities. In addition, Lincoln Hospital developed strong ties with the Duke Endowment beginning in 1925, and with Duke University School of Medicine when it opened in 1930. Dr. Warren helped found other important institutions in Durham such as Mechanics and Farmers Bank and the African-American public library. Lincoln Hospital remained the focus of his civic duty and is a legacy of his leadership. (Courtesy of Selena Warren Wheeler.)

William Rich served as superintendent of Lincoln Hospital from 1934 to 1959. During his tenure he oversaw a $1.5-million capital expansion and reduction in the charity case load from 82 to 38 percent. Mr. Rich was respected highly by officials of the Duke Endowment as well as the leadership of the Durham community. In partnership with the Duke Endowment, he hosted annually a conference at Lincoln Hospital on the principles of record-keeping and accounting. He worked closely with Sample Forbus, superintendent of Watts Hospital, and the civic leadership to increase government contributions, secure federal funds, and improve clinical facilities. (Courtesy of Carolyn Henderson.)

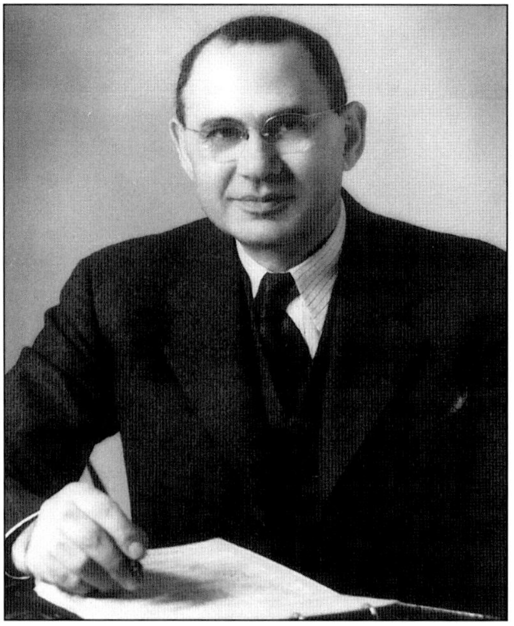

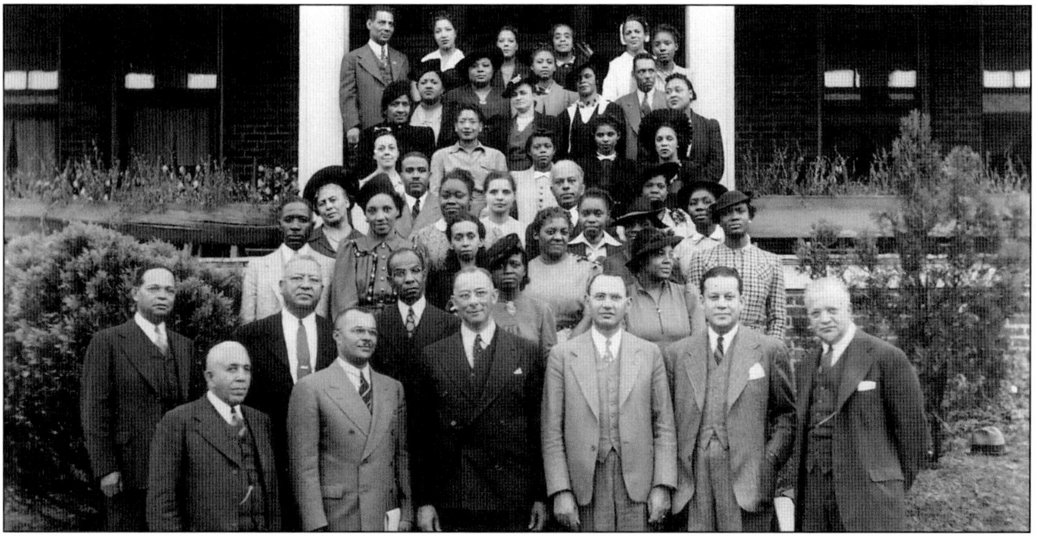

Lincoln Hospital often served as host to meetings of the administrators of the African-American hospitals in the Carolinas. Conferences would be organized periodically at the suggestion of George Harris of the Duke Endowment or Dr. Midian O. Bousfield, director of the Negro Health Division of the Julius Rosenwald Fund. The African-American hospitals in North Carolina in 1940 included Community Hospital, Wilmington; Gaston County Hospital, Gastonia; Good Samaritan Hospital, Charlotte; Jubilee Hospital, Henderson; Lincoln Hospital, Durham; Mercy Hospital, Wilson; L. Richardson Memorial Hospital, Greensboro; St. Agnes Hospital, Raleigh; and Susie Cheatham Memorial Hospital, Oxford. Those in South Carolina included Arthur B. Lee Hospital, Summerville; Brewer Hospital, Greenwood; Good Samaritan Hospital-Waverly, Columbia; Hospital and Training School, Charleston; and Working Benevolent Hospital, Greenville. (Courtesy of Margaret Kennedy Goodwin and photographer C.W. Richardson.)

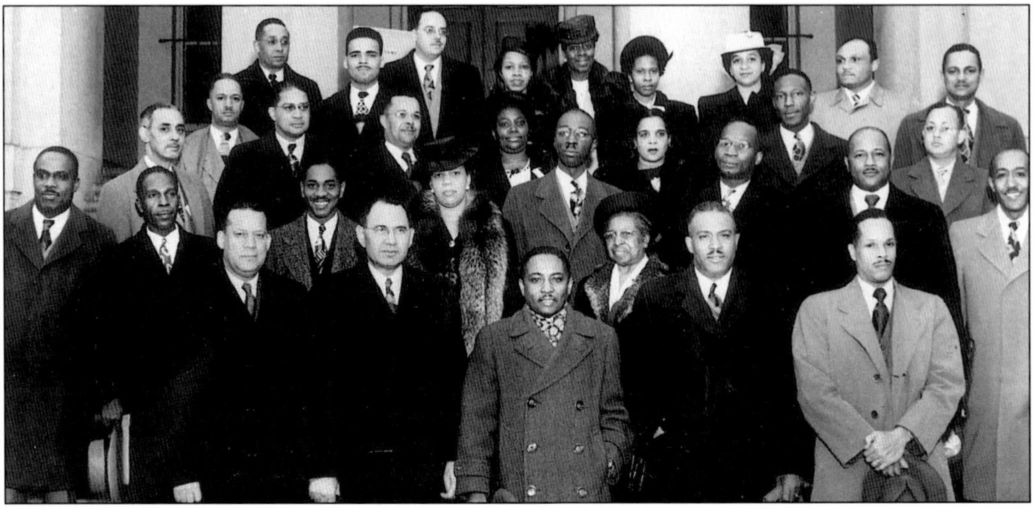

William Rich enjoyed membership in the American College of Hospital Administrators, the American Hospital Association, and the National Hospital Association. The National Hospital Association was founded in 1923 as a way to represent the needs of African-American hospitals throughout the country. The organization worked with the National Medical Association (the professional organization for African-American physicians) as well as with the American Hospital Association in its efforts to upgrade the quality of African-American hospitals. Pictured here are attendees of the 1948 National Conference of Hospital Administrators taken on the steps of Freedmen's Hospital in Washington, D.C. (Courtesy of Carolyn Henderson and photographer/lab Fletcher Foto.)

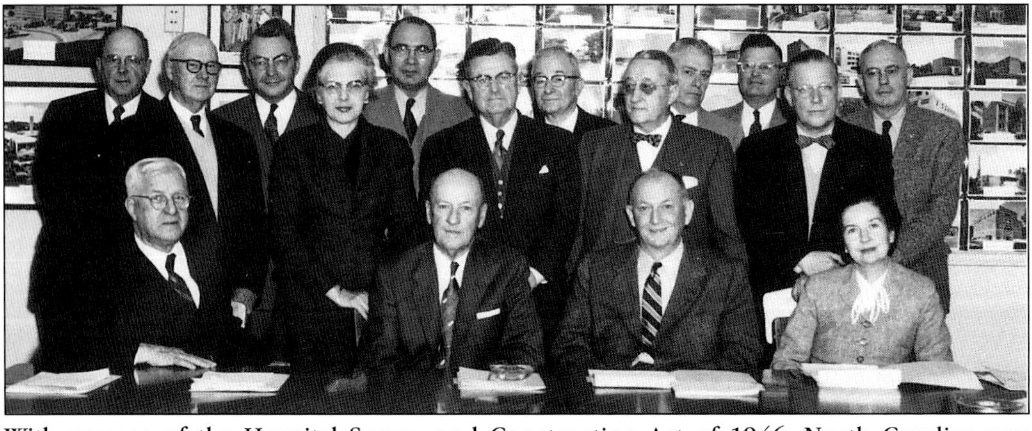

With passage of the Hospital Survey and Construction Act of 1946, North Carolina was charged to establish a state agency to survey the need for hospitals in rural and urban areas and to allocate federal funds for hospital construction. William Rich joined three other Durham citizens as members of the North Carolina Medical Care Commission. He was the only African American invited to join the original group of commissioners. Members of the commission, from left to right, are (seated) Dr. John A. Ferrell, Mr. James H. Clark, Dr. George L. Carrington, and Dr. Ellen B. Winston; (standing, front row) Dr. Walter Jackson, Miss Flora Wakefield, Dr. William Coppridge (Durham), Mr. E.C. Daniel, and Dr. Paul F. Whitaker; (standing, back row) Dr. W. Raney Stanford (Durham), Mr. Claude F. Gaddy, Mr. William Rich (Durham), Dr. John Hamilton, Dr. Harry Johnson, Mr. Sample Forbus (Durham), and Dr. J. Street Brewer. (Courtesy of Margaret Kennedy Goodwin.)

Charles Clinton Spaulding, shown *c.* 1950, was the first member of the Lincoln Hospital Board of Trustees elected as chair of the finance committee. In that role he worked closely with Dr. Robert L. Flowers to secure grants from the Duke Endowment and contributions from the Duke family. Within Durham he was the most distinguished African-American citizen and served as president of the North Carolina Mutual Life Insurance Company. Under his leadership, the Mutual rose to become the largest insurance company in the world owned by African Americans. Mr. C.C. Spaulding served Lincoln Hospital as president of the board of trustees with the death of Dr. Warren in 1940 until his own death in 1952. (Courtesy of Charles D. Watts.)

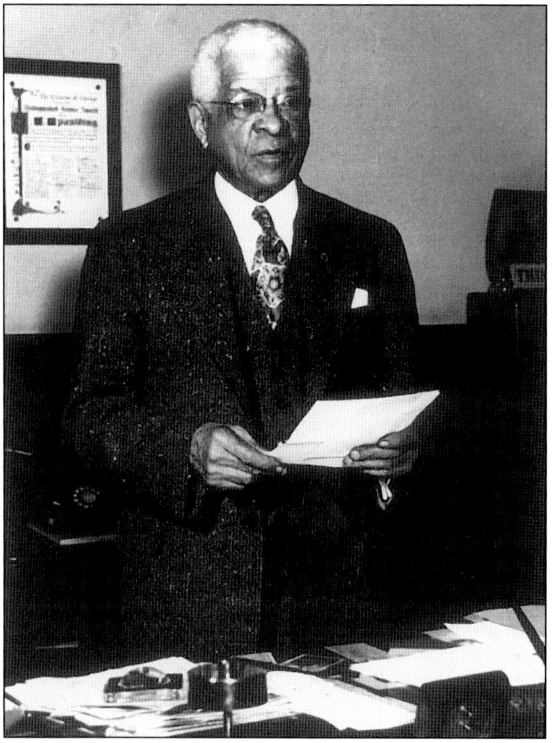

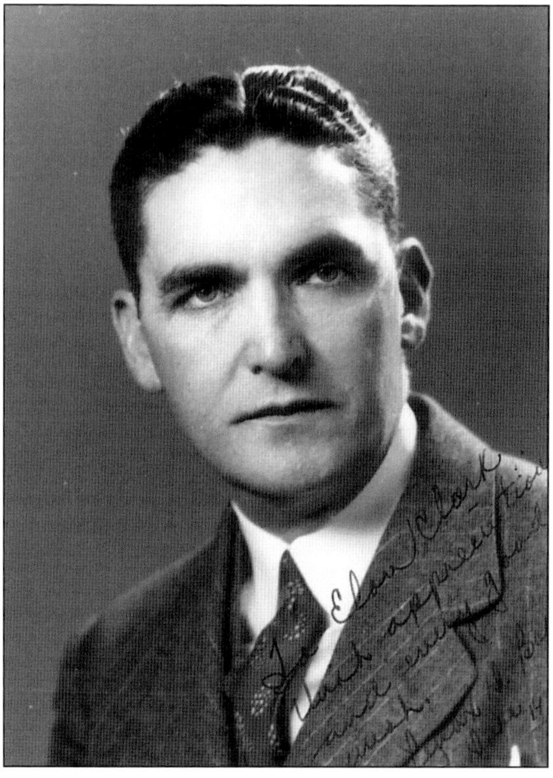

Lenox Baker Sr., M.D., chief of orthopedic surgery at Duke Hospital, was the son-in-law of Duke University president Dr. Robert L. Flowers. He established the Lenox Baker Hospital, dedicated to the care of children with orthopedic problems, which was racially integrated from its opening in 1950. Dr. Baker continued the family tradition of dedication to Lincoln Hospital, serving as trustee from 1940 until 1976. He was active as a member of the executive committee of the board of trustees and worked with Duke Endowment officials to strengthen Lincoln Hospital's financial and clinical programs. (Courtesy of Duke University Medical Center Archives.)

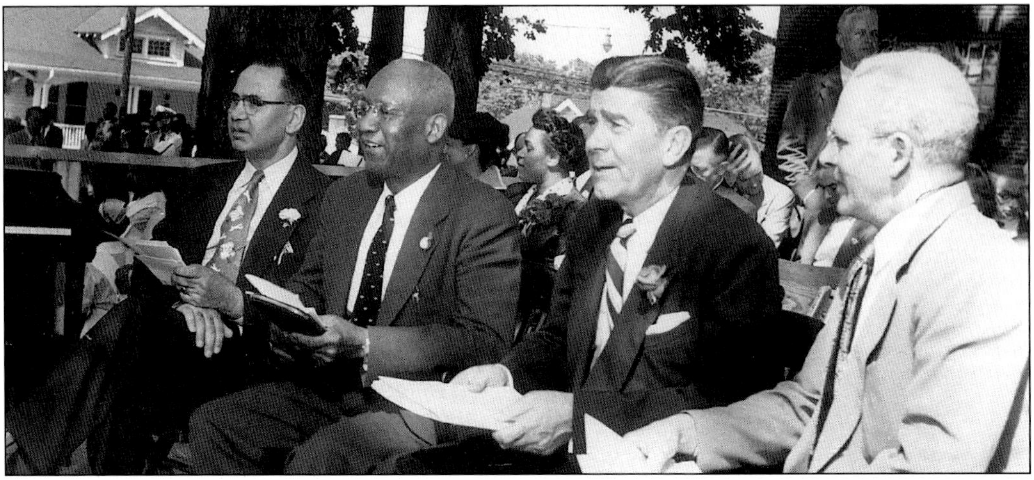

Seated are the speakers for the dedication of the 1953 wing of Lincoln Hospital. They are, from left to right, as follows: William Rich, superintendent of Lincoln Hospital; William Jesse Kennedy Jr., president of the North Carolina Mutual Life Insurance Company, Dr. Hollis A. Edens, president of Duke University, and Dr. Alphonso Elder, president of North Carolina College. The event drew hundreds of people from the area with guests from neighboring cities and states. Dr. Hollis Edens praised the community for its cooperative efforts to expand the hospitals for both African-American and white residents of Durham. (Courtesy of Margaret Kennedy Goodwin.)

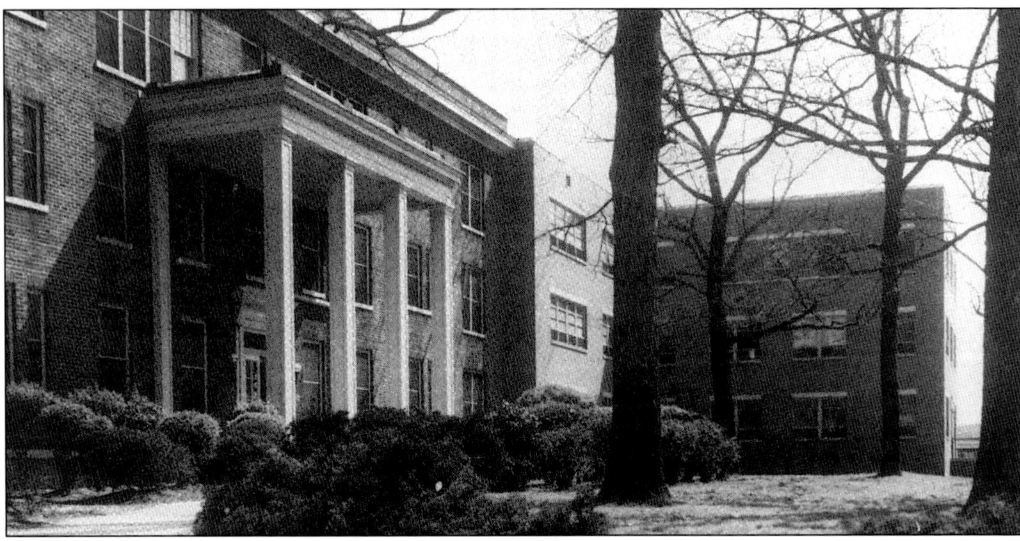

Sample Forbus, superintendent of Watts Hospital, and William Rich, superintendent of Lincoln, jointly submitted a proposal to the North Carolina Medical Care Commission for expansion of both hospitals using federal funds. The campaign to secure passage of the 1950 bond issue was heralded as the largest voter registration drive within the African-American community. In November citizens passed a $2.2-million bond issue that provided $1.6 million to Watts Hospital and $333,700 to Lincoln Hospital. These dollars were matched by federal Hill-Burton funds totaling $950,000. Lincoln Hospital used its $592,400 grant to construct a new wing that added 35 beds for a total of 125. The operating suites and radiology and laboratory departments were modernized. (Courtesy of *The Scalpel*, 1958.)

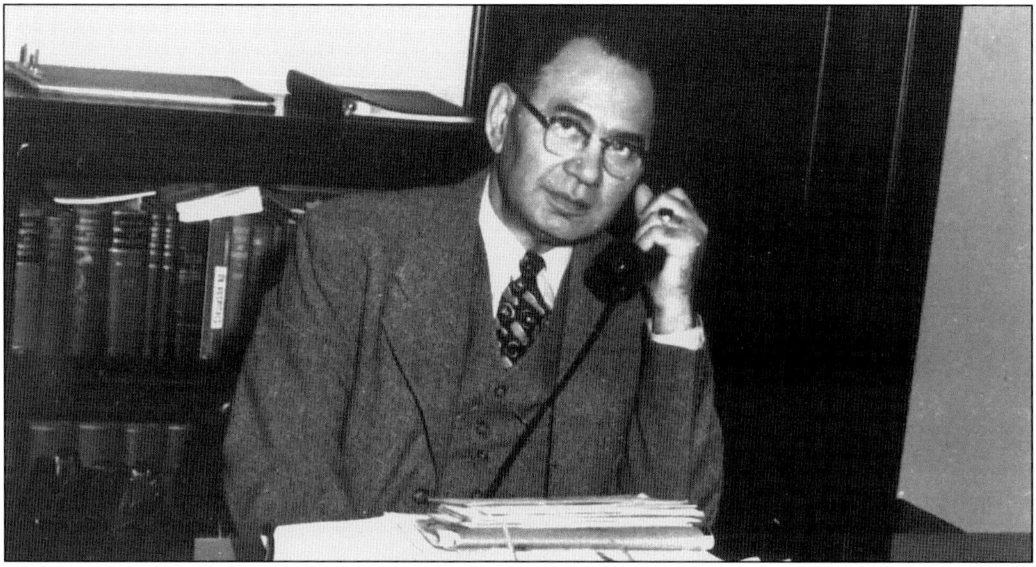

As hospital superintendent, William Rich was responsible for keeping Lincoln Hospital financially afloat. Accordingly, he worked with the hospital trustees as well as Sample Forbus of Watts Hospital when making appeals to the city and county governments for increased allocations. Beginning in 1954, Lincoln and Watts Hospitals received monies from a tax levy to support increased costs of operating both hospitals resulting from inflation caused by the Korean War. (Courtesy of Margaret Kennedy Goodwin.)

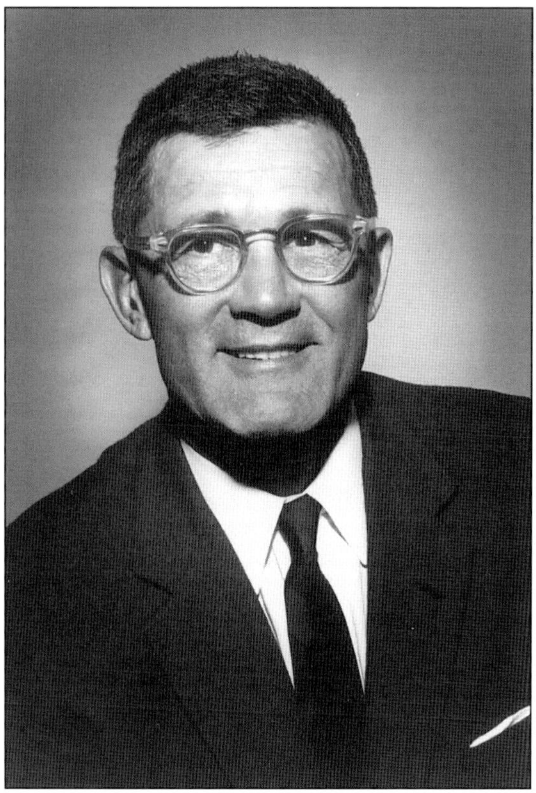

H. Max Schiebel, M.D., an honors graduate of Johns Hopkins School of Medicine and the Duke Hospital surgical residency program, joined the Lincoln Hospital staff in 1940. As chief of surgery at Lincoln Hospital from 1944 to1973, he worked closely with the nursing and hospital administration to recruit essential staff, review clinical statistics to maintain the hospital's accreditation, and establish a four-year fully accredited surgery residency program. In 1949, he started several cancer screening clinics held throughout the Durham community under the auspices of the American Cancer Society. (Courtesy of H. Max Schiebel and photographer Burnie Bachelor Studio, Inc.)

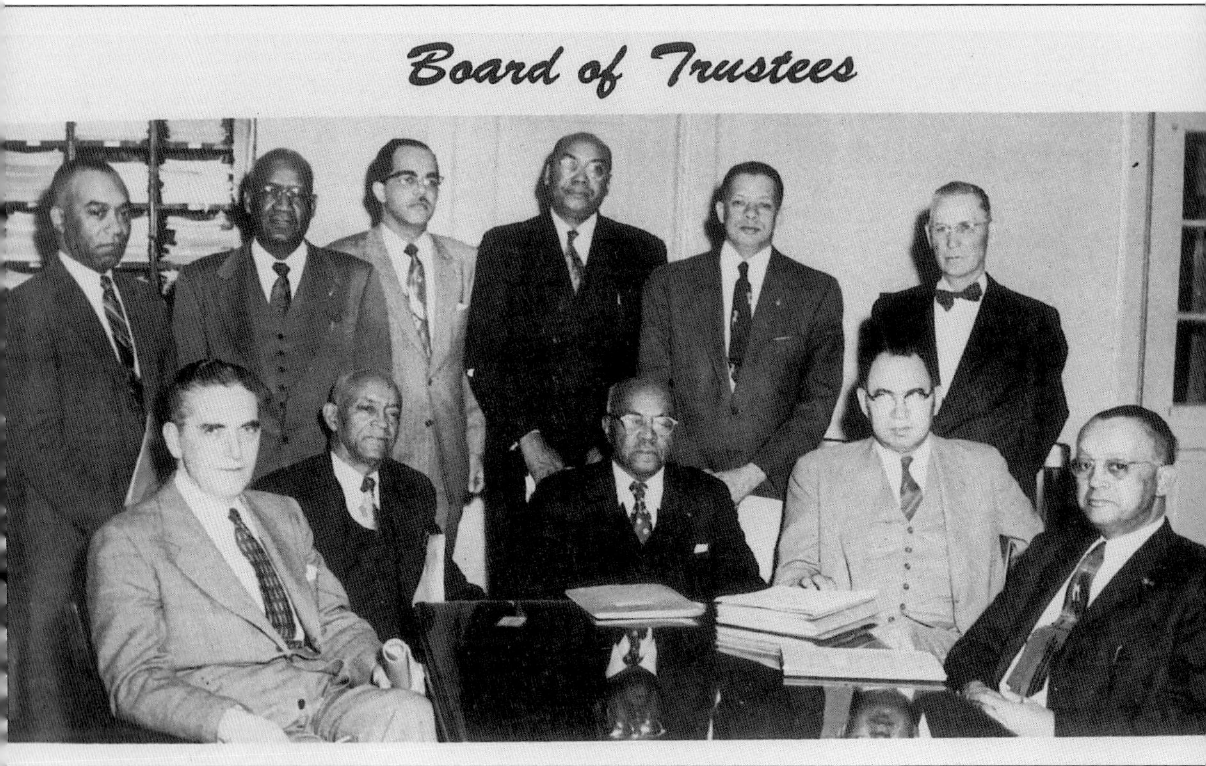

Beginning as early as 1921, the Lincoln Hospital Board of Trustees was bi-racial with one-third of the trustees selected from the white community. Similar to Watts Hospital, trustees were chosen as representatives of leading institutions and families in Durham and the local city and county governments. Once a member of the board, individuals often served for many years. Pictured here, from left to right, are (sitting) Lenox Baker, M.D.; A.S. Hunter, D.D.S.; J.N. Mills, M.D.; William Rich; and Edward R. Merrick; (standing) H.M. Michaux; William J. Kennedy Jr.; Frank W. Scott; Rev. S.P. Perry, John H. Wheeler, and L.G. Kirkland. Those not pictured are Rencher H. Harris, Mary D.B.T. Semans, Dr. Alphonso Elder, Vance Fisher, and Dr. Clyde Donnell. (Courtesy of *The Scalpel*, 1956.)

The retirement of William Rich after 25 years of service to Lincoln Hospital drew representatives from over 50 organizations in Durham spanning the business, medical, education, and religious communities. The Biltmore Hotel banquet room was filled with people honoring the work of Mr. Rich in making Lincoln Hospital unique among African-American hospitals for its efficiency of operation, the high quality of its medical and nursing personnel, and the cooperation that existed among the area hospitals. (Courtesy of Margaret Kennedy Goodwin.)

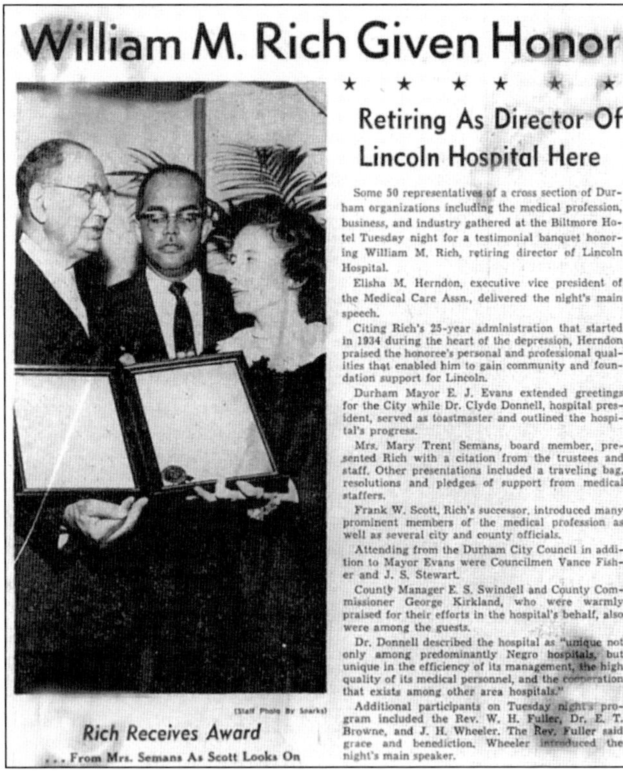

William M. Rich Given Honor

Retiring As Director Of Lincoln Hospital Here

Some 50 representatives of a cross section of Durham organizations including the medical profession, business, and industry gathered at the Biltmore Hotel Tuesday night for a testimonial banquet honoring William M. Rich, retiring director of Lincoln Hospital.

Elisha M. Herndon, executive vice president of the Medical Care Assn., delivered the night's main speech.

Citing Rich's 25-year administration that started in 1934 during the heart of the depression, Herndon praised the honoree's personal and professional qualities that enabled him to gain community and foundation support for Lincoln.

Durham Mayor E. J. Evans extended greetings for the City while Dr. Clyde Donnell, hospital president, served as toastmaster and outlined the hospital's progress.

Mrs. Mary Trent Semans, board member, presented Rich with a citation from the trustees and staff. Other presentations included a traveling bag, resolutions and pledges of support from medical staffers.

Frank W. Scott, Rich's successor, introduced many prominent members of the medical profession as well as several city and county officials.

Attending from the Durham City Council in addition to Mayor Evans were Councilmen Vance Fisher and J. S. Stewart.

County Manager E. S. Swindell and County Commissioner George Kirkland, who were warmly praised for their efforts in the hospital's behalf, also were among the guests.

Dr. Donnell described the hospital as "unique not only among predominantly Negro hospitals, but unique in the efficiency of its management, the high quality of its medical personnel, and the cooperation that exists among other area hospitals."

Additional participants on Tuesday night's program included the Rev. W. H. Fuller, Dr. E. T. Browne, and J. H. Wheeler. The Rev. Fuller said grace and benediction. Wheeler introduced the night's main speaker.

(Staff Photo By Sparks)

Rich Receives Award

... From Mrs. Semans As Scott Looks On

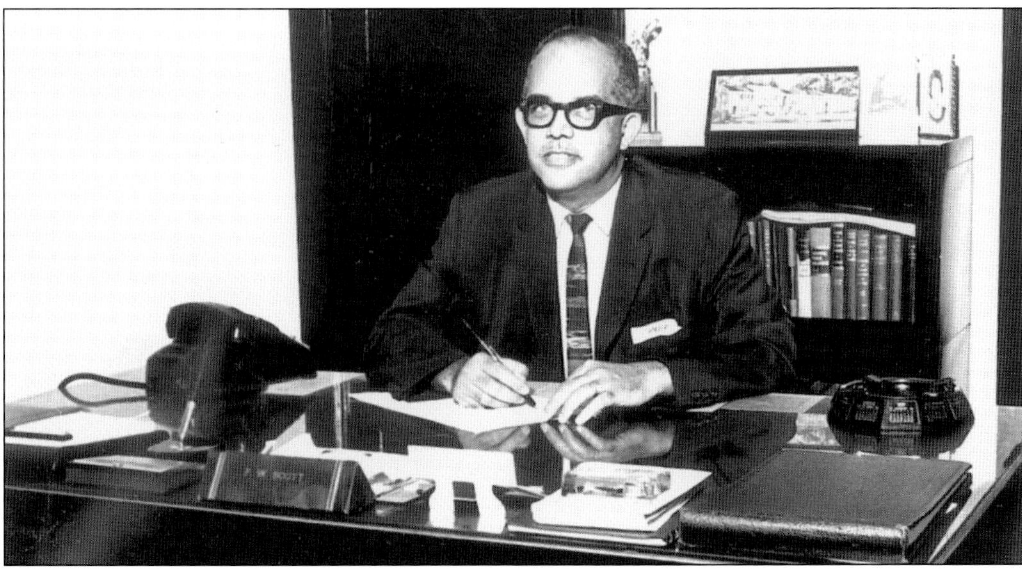

Frank W. Scott, the nephew of William Rich, was recruited to Lincoln Hospital in 1950 as assistant superintendent. He succeeded Mr. Rich as superintendent beginning officially on January 1, 1960. Mr. Scott led the institution through the early era of racial integration in hospital patient care under Medicare and defeat of the 1966 hospital bond issue before assuming a senior position in a large hospital system in New Jersey in 1968. (Courtesy of Margaret Kennedy Goodwin.)

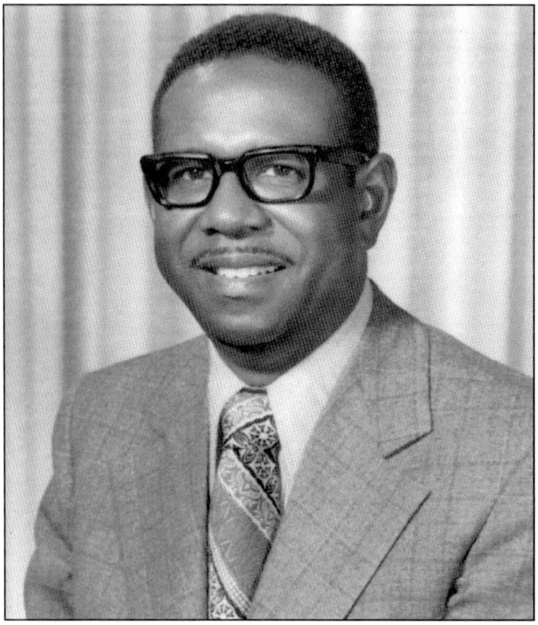

Dr. Robert E. Dawson, after completing residency training at Homer G. Phillips in St. Louis, moved to Durham in 1946. His clinical practice focused mainly on ophthalmology, for which he was board certified in 1963. From 1965 to 1970, Dr. Dawson served as medical director of Lincoln Hospital, restoring a physician's voice to its administrative leadership. As medical director he launched the Private Diagnostic Clinic at Lincoln Hospital with assistance from administrators of Duke Hospital. He served as president of the National Medical Association in 1979–1980 and as a Lifetime Trustee of Meharry Medical College. (Courtesy of Robert E. Dawson.)

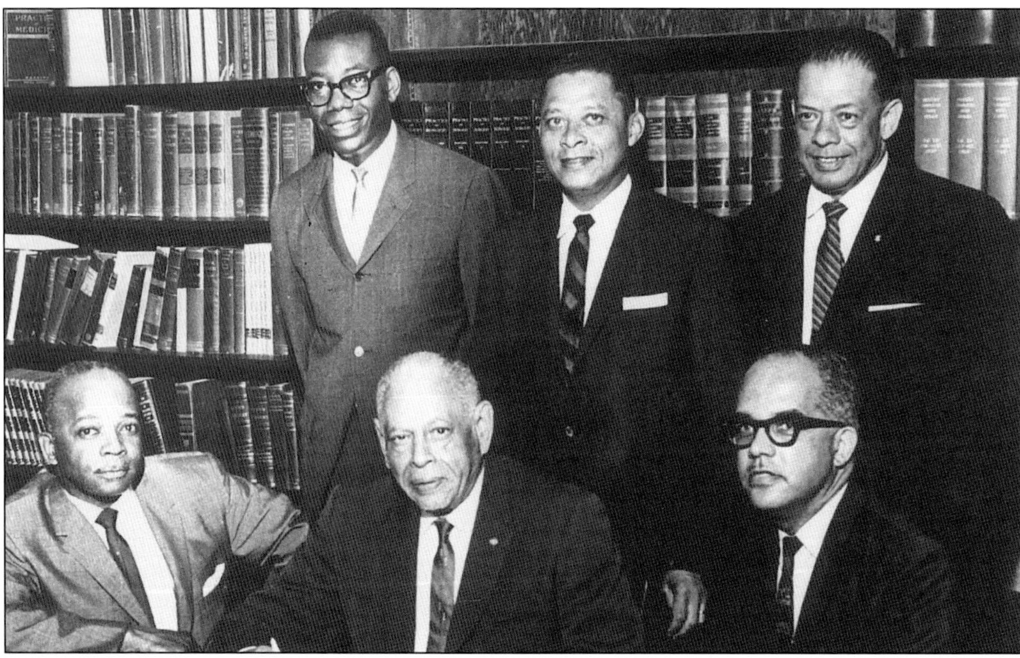

The Board of Trustees of Lincoln Hospital gained the expertise of the leadership of two important institutions in Durham—Mechanics and Farmers Bank and the North Carolina Mutual Life Insurance Company. Trustees who came with skills in finance and insurance shown in this *c.* 1964 photograph are, from left to right, (standing) Larkin Teasley, assistant actuary, NC Mutual; Thad Gaillard, assistant agency director; and John Wheeler, president, Mechanics and Farmers Bank; (sitting) Noah Bennett, actuary, NC Mutual; Dr. Clyde Donnell, medical director, NC Mutual; and Frank Scott, superintendent of Lincoln Hospital. (Courtesy of Margaret Kennedy Goodwin and photographer Nat Purefoy.)

Three

PATIENTS COME FIRST

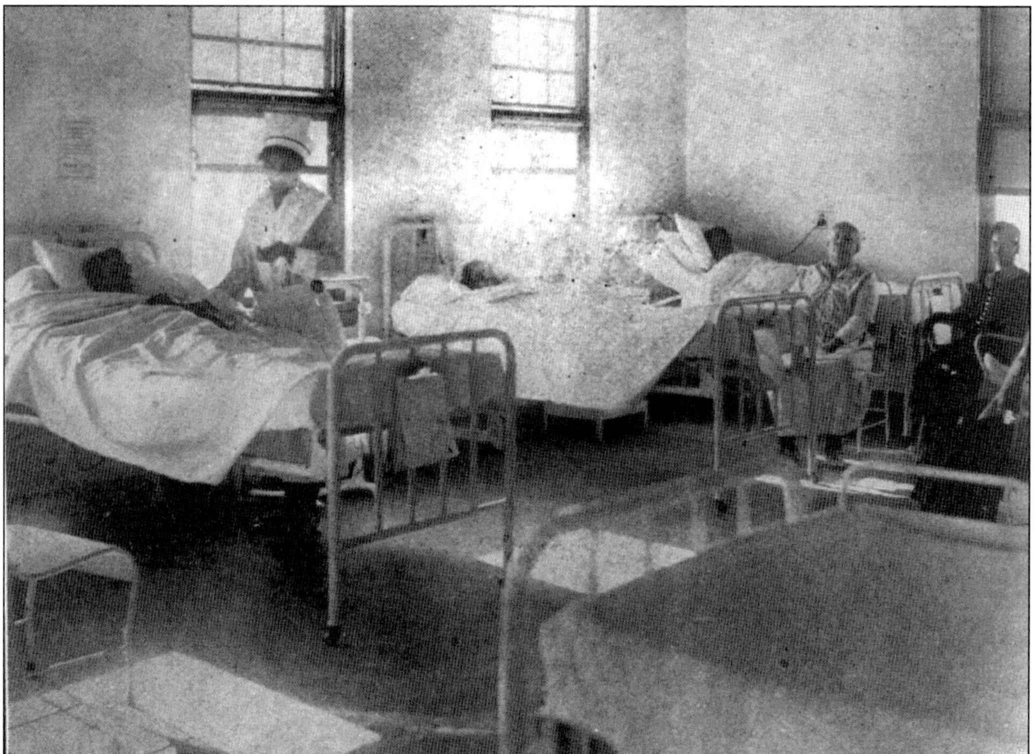

When Lincoln Hospital opened in 1901, it focused its primary mission on patient care. Only later did it establish a nurses training school and, years later, internship training opportunities. With the opening of the new hospital in 1925, Lincoln Hospital segregated patients into female wards, male wards, and pediatric beds. The goal was to decrease the spread of infection and to enable nurses to care for patients with similar illnesses. (Courtesy of *Modern Hospital*.)

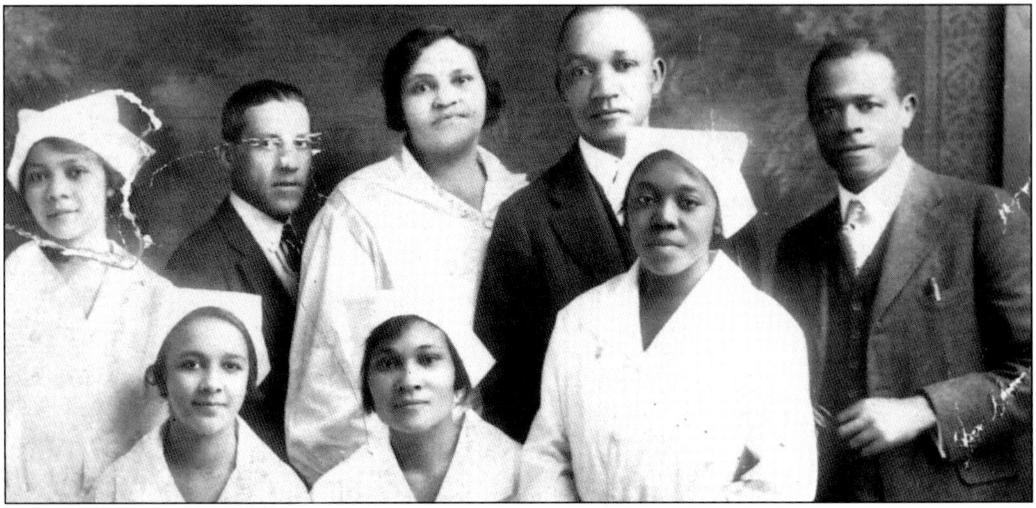

Patricia Hawkins Carter was born in 1875. She was the daughter of Hawkins W. Carter who served Warren County as a representative and as a state senator during the Reconstruction era. Her advanced preparation was obtained from Shaw University, St. Agnes Hospital, and Lincoln Hospital in New York City. Before coming to Durham in 1911 as director of nursing, Miss Carter taught school in Warren County and served as director of nursing at Leonard Hospital. Miss Carter (middle, back row) worked closely with Dr. Charles Shepard (far right) to transform Lincoln Hospital into a modern institution. They succeeded through establishing a medical records department, implementing standards for patient admission work-ups, expanding laboratory and x-ray tests, and maintaining standards in nursing and internship training. (Courtesy of Margaret Kennedy Goodwin.)

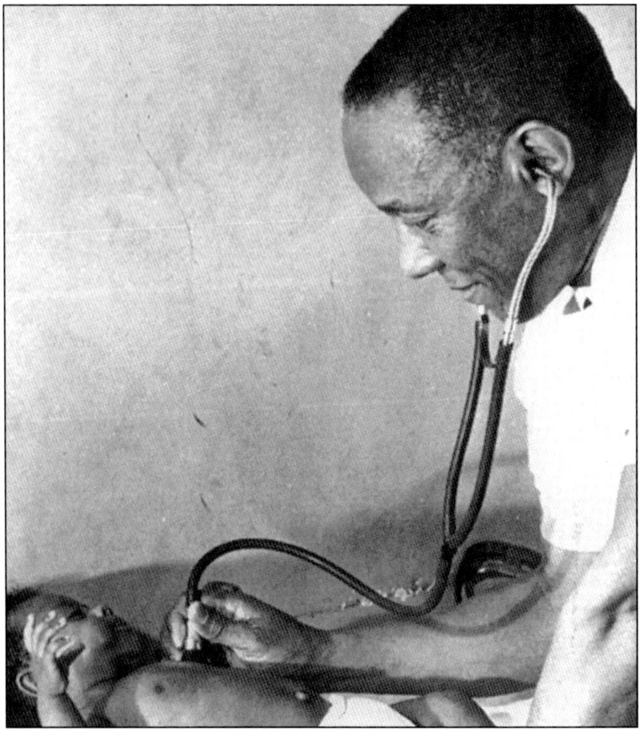

Dr. William A. Cleland, the first African-American pediatrician in Durham, required all children registered in one of his four well-baby clinics to be immunized with vaccines provided by the North Carolina State Board of Health. The state later calculated the rate of infection among his African-American children to be dramatically lower than among the white children in Durham. Dr. Cleland's success in preventing childhood illnesses led to legislation requiring all children to be immunized before starting school. (Courtesy of *The Scalpel*, 1963.)

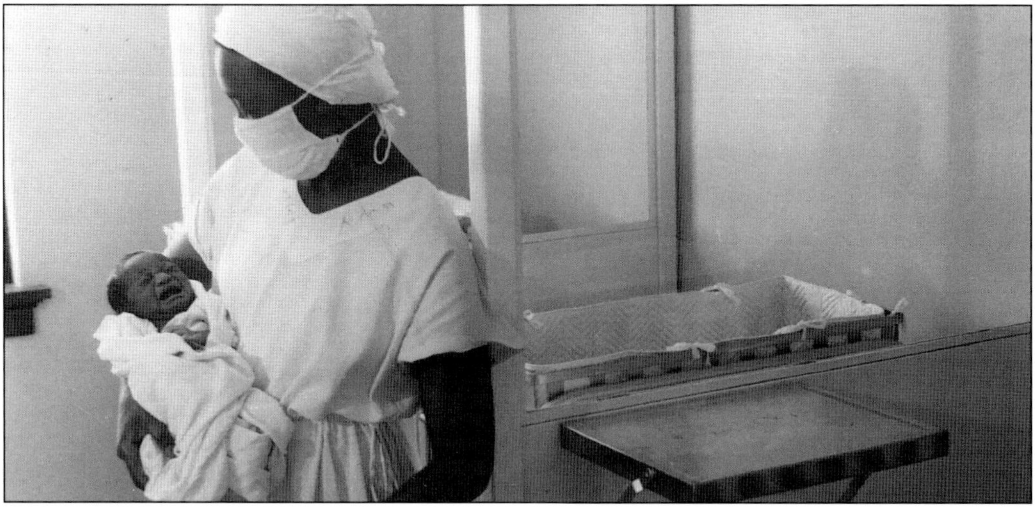

Delivery of a baby at Lincoln Hospital occurred often in the operating suites under the direction of an obstetrician and the surgical nurses. It would not be until Lincoln Hospital closed and the staff moved into Durham County General Hospital in 1976 that obstetrical nurses would oversee Cesarean and vaginal deliveries. The babies stayed in the newborn nursery until they were ready to go home. Pictured here is Elizabeth William Thorpe, R.N. (Courtesy of Margaret Kennedy Goodwin.)

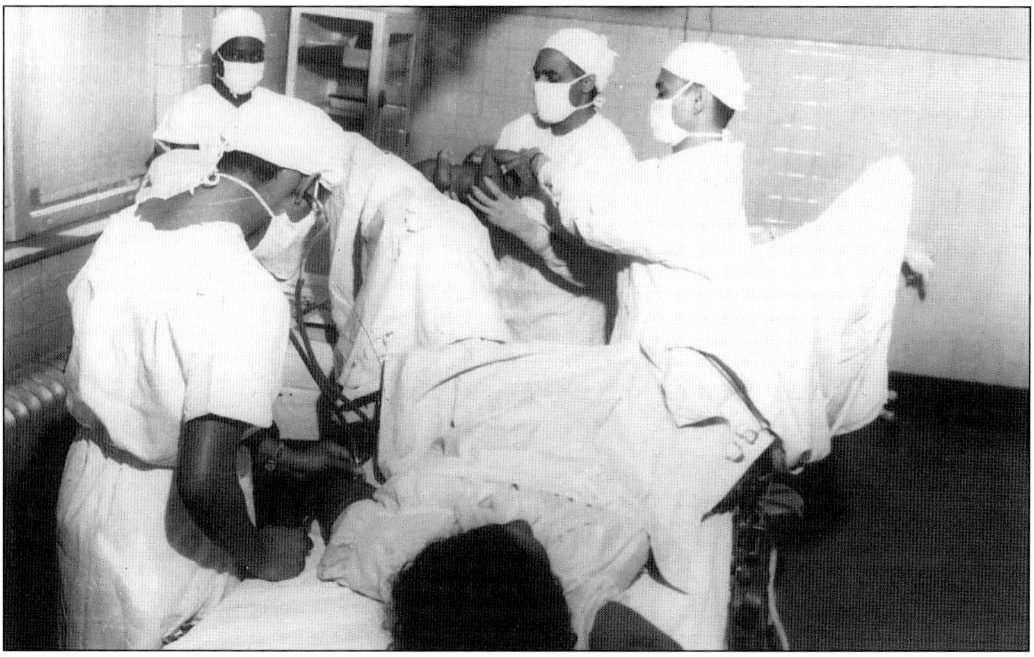

African-American women could not deliver their babies at Watts and Duke Hospitals. Consequently, Lincoln Hospital played an important role in moving obstetrics out of the home and into the hospital and the hands of a physician. Beginning in 1933 with the help of public health nurses who identified poor women, Lincoln Hospital operated pre-natal and post-natal clinics for them in an effort to reduce complications and maternal and newborn illnesses. (Courtesy of Carolyn Henderson and photographer Bob Lawson.)

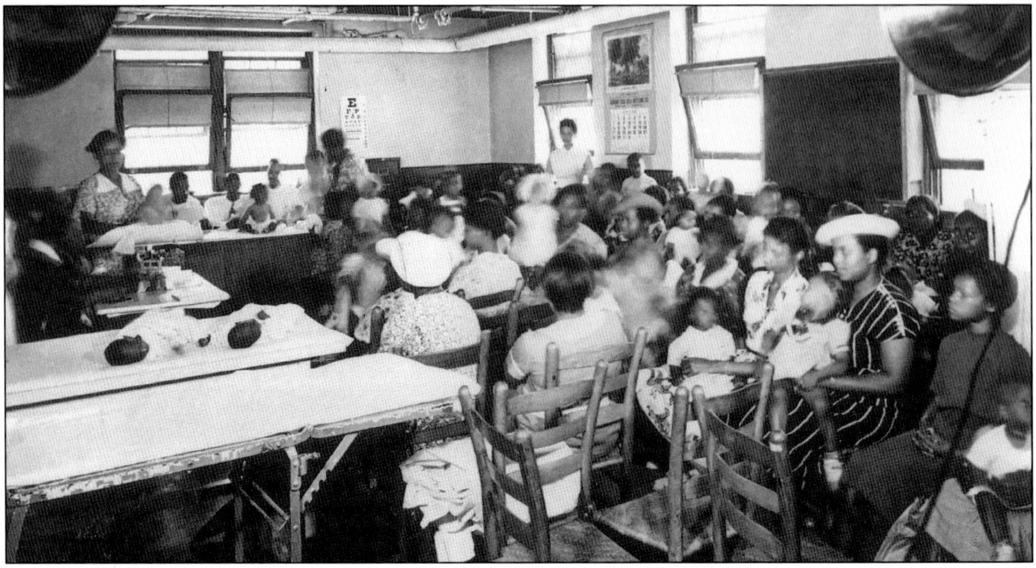

The well-baby clinic at Lincoln Hospital was originally established by Dr. Baird U. Brooks, a white pediatrician in Durham. Each baby's height and weight were recorded to assess nutritional status and overall health. Dr. Cleland continued this clinical assessment and, in the 1950s, determined that by school age, all of his children had caught up to the growth parameters of babies born in the white community. (Courtesy of Margaret Kennedy Goodwin and photographer C.W. Richardson.)

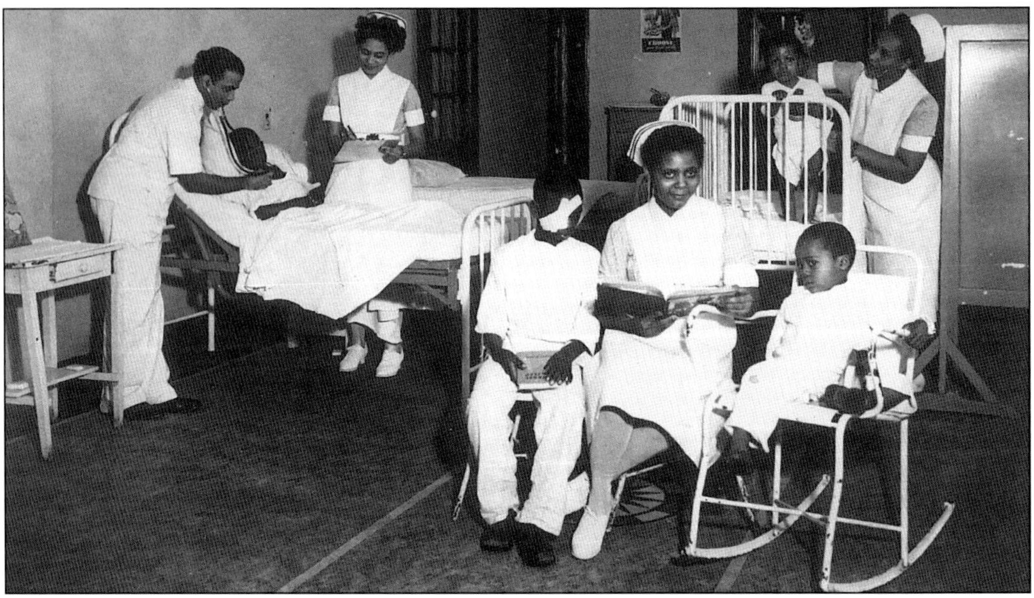

The original pediatric ward was carved out of half of the library located on the first floor of the hospital. Seen here is Dr. George Jackson, an intern, examining a child. Dr. Cleland helped obtain advanced training for all the nurses in the photograph; one went to the University of Pennsylvania and later returned to serve as a head nurse at the University of North Carolina–Chapel Hill. (Courtesy of Margaret Kennedy Goodwin and photographer C.W. Richardson.)

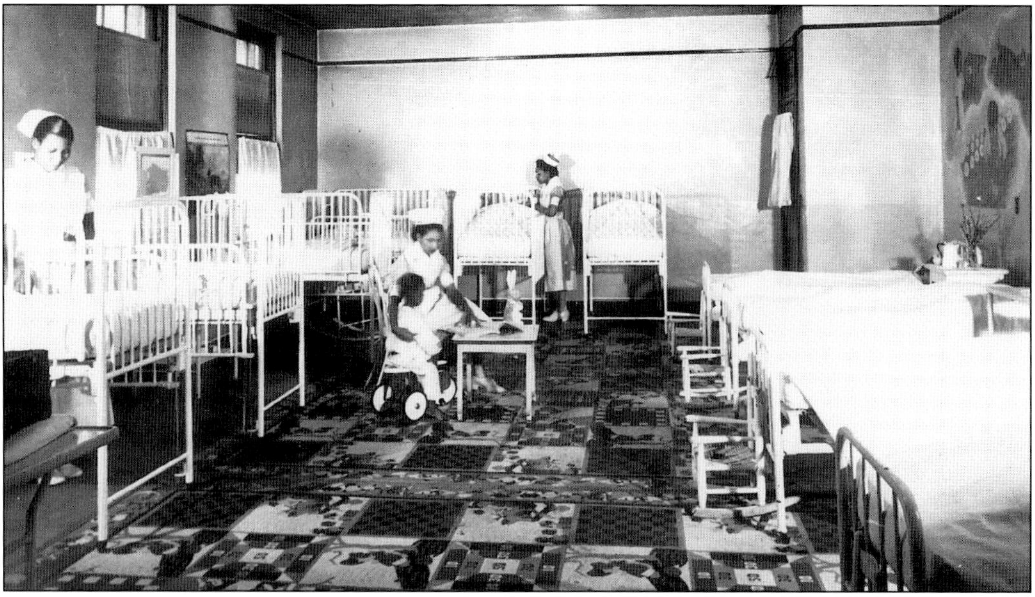

In 1938, the pediatric ward was moved to the second floor and renovated with wall murals and space for the children to play. The ward was enlarged to accommodate ten patients thus also enabled student nurses to acquire specialized pediatric instruction. That year, 389 children under the age of 14 years were discharged from Lincoln Hospital and only 13 died. (Courtesy of Margaret Kennedy Goodwin and photographer C.W. Richardson.)

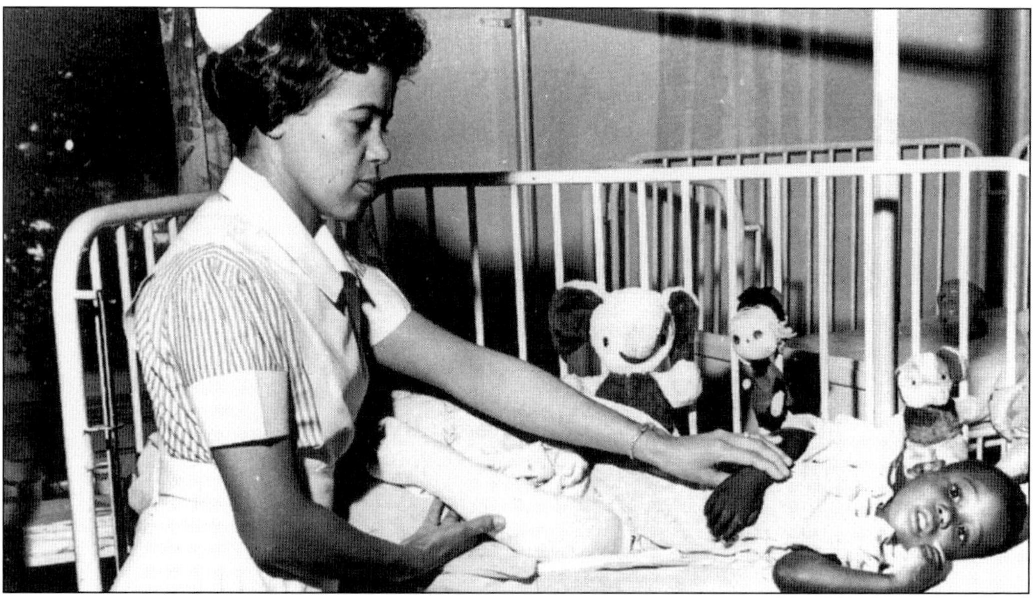

Lincoln Hospital admitted children under the Crippled Children's Program established by Dr. Al Shands, chief of orthopedic surgery at Duke Hospital. The orthopedic team of Dr. Everett Bugg and Dr. Ralph Coonrad cared for, on average, five of these special children at any one time at Lincoln Hospital. Round the clock nursing care was essential to prevent them from developing pressure sores and other problems from casts, braces, and traction devices. (Courtesy of *The Scalpel*, 1963.)

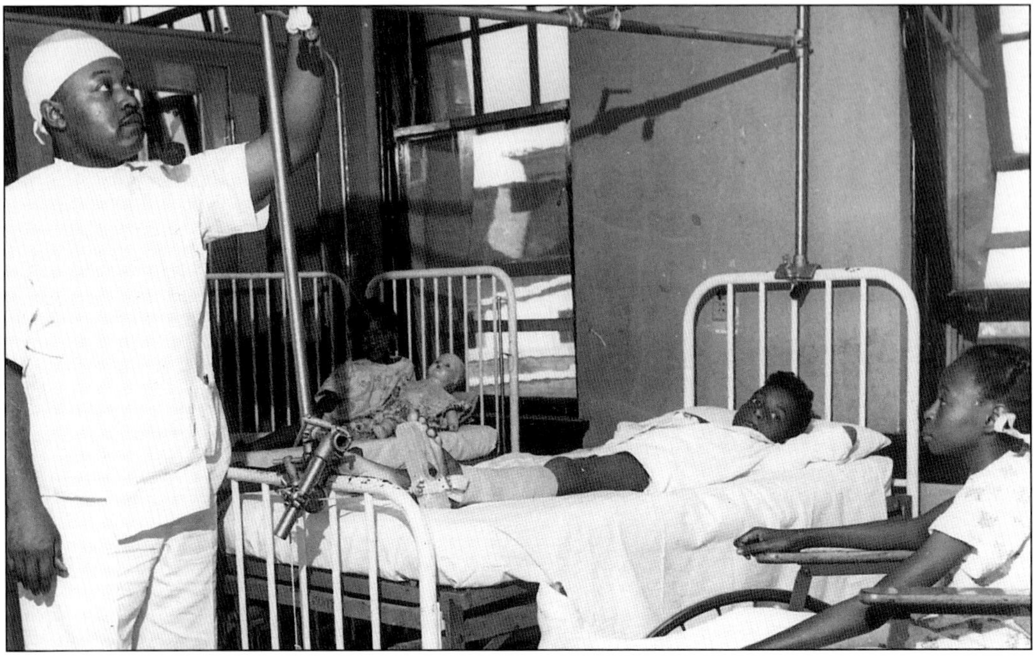

Lincoln Hospital had a large orthopedic patient population because of the Crippled Children's Program and the clinical activity of two Durham surgeons, Dr. Everett Bugg and Dr. Ralph Coonrad. Pictured here is Dr. Elroy Young, a surgery resident, making rounds on these patients. (Courtesy of Margaret Kennedy Goodwin.)

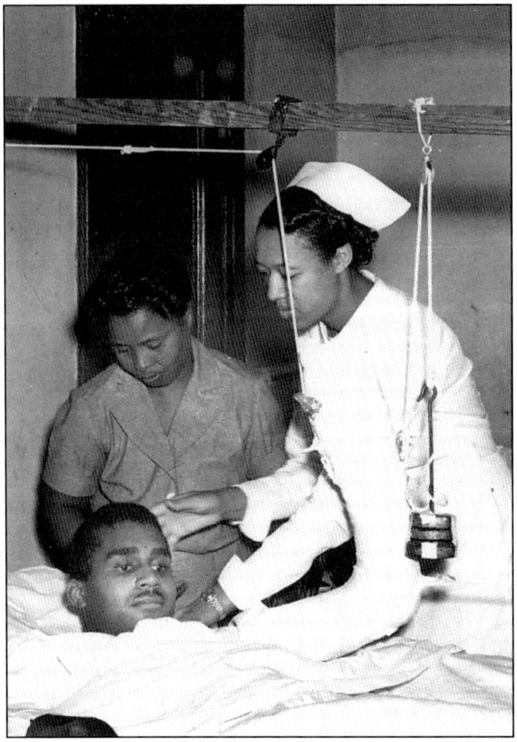

Lincoln Hospital's nursing and physician staff often had to improvise as seen with the simple traction apparatus for this patient. William Rich rarely had adequate resources to purchase the most modern equipment, and at times, there were insufficient funds to obtain essential supplies. Doctors and nurses made do. As a former Lincoln nursing student recalled, when compared to students from other programs, the Lincoln Hospital students may have been weaker on theory, but they were stronger in practical skills of bedside nursing because of the necessity to figure out the how, if not always the why. (Courtesy of Carolyn Henderson.)

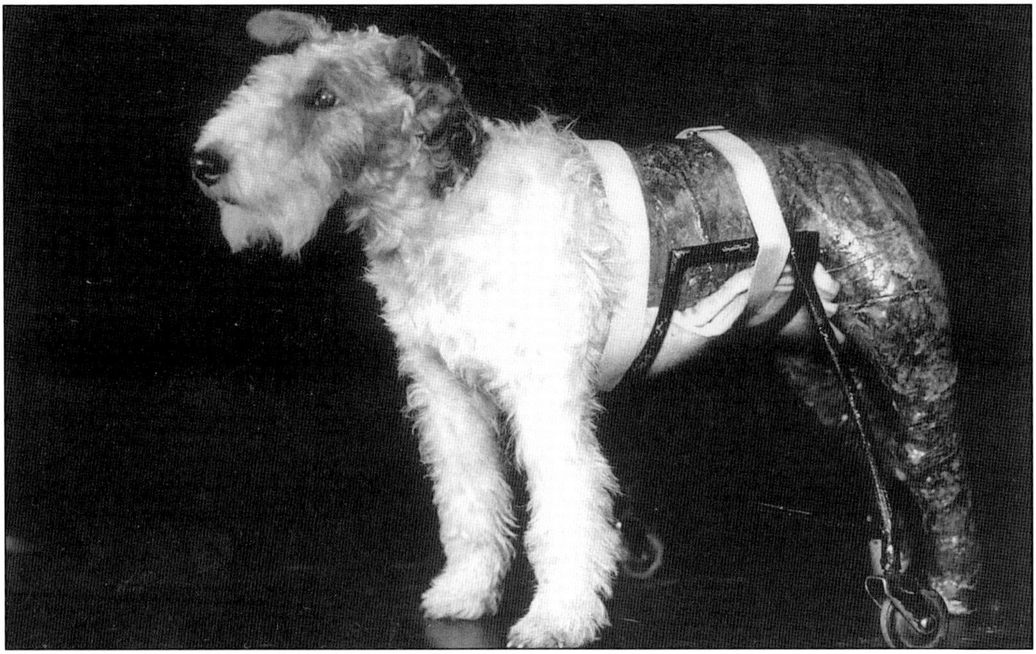

Dr. Max Schiebel's wire-haired terrier often rode with him around town. One day in 1940–1941, a truck ran over her in front of Lincoln Hospital, fracturing one back leg and crushing her pelvis. Dr. Schiebel took her into Lincoln Hospital, set her fractures and applied this plaster cast. The Duke brace shop made the frame with wheels allowing her to walk. She recovered and lived to old age. (Courtesy of H. Max Schiebel.)

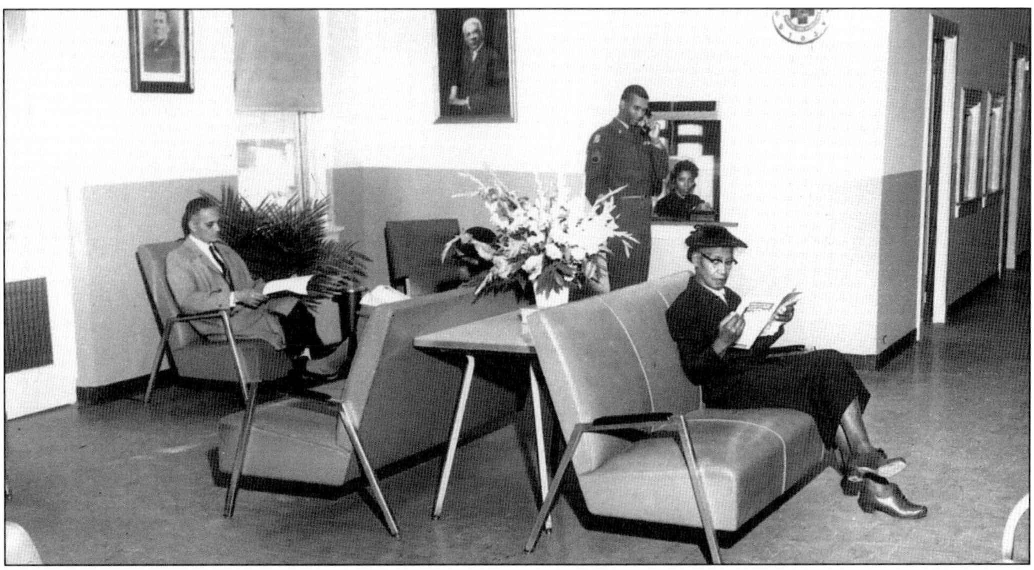

The Lincoln Hospital front lobby was the reception area for all individuals waiting to see patients and family members. The hospital did not have formal waiting hours and, thus, was open nearly all day and evening. When arriving one would use the telephone in the front lobby to call up to the floor to gain permission to visit a patient. (Courtesy of Margaret Kennedy Goodwin.)

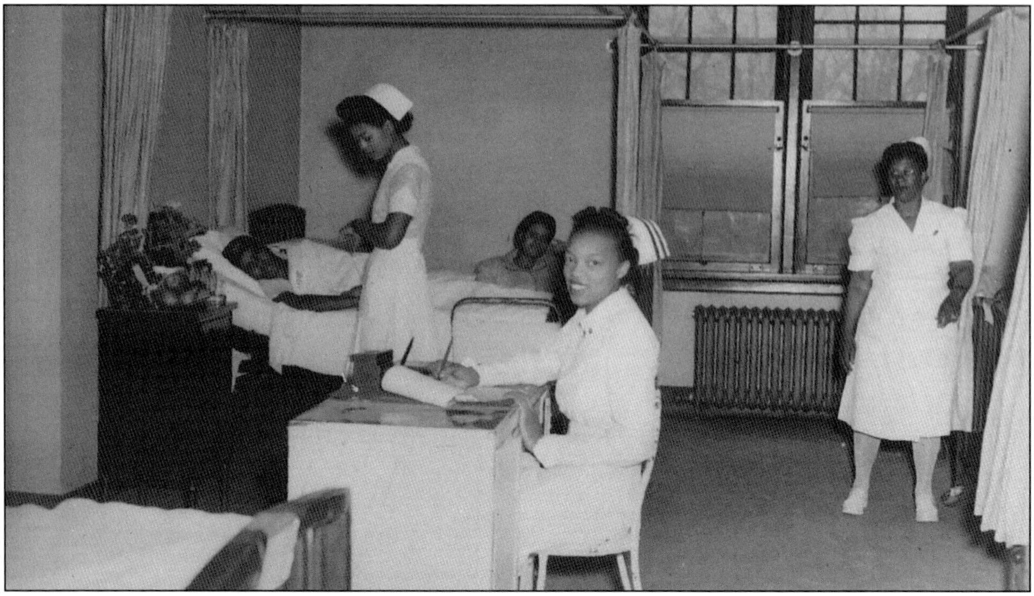

Nursing students learned on the job as well as in the classroom. After the first year of school, nursing students worked side by side with graduate nurses on the wards caring for patients. Their service was an inexpensive and irreplaceable source of bedside care. (Courtesy of Margaret Kennedy Goodwin.)

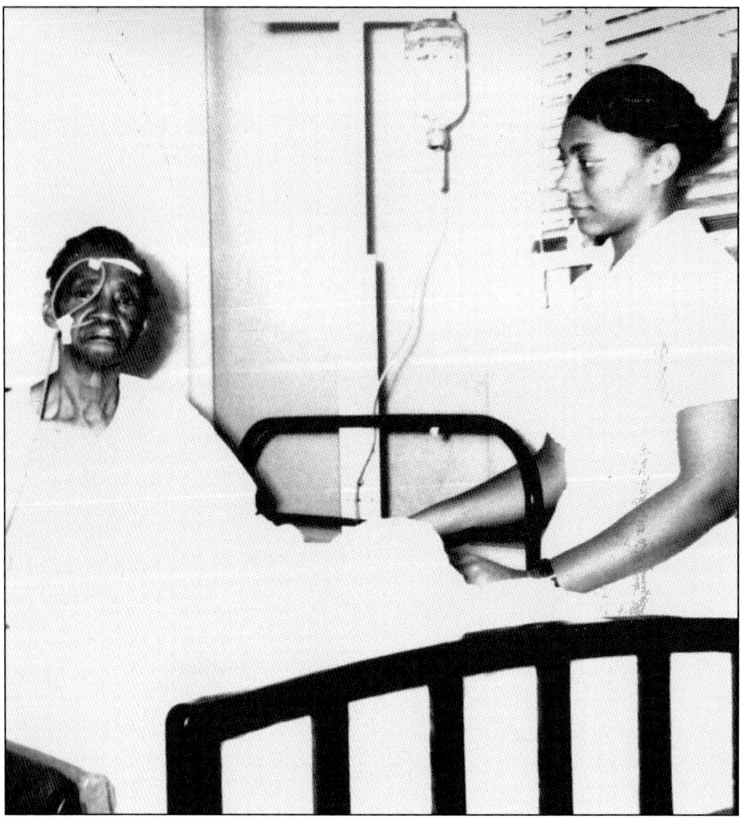

Lincoln Hospital admitted all patients regardless of their ability to pay and often with advanced illness when little could be offered in terms of a cure. Compassion and comfort were administered in heavy doses to provide what little hope remained. (Courtesy of Margaret Kennedy Goodwin.)

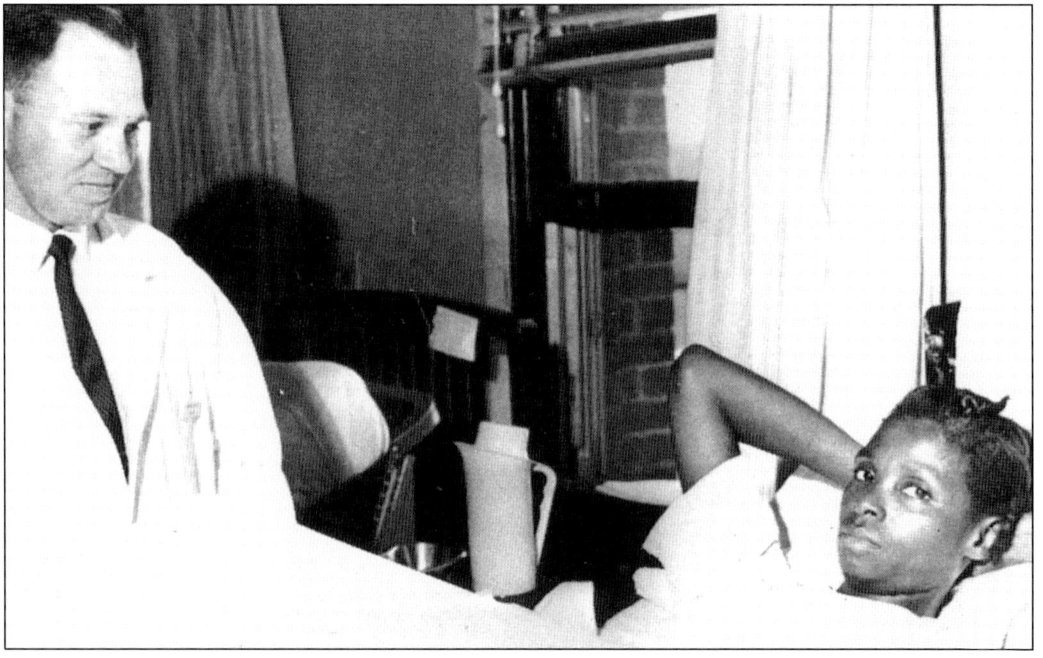

The medical and surgical staff rotated monthly the responsibility for admitting charity cases, those patients who had no physician and little financial resources. Doctors who admitted their private patients to Lincoln Hospital rounded on both the public and private patients usually twice a day, once in the morning and again after dinner. (Courtesy of Carolyn Henderson.)

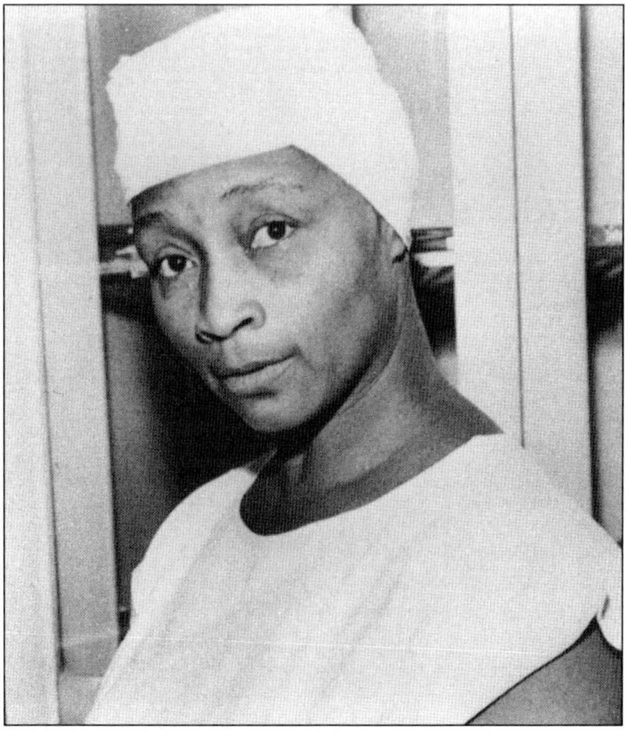

Mrs. Lelia Thompson Miller, supervisor of the operatiing room, ran a tight ship and garnered genuine respect from everyone. She joined the Lincoln Hospital staff in 1950 and retired from Durham County General Hospital in 1981 after more than 30 years of service. Mrs. Miller served as mentor to many student nurses who followed her into careers in surgical nursing. (Courtesy of *The Scalpel*, 1962.)

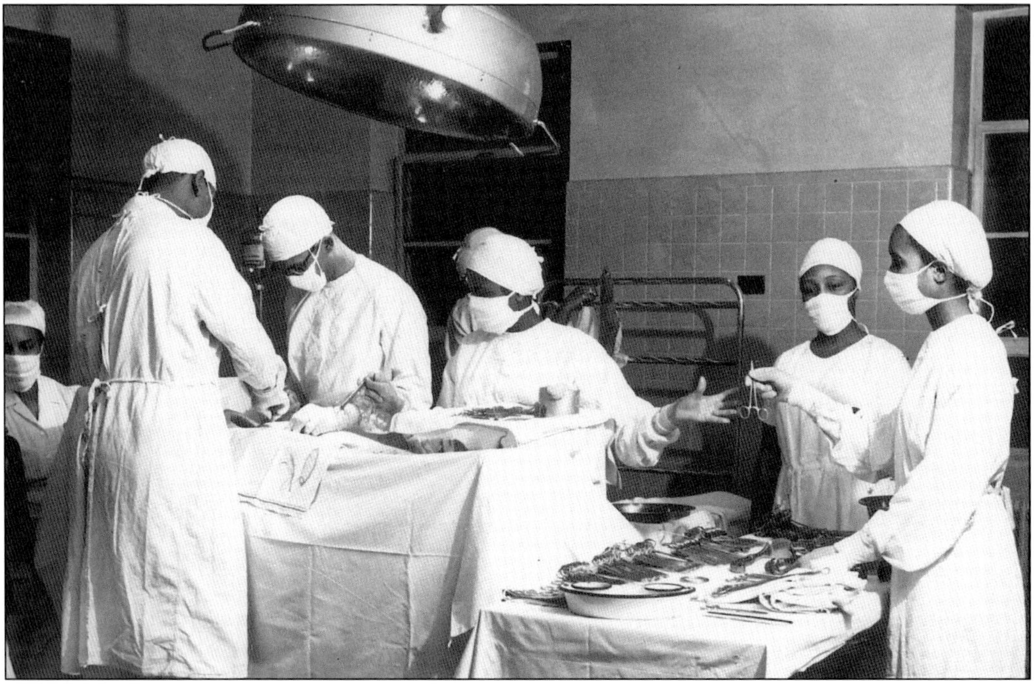

Pictured here are L.B. Thompson Miller, R.N., OR nurse supervisor; Dr. E.L. Bradock, surgeon; Dr. W.W. Adams, assistant surgeon; Louise LeVielle, R.N., anesthetist; Etta Young, R.N., first instrument nurse; and Sylvia McNeil, R.N., second instrument nurse. The operating room was busy with scheduled major and elective surgeries as well as emergency operations. It was an efficient team that worked well together. (Courtesy of Margaret Kennedy Goodwin.)

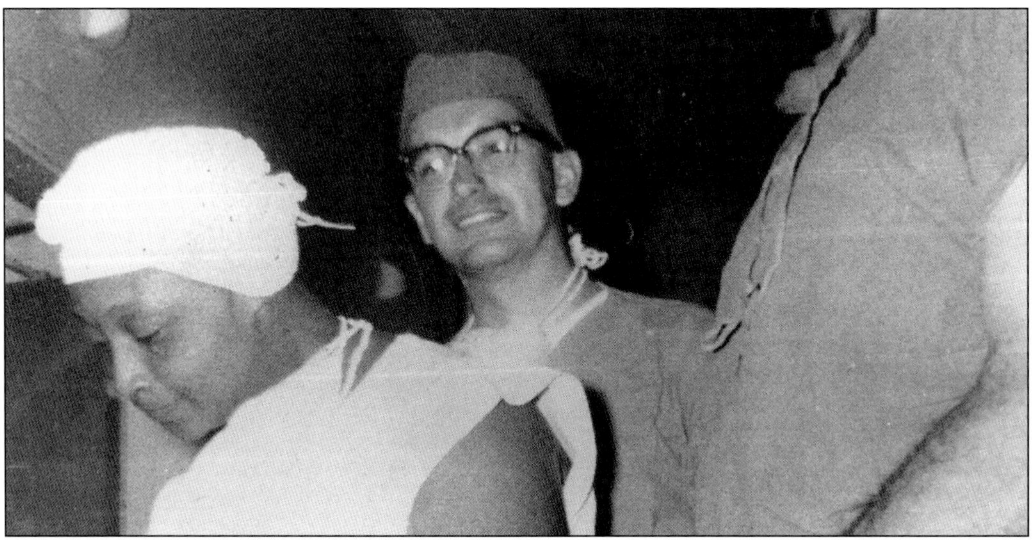

Pictured here is Duke Hospital's orthopedic resident Wayne Venters, M.D., going into surgery with Mrs. Lelia Thompson Miller, R.N. Dr. Venters now practices in Jacksonville, North Carolina. The Duke Departments of Pathology, Radiology, and Surgery rotated residents through Lincoln Hospital until the 1960s when the Departments of Medicine and Pediatrics became involved directly in te teaching programs there. (Courtesy of *The Scalpel*, 1962.)

Mrs. Elizabeth Thorpe, R.N. was head nurse for obstetrics. She was in charge of the delivery suites and scheduling the operating room for elective Cesarean sections. She also served as clinical instructor teaching the nursing students principles of labor and delivery. (Courtesy of *The Scalpel*, 1962.)

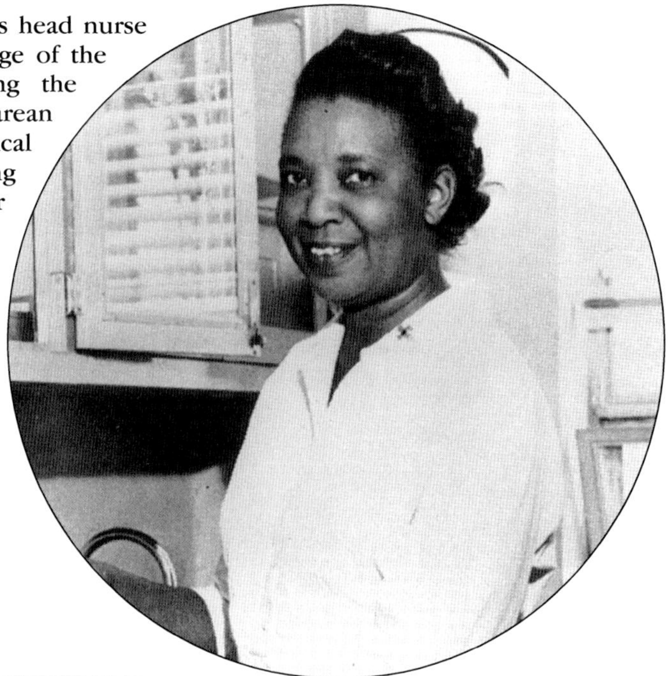

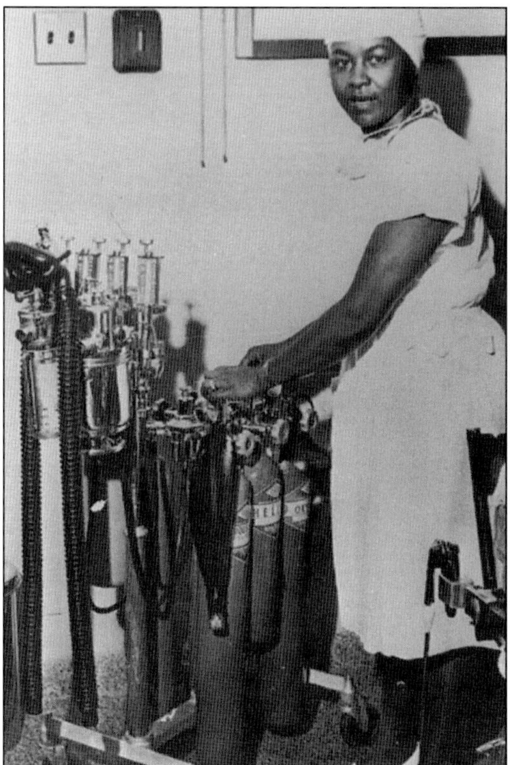

Mrs. Yellock

William Rich responded to the continued pleas of Dr. Max Schiebel for another nurse anesthetist. Prior to Mrs. Georgia Yellock's recruitment, Schiebel and other surgeons would often administer their own anesthesia on patients. As standards of care rose in hospitals around the country, Lincoln Hospital responded with its own cadre of well-trained professionals. (Courtesy of *The Scalpel*, 1963.)

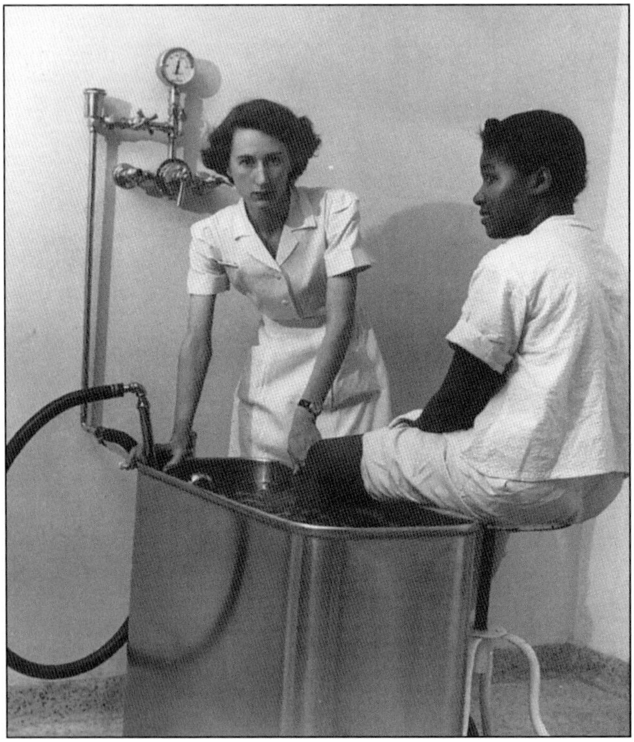

Jean Gordon, P.T., was the first trained physical therapist at Lincoln Hospital. Pictured here *c.* 1953, she was an essential member of the team caring for many of the orthopedic patients after the removal of casts and braces and when injured with sprained ankles and dislocated joints. She also provided water baths, massage, and electrotherapy, including diathermy and ultraviolet lights. (Courtesy of Margaret Kennedy Goodwin.)

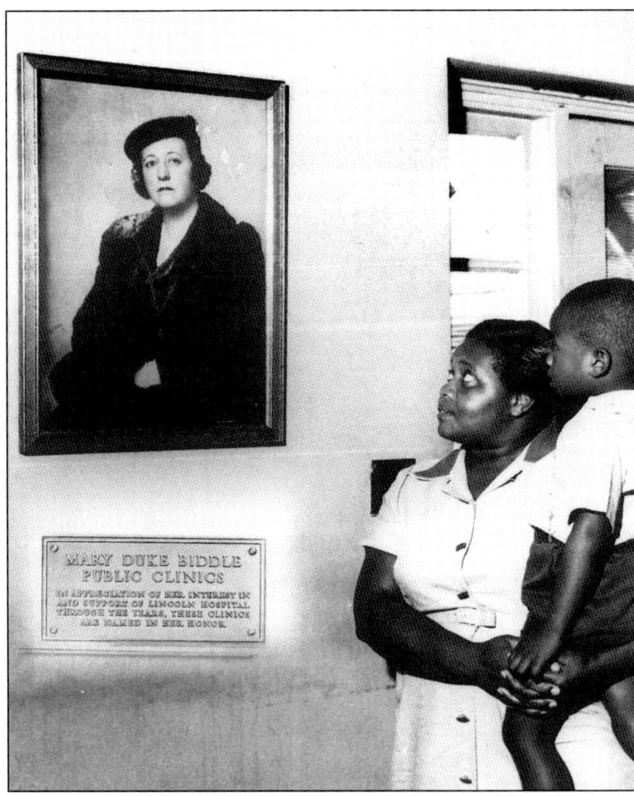

The Lincoln Hospital outpatient clinic was named in honor of Mrs. Mary Duke Biddle, the daughter of Benjamin N. Duke, because of her long-standing devotion to Lincoln Hospital and her regular appearance in the waiting room. Mrs. Biddle would often sit in the outpatient waiting room knitting away while talking to patients asking about their children's progress in school. (Courtesy of Margaret Kennedy Goodwin.)

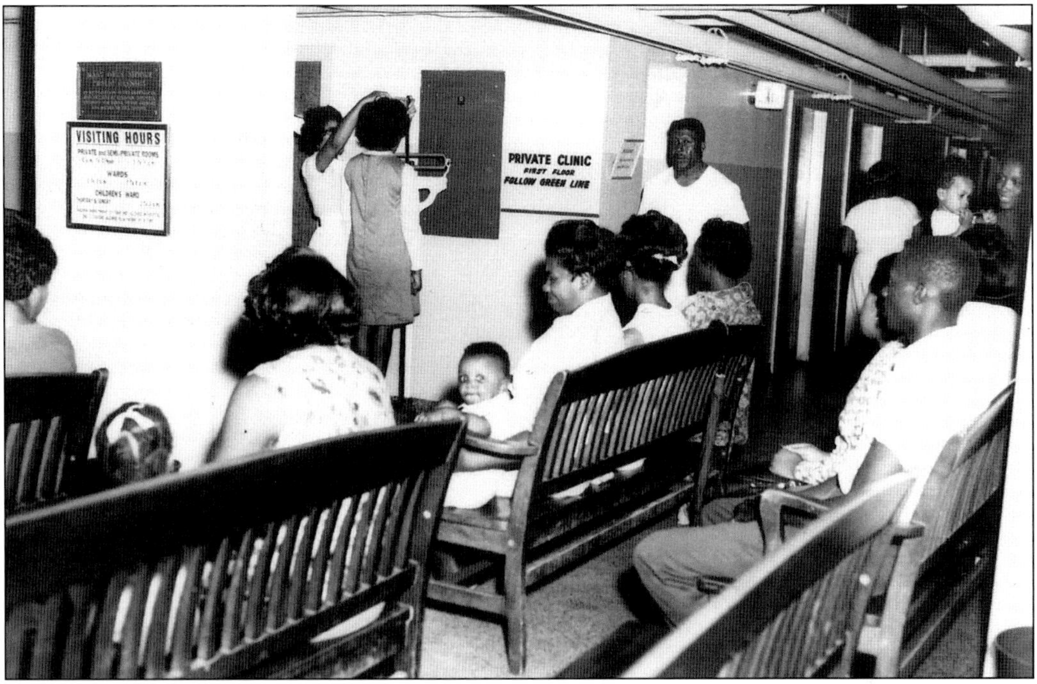

Lincoln Hospital worked closely with the Durham County Health Department offering clinics in tuberculosis and venereal disease prevention. In addition, the clinical services operated sessions devoted to gynecology, orthopedics, general surgery, urology, cancer, medicine, and well-baby care. (Courtesy of Margaret Kennedy Goodwin.)

The full-time radiologists at Watts and Duke Hospitals directed the service at Lincoln Hospital, rotating the responsibility every six months. As such they began their day by reading films at Lincoln Hospital. The arrangement provided Lincoln with qualified supervision, but without on-site expertise. If an emergency arose, someone carried the x-rays to the radiologist-on-call. The same arrangement existed for the supervision of laboratory services. Pictured here, from left to right, are Dr. Robert Reeves, chair of Duke Radiology, and a Duke radiology resident. (Courtesy of *The Scalpel*, 1956.)

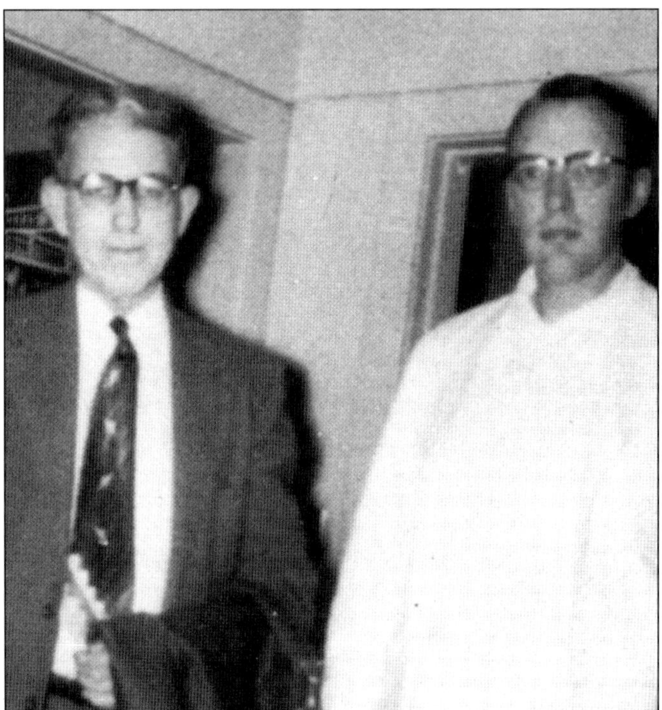

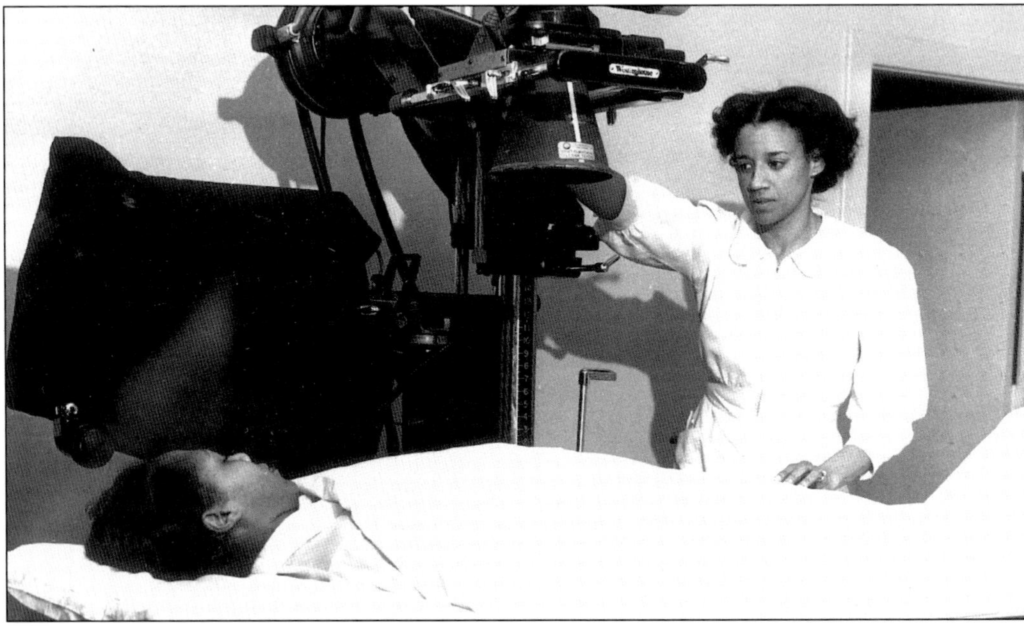

Mrs. Margaret Kennedy Goodwin graduated from Talladega College in 1938 with a major in chemistry. With aspirations for a career in science, she was pulled into Lincoln Hospital by a plea for help running the x-ray department. Margaret Goodwin obtained specialized training at Duke Hospital and at Philadelphia General Hospital and was registered with the American Registry of Radiologic Technicians in 1947. She was the first African American elected to membership in the North Carolina Society of Radiology Technology and the first African American elected president of the group. Mrs. Goodwin continued as director of radiology of the Lincoln Community Health Center until 1982 when she retired with 40 years of service. (Courtesy of Margaret Kennedy Goodwin.)

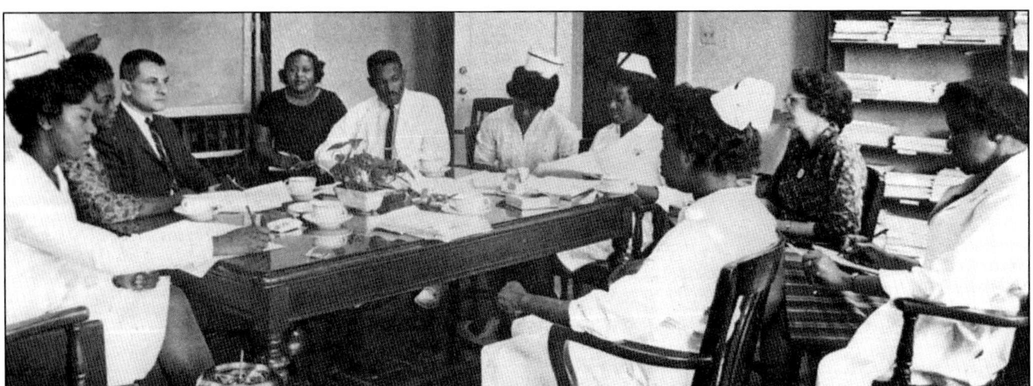

Dr. Max Schiebel, as chief of surgery at Lincoln and Watts Hospitals, met monthly with the Lincoln Hospital nursing and administrative staff to review mortality and morbidity statistics, the incidence of wound infection and post-operative complications, and any other problem that arose. It was this systematic supervision the Duke Endowment endorsed as a means of keeping complications to a minimum. Pictured here is Dr. Havel Cleaver, partner of Dr. Schiebel in general and thoracic surgery, conducting the monthly review. (Courtesy of *The Scalpel*, 1963.)

Four

Physicians and Residency Training

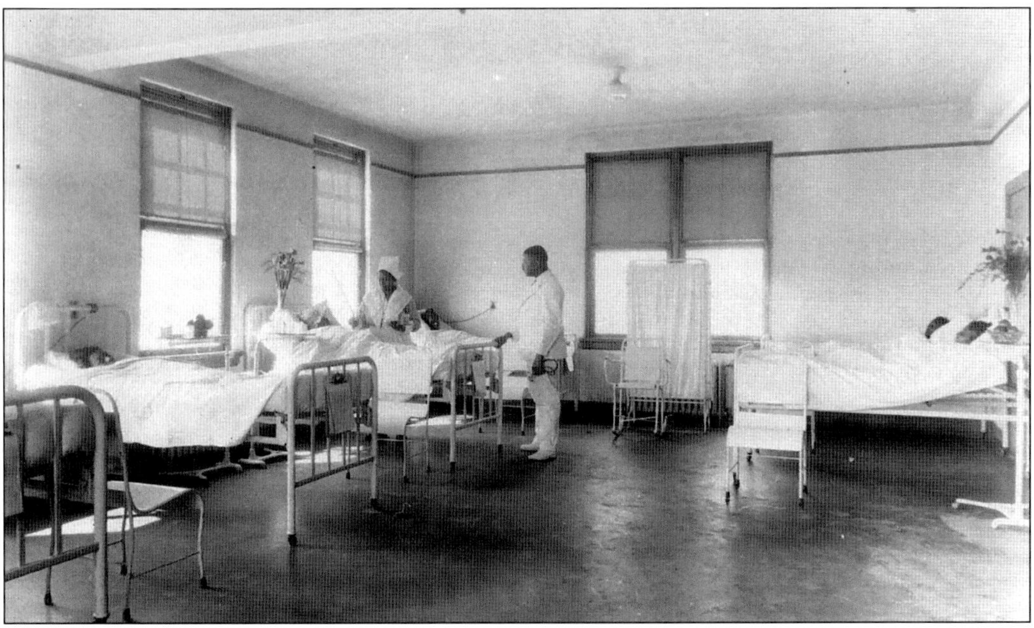

By 1930 Lincoln Hospital was secure in the community. That year 1,556 patients were admitted with 61 percent classified as charity cases. The bed capacity had grown from 86 beds and 7 bassinets to 95 beds and 9 bassinets. The medical staff increased from 53 to 97 physicians with 14 listed as regular. The annual report for the year 1933 reported 5 graduate nurses, 33 student nurses, and 3 interns. (Courtesy of Margaret Kennedy Goodwin.)

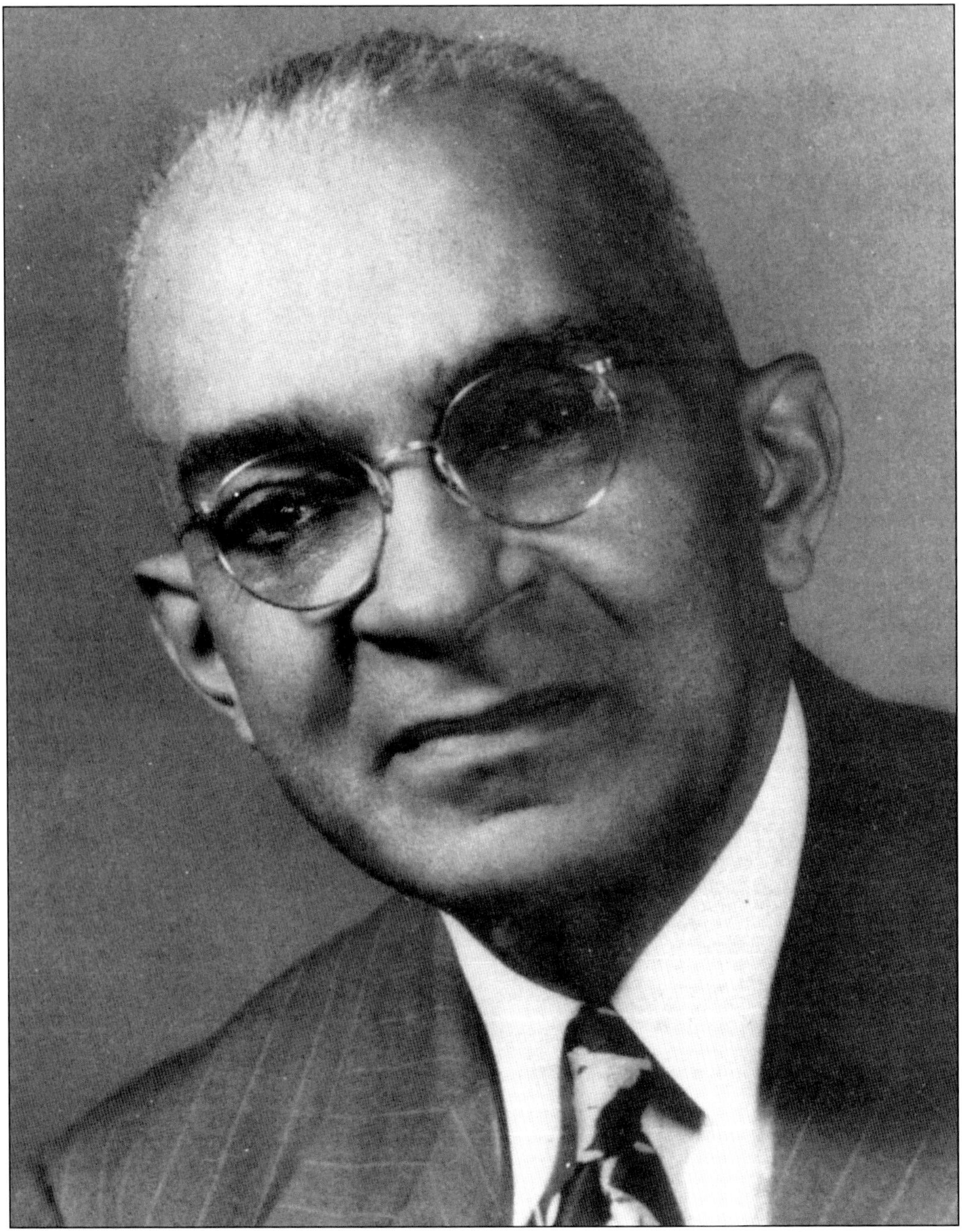

John Walter Vincent Cordice Sr. was born in St. Vincent, British West Indies, in 1881. He studied pharmacy before matriculating into Howard University. An honors student at Howard, Cordice graduated from medical school in 1911 and completed his internship at Freedmen's Hospital in Washington, D.C. He worked as a surgeon in the U.S. Public Health Service in Aurora, North Carolina, before joining the staff of Lincoln Hospital in 1925. Dr. Cordice practiced only general surgery, becoming the hospital's first African-American specialist physician. (Courtesy of *Nightingale*, 1958.)

Joseph Napolean Bonaparte Mills was a graduate of Leonard Medical School of Shaw University. He concentrated his practice in medical gynecology and diseases of women. Dr. J.N. Mills was a very popular physician and developed one of the largest practices in the community. In 1940 and again in 1942 he ran for a seat on the board of county commissioners. Dr. Mills was well-known for his leadership in the medical community serving as a Lincoln Hospital trustee and chief of its medical staff, assistant medical director of the North Carolina Mutual Life Insurance Company, and school physician for the North Carolina College of Negroes. (Courtesy of *The Scalpel*, 1946.)

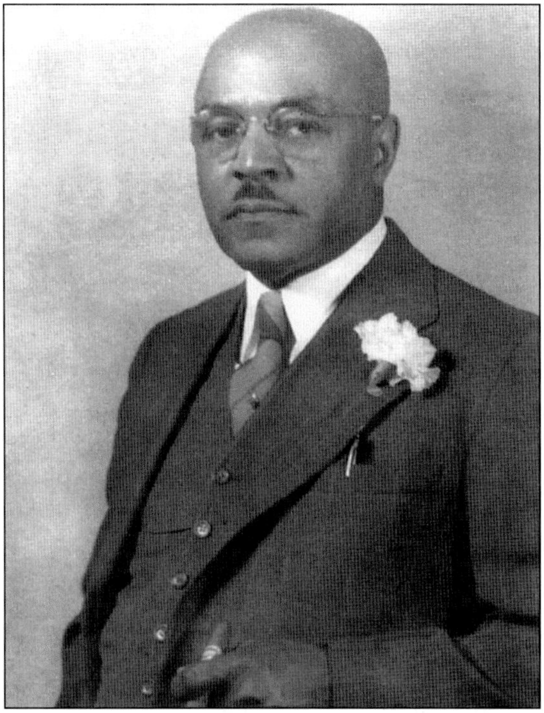

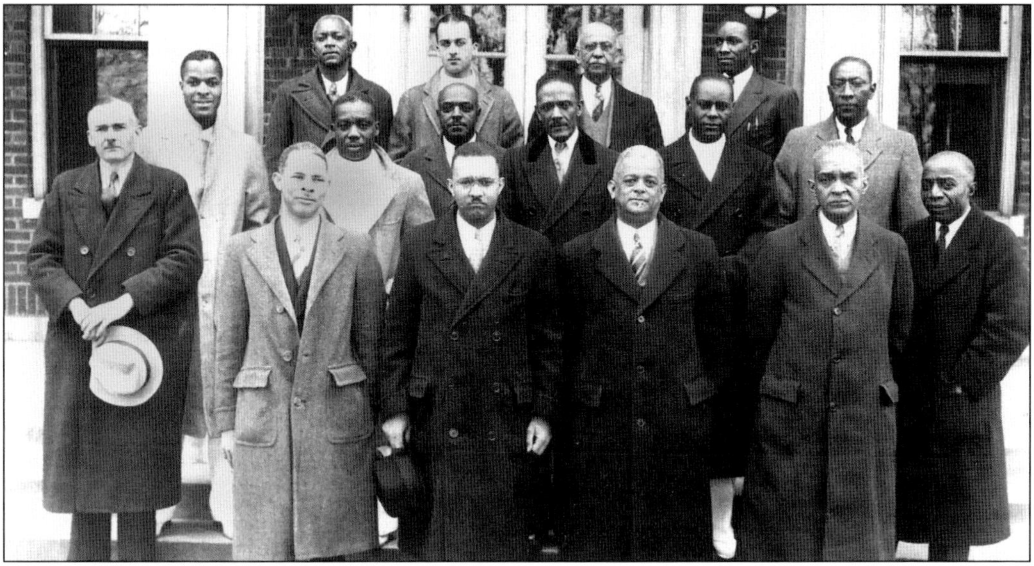

Lincoln Hospital served as a magnet for well-trained African-American physicians. By the late 1930s there were nearly 20 African-American physicians on staff. These physicians worked together with white physicians from Watts and Duke Hospitals to care for patients and teach the interns. Pictured in this *c*. 1938 photograph are, from left to right, (front row) Dr. Ezra Turner, Dr. R.P. Randolph, Dr. J.O. Plummer, and Dr. J.W.V. Cordice; (second row) Dr. E.P. Norris and Dr. J.S. Thompson; (third row) intern, intern, Dr. J.N.B. Mills, Dr. Norman Cordice, intern, and Dr. J.M. Hubbard; (fourth row) Dr. A.S. Hunter, intern, Dr. S.L. Warren, and Dr. W.A. Cleland. (Courtesy of Margaret Kennedy Goodwin.)

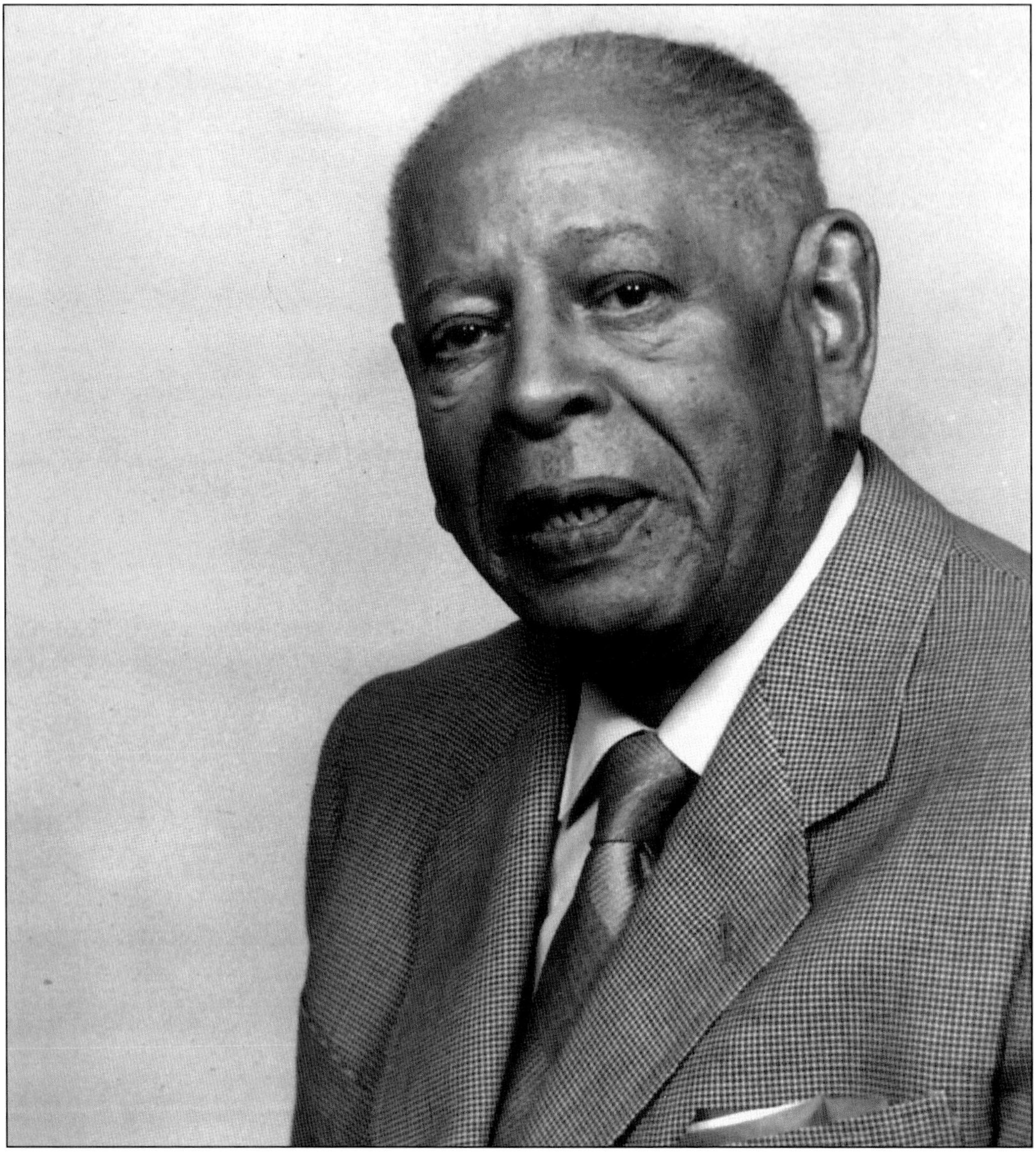

Clyde Donnell was born in 1890 in Greensboro, North Carolina. He earned a B.S. degree in 1907 from A&T College in Greensboro and a B.A. from Howard University in 1911 before entering Harvard medical school, from which he graduated in 1915 near the top of his class. Similar to another African-American classmate at Harvard, Dr. Donnell was refused an internship from every Boston training program. A sympathetic faculty arranged for him to work as a junior house officer in medicine at Boston City Hospital. Dr. Donnell returned to North Carolina, joining Dr. Aaron Moore in general practice in 1917. When Dr. Moore became president of the North Carolina Mutual in 1920, Dr. Donnell filled his position as medical director. Dr. Donnell set as a priority the continuing education of African-American professionals. He founded the Durham Academy of Medicine and served for 32 years as secretary-treasurer of the Old North State Medical Society. In these roles he organized dozens of conferences for practicing physicians in North Carolina and surrounding states. (Courtesy of Charles D. Watts.)

Beginning in 1935, Lincoln Hospital annually hosted the Lincoln Hospital Post-Graduate Clinic. The faculty were physicians from the top medical institutions in the state and the North Carolina State Board of Health. Physicians from around North Carolina attended and when invited, physicians from neighboring states participated. The original committee that organized the post-graduate clinic reflected bi-racial cooperation between Dr. Clyde Donnell and other medical leadership throughout North Carolina. (Courtesy of William A. Cleland.)

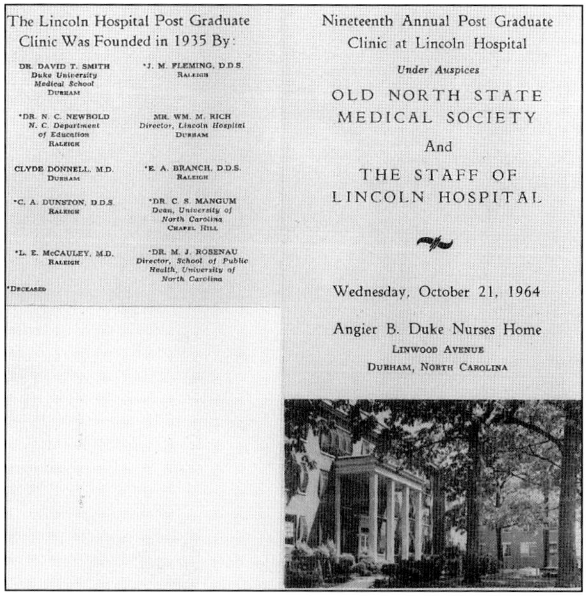

The Lincoln Hospital Post Graduate Clinic Was Founded in 1935 By:

DR. DAVID T. SMITH
Duke University Medical School
DURHAM

*J. M. FLEMING, D.D.S.
RALEIGH

*DR. N. C. NEWBOLD
N. C. Department of Education
RALEIGH

MR. WM. M. RICH
Director, Lincoln Hospital
DURHAM

CLYDE DONNELL, M.D.
DURHAM

*E. A. BRANCH, D.D.S.
RALEIGH

*C. A. DUNSTON, D.D.S.
RALEIGH

*DR. C. S. MANGUM
Dean, University of North Carolina
CHAPEL HILL

*L. E. McCAULEY, M.D.
RALEIGH

*DR. M. J. ROSENAU
Director, School of Public Health, University of North Carolina

*DECEASED

Nineteenth Annual Post Graduate Clinic at Lincoln Hospital

Under Auspices

OLD NORTH STATE MEDICAL SOCIETY

And

THE STAFF OF LINCOLN HOSPITAL

Wednesday, October 21, 1964

Angier B. Duke Nurses Home
LINWOOD AVENUE
DURHAM, NORTH CAROLINA

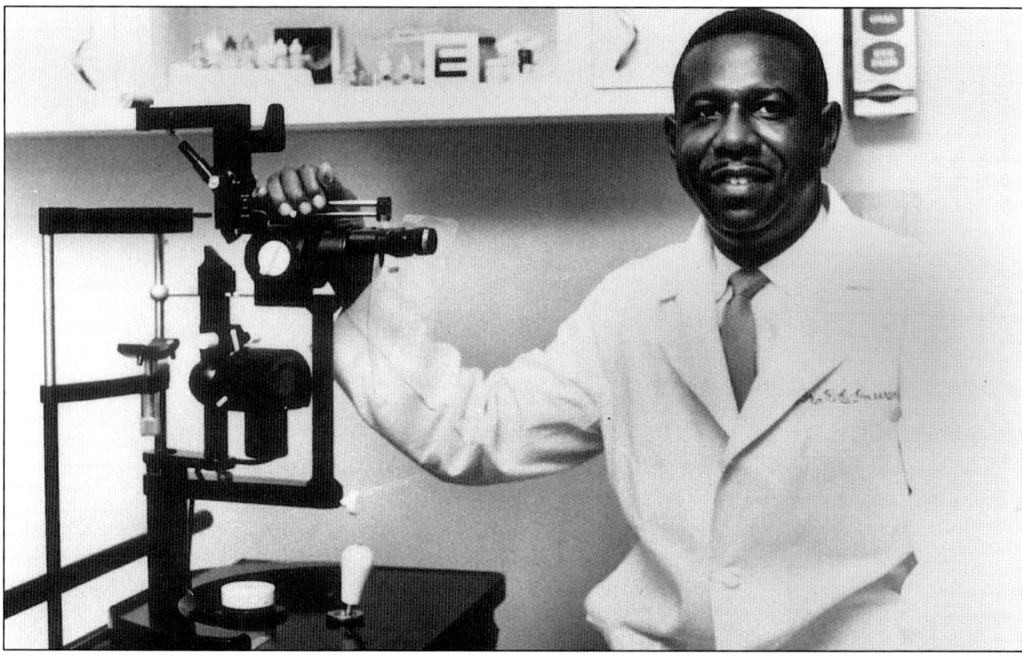

Robert E. Dawson was born in 1918 in Rocky Mount, North Carolina, and grew up in Florence, South Carolina. He graduated from Clark College with honors in 1939 and from Meharry Medical College with honors in 1943. World War II provided Dr. Dawson increased opportunities for training. He spent three years at Homer G. Phillips in St. Louis as a resident in ophthalmology and in ear, nose, and throat surgery. He moved to Durham in 1946 where he opened a private practice and worked with Dr. Banks Anderson Sr. at Duke Hospital. For many years he precepted Duke ophthalmology residents at Duke Hospital, Lincoln Hospital, and in his office practice. (Courtesy of Margaret Kennedy Goodwin and photographer Nat Purefoy.)

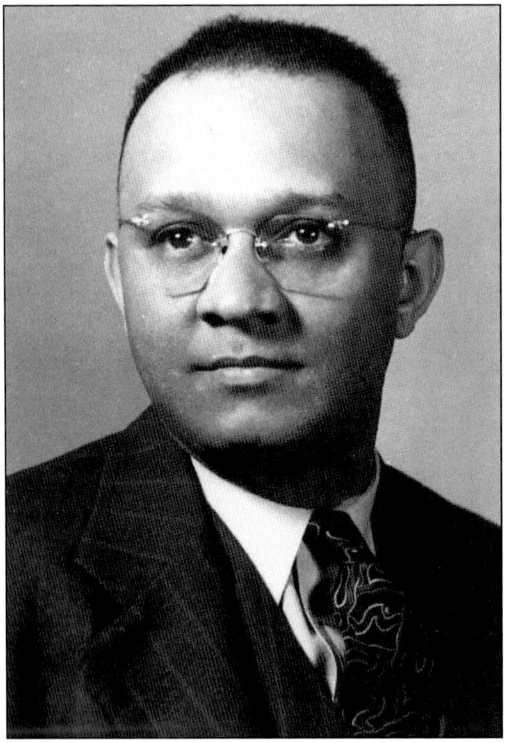

Robert P. Randolph joined the staff after completing an internship at Lincoln Hospital in 1935. Dr. Randolph was one of the earliest African-American physicians in Durham to concentrate his practice exclusively in internal medicine. He was respected widely for his thorough approach to the patient. In 1951 he requested clinical privileges to see patients in the Duke Hospital outpatient clinic that he did weekly for many years. Dr. Randolph married Emma Elizabeth Lee RN, a graduate of Tuskegee Institute's nursing program, who served as operating room supervisor at Lincoln Hospital beginning in 1935, and later as a nurse at North Carolina College. (Courtesy of Carolyn Henderson.)

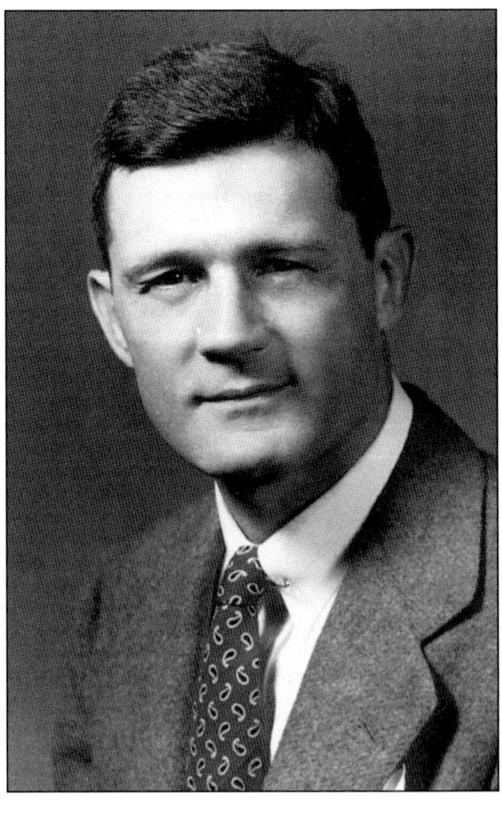

H. Max Schiebel was born in 1909 in Baltimore, Maryland. He graduated from Johns Hopkins University with honors in 1929 and Johns Hopkins University School of Medicine with honors in 1933. After finishing his residency training in surgery at Duke in 1939, the Duke Hospital administrator asked him to perform elective surgery at Lincoln Hospital on African-American patients waiting to be admitted to Duke Hospital. From 1940 through 1943 he performed 295 surgeries at Lincoln Hospital. Dr. Schiebel earned the respect of the African-American physicians and was asked to assume the role of chief of surgery, a position he held from 1944 to 1973. (Courtesy of Carolyn Henderson.)

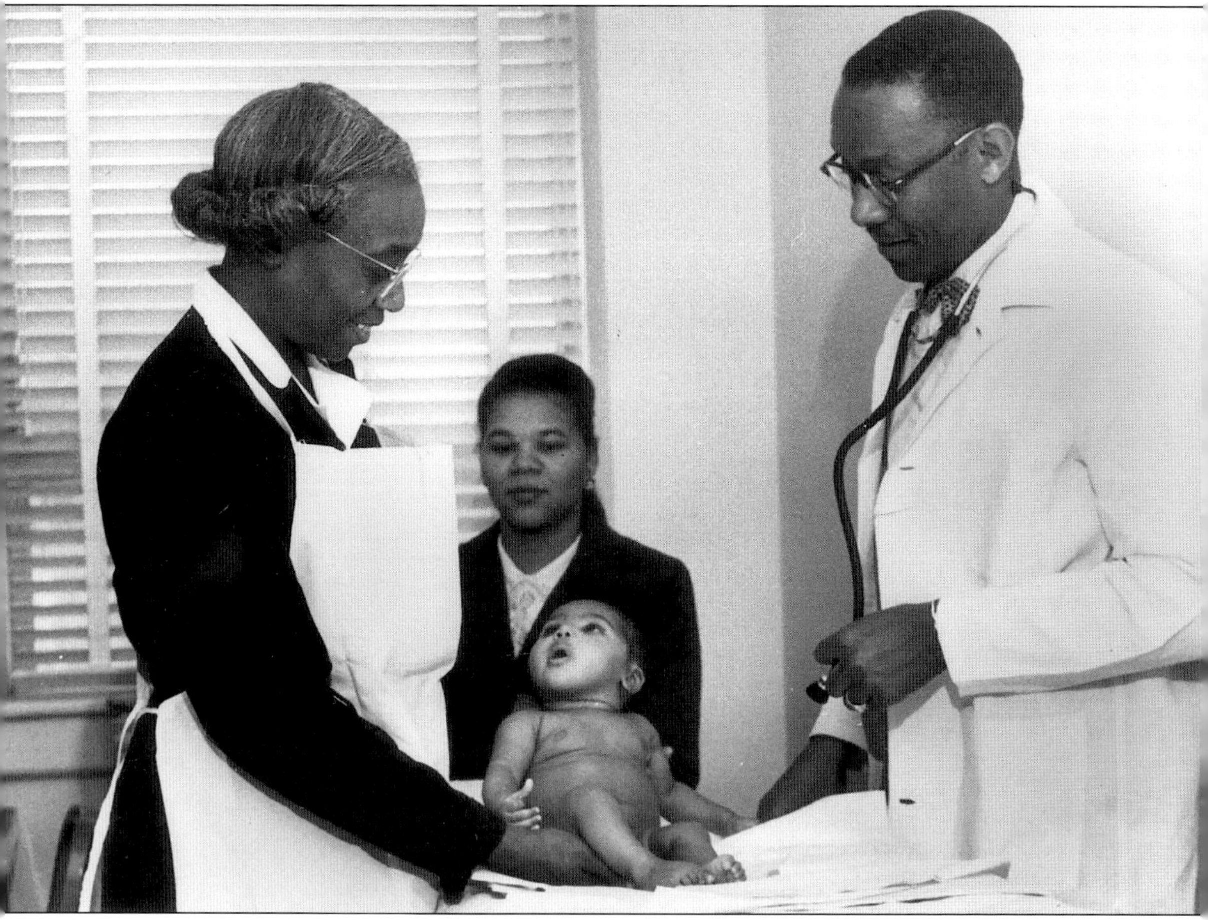

William A. Cleland was born in 1907 in Hickory, North Carolina and grew up in Durham where his father served as minister of St. Joseph's A.M.E. Church. After finishing high school, he worked in New Jersey for 14 months before returning to complete his education at Kittrell College. Cleland graduated from Howard University and then its School of Medicine in 1933 before doing an internship at Freedmen's Hospital. With support from Dean Wilburt Davison of Duke medical school and Dr. Clyde Donnell, in 1936, Dr. Cleland obtained a Julius Rosenwald Fund fellowship for training in pediatrics at New York University. Upon his return Dr. Cleland was the first African-American pediatrician in Durham. He assumed responsibility for the well-baby clinic at Lincoln Hospital. Pictured from left to right are Nora T. Allen, R.N., Dorothy Prince, and Dr. Cleland. (Courtesy of William A. Cleland and *Durham Herald-Sun*.)

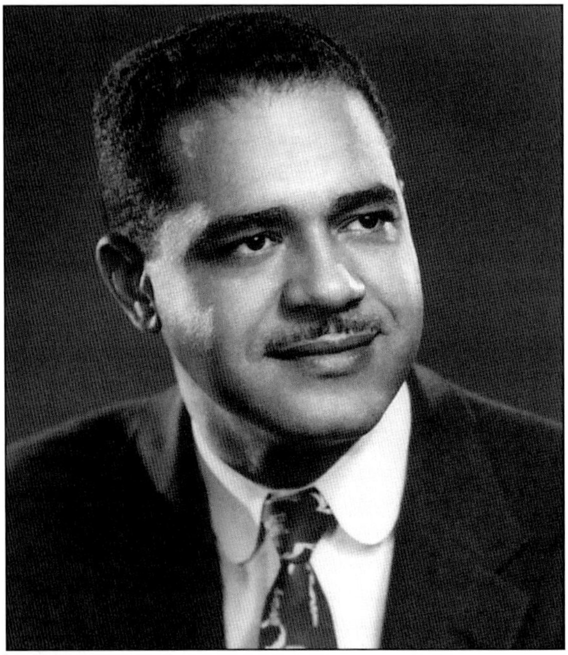

Charles D. Watts was born in 1917 in Atlanta, Georgia. He attended Atlanta University Laboratory High School, which was designed to prepare exceptional students for college. He graduated with honors and a scholarship to college. After four years at Morehouse College, Watts entered Howard University Medical School and graduated in 1943. He completed his surgery residency under the world-renowned Dr. Charles Drew at Freedmen's Hospital, and he then served as an instructor on the faculty at Howard. In 1950 Dr. Watts became a diplomat of the American Board of Surgery, the first African-American surgeon in North Carolina certified by the specialty board. (Courtesy of Charles D. Watts.)

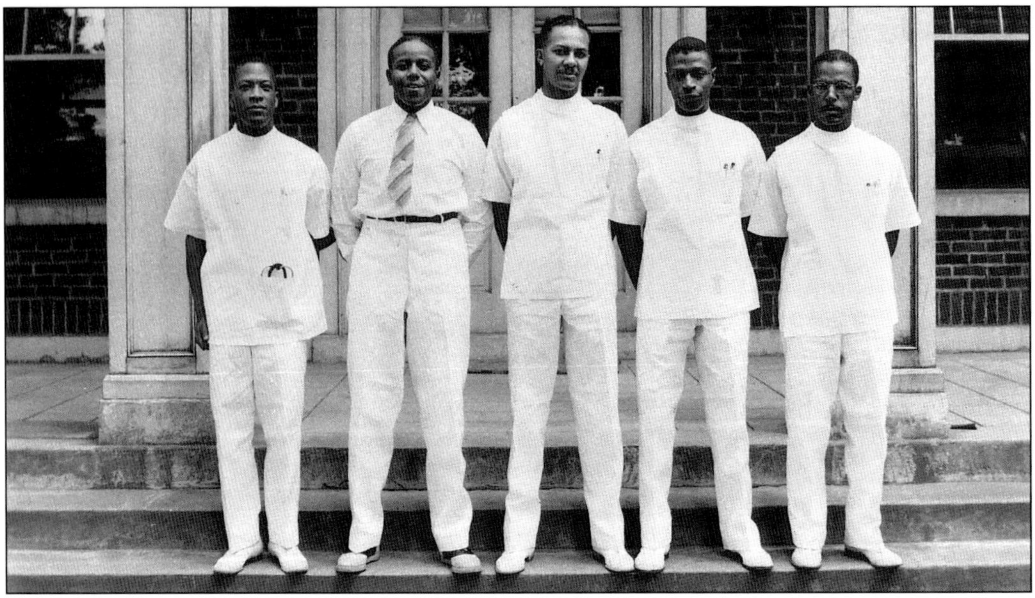

Lincoln Hospital was accredited by the American Medical Association for internship training in 1925 and by the American College of Surgeons for surgical residency training in October 1933. Under the leadership of Dr. Max Schiebel, Lincoln Hospital earned full accreditation for a four-year surgical residency leading to board certification in 1950. With very few internship and residency positions available for African Americans in hospitals throughout the country, those offered at Lincoln Hospital met a national demand for residency training. Pictured here in 1938 is Dr. Leroy Swift, surgery resident, standing second from the left. The interns that year were Drs. Leroy W. Upperman Jr, Joseph A. Sylvester, William A. Atkinson, and Albert E. Nesbitt. (Courtesy of Margaret Kennedy Goodwin.)

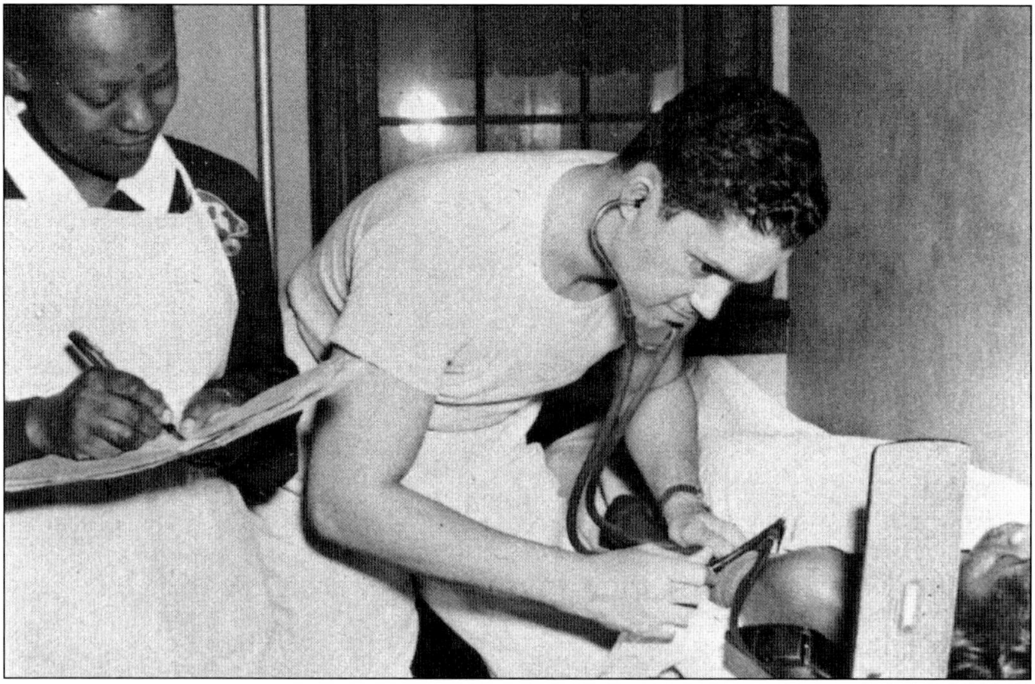

Dr. William Henry Bruce was chief resident at Lincoln Hospital in 1948. After finishing his residency, he completed a fellowship in OB-Gyn at the Margaret Hague Maternity Hospital in Jersey City, New Jersey from 1949-1950. He then moved to Winston-Salem where he engaged in the specialty practice of obstetrics and gynecology. (Courtesy of *The Scalpel*, 1948.)

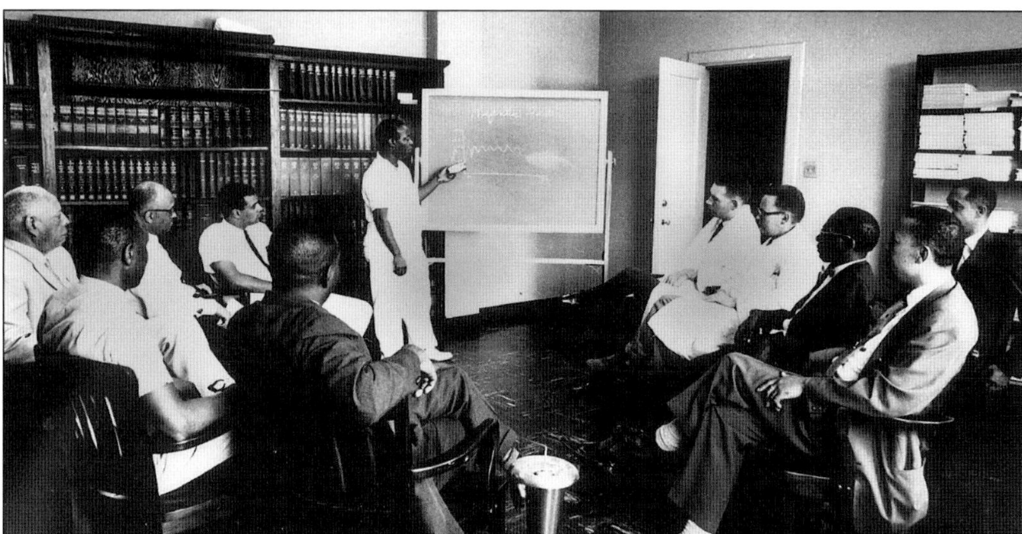

Every week the medical staff assembled for grand rounds. A lecture usually was given by one of the residents. This was a time of instruction and dialogue between the residents and staff physicians at Lincoln Hospital, many of whom held busy clinical practices at Watts and Duke Hospitals, as well as the University of North Carolina–Chapel Hill. (Courtesy of Margaret Kennedy Goodwin.)

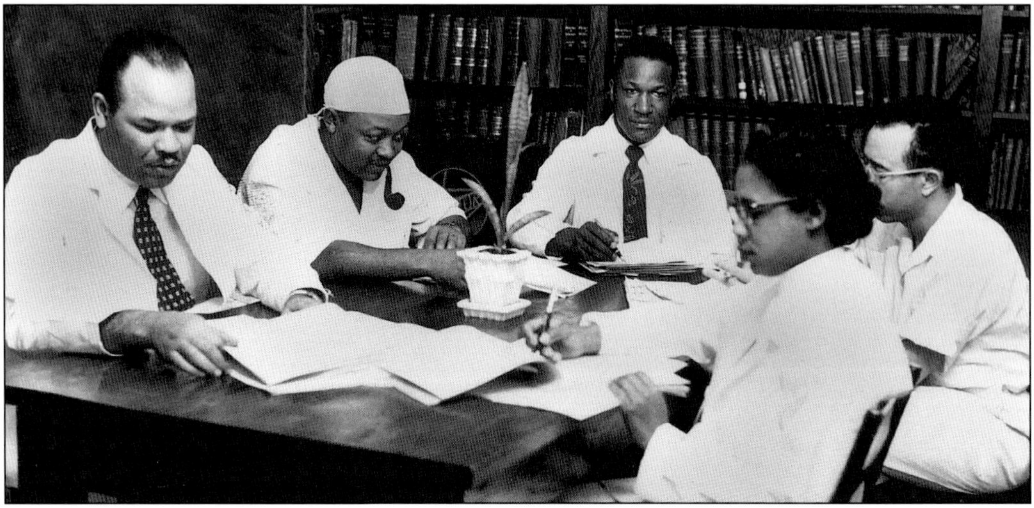

To meet accreditation standards, the medical library had to be accessible to the residents and include up-to-date medical journals and textbooks. Dean Wilburt Davison of Duke medical school donated journals and textbooks. Contributions also came in from members of the medical staff. The library served as a place of study and also the location for monthly meetings of the medical staff and board of trustees. (Courtesy of Margaret Kennedy Goodwin.)

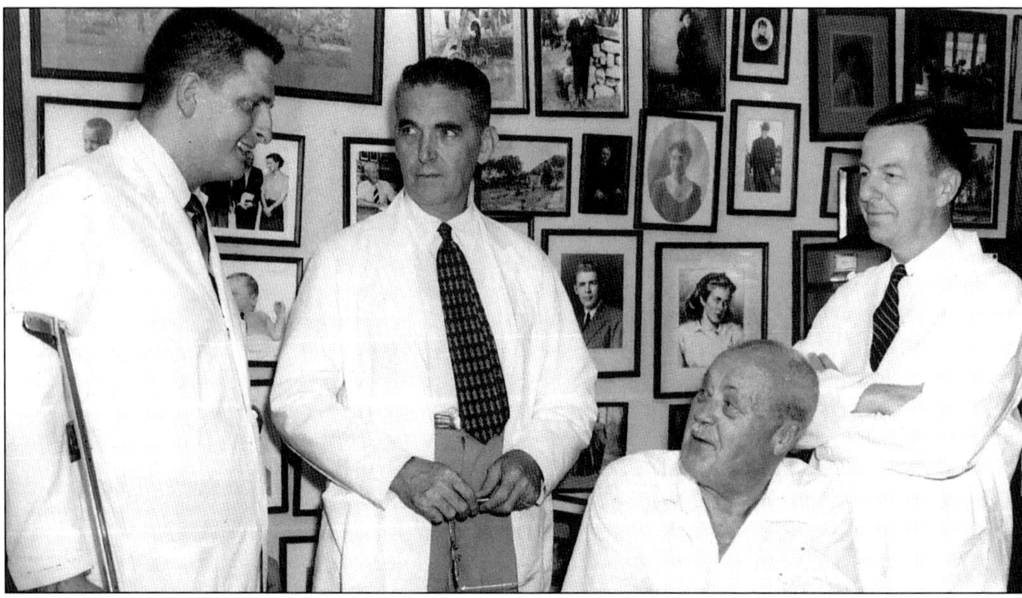

After completing medical school at Duke University and orthopedic residency training at Johns Hopkins Hospital, Dr. Lenox Baker Sr. returned to Duke in 1937 as chief of orthopedic surgery. He expanded North Carolina's Crippled Children's Program, which in 1938 provided over 1,530 days of care to children at Lincoln Hospital with funding from the state and federal governments. From 1939 through 1943, Dr. Baker performed 82 orthopedic operations and procedures at Lincoln Hospital. He also rotated Duke orthopedic residents through Lincoln. Pictured, from left to right, are a Duke orthopedic resident, Dr. Lenox Baker Sr., Dean Wilburt Davison, and Dr. James Semans. (Courtesy of Robert F. Baker.)

Dr. Everett Bugg, left, completed his orthopedic residency at Johns Hopkins Hospital before establishing a private practice in Durham. Dr. Ralph Coonrad, right, grew up as the son of missionaries in China. He completed his orthopedics residency at Duke Hospital and joined Dr. Bugg in practice. As partners, they developed a large clinical service at Lincoln Hospital, seeing, on average, 18 inpatients a day. In addition, as Duke faculty and staff of Lincoln Hospital, they helped train surgery and orthopedic residents at Lincoln. (Courtesy of Ralph Coonrad.)

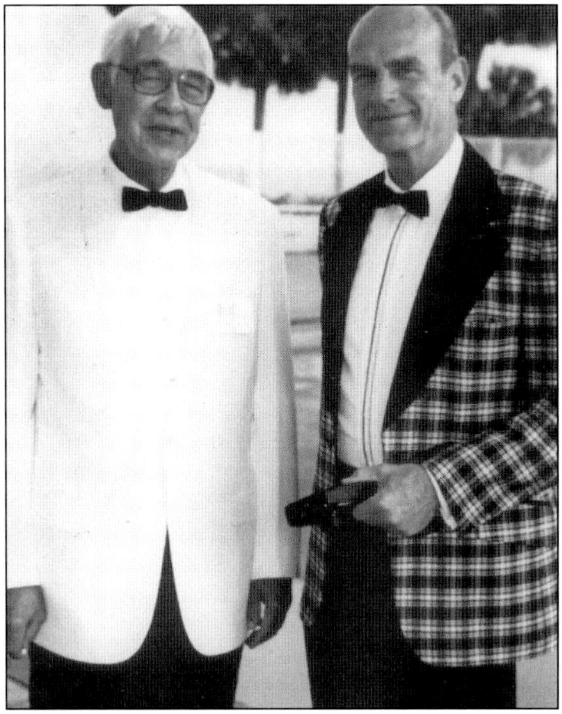

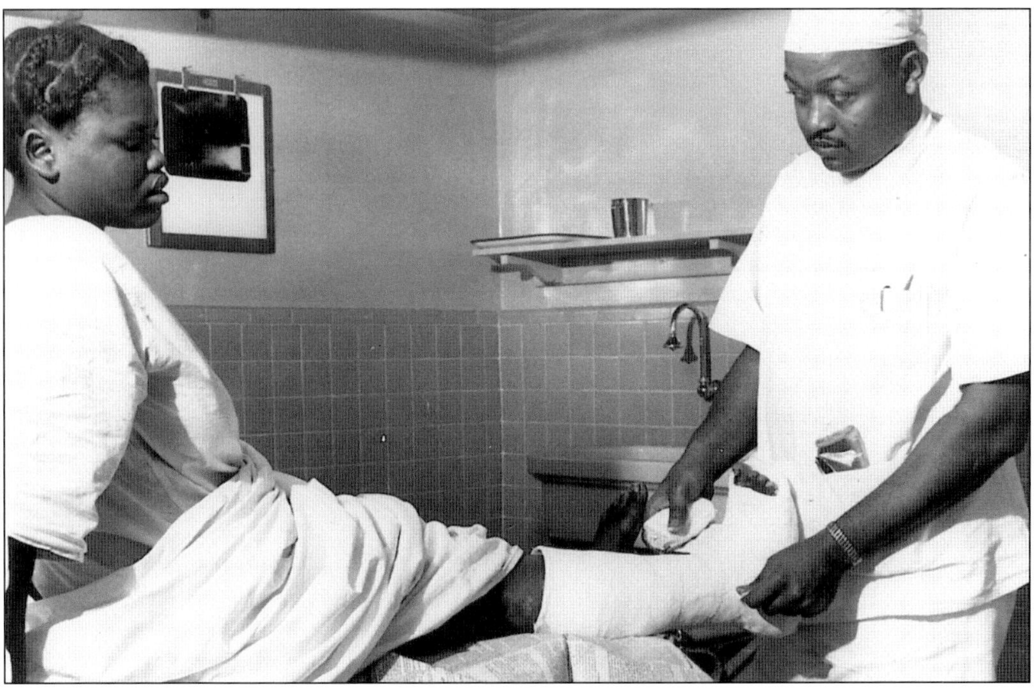

Dr. Elroy Young completed his general surgery internship and residency at Lincoln Hospital and requested further training in orthopedics. He continued on under the direction of Dr. Everett Bugg and Dr. Ralph Coonrad. Dr. Young is remembered as the first African-American orthopedic resident at Lincoln Hospital. (Courtesy of Margaret Kennedy Goodwin.)

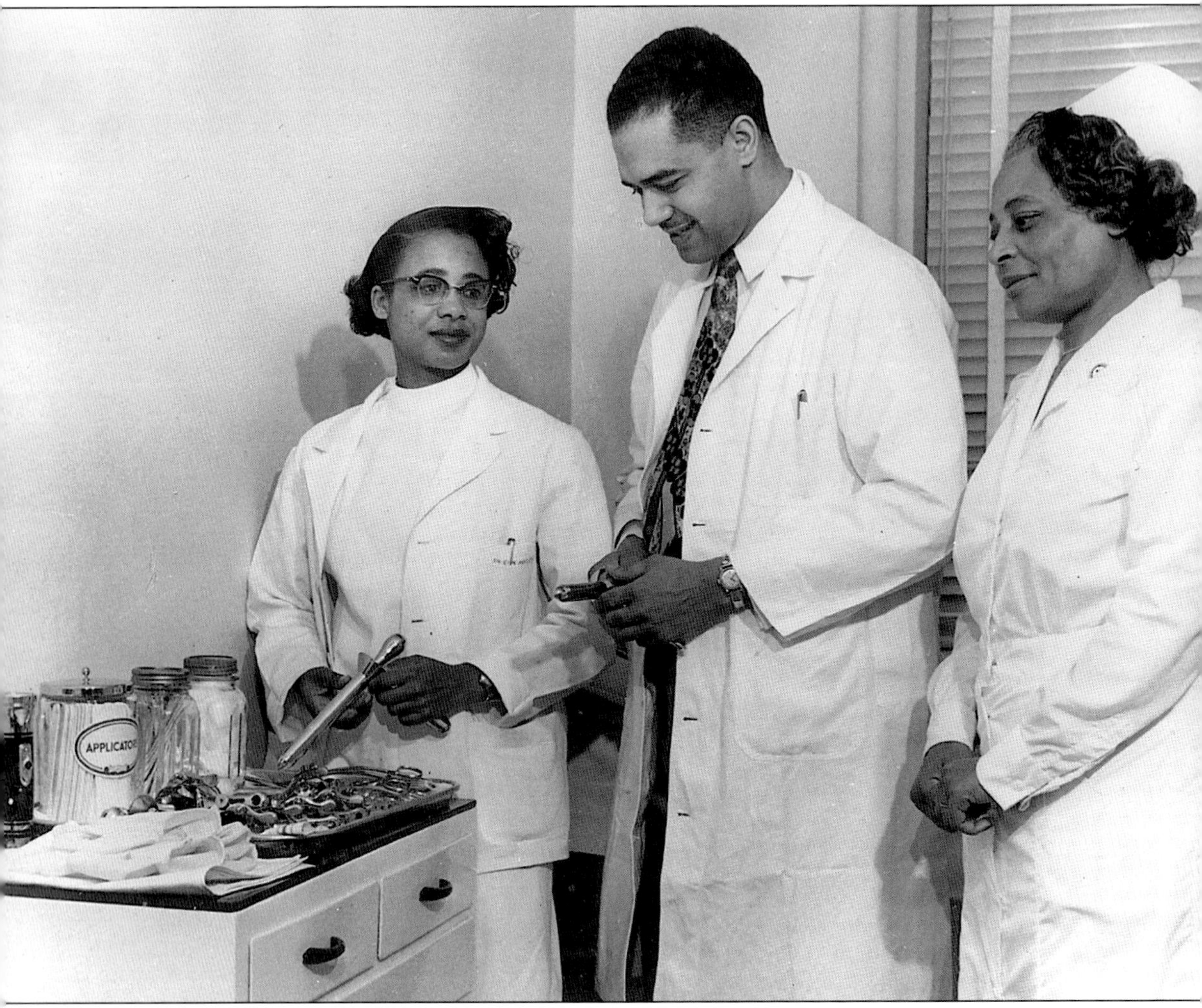

The surgery residents had to perform a minimum number of major and minor operations and follow patients in the clinic. The surgery program enabled residents to be board eligible with letters of recommendations by board-certified surgeons who included Dr. Charles Watts, Dr. Max Schiebel, Dr. Havel Cleaver, Dr. Everett Bugg, and Dr. Ralph Coonrad. Pictured in the outpatient clinic are Catherin McCottry, MD, surgery resident (left), Dr. Charles Watts (middle), and Eugenia Cordice, R.N. (right). (Courtesy of Charles D. Watts.)

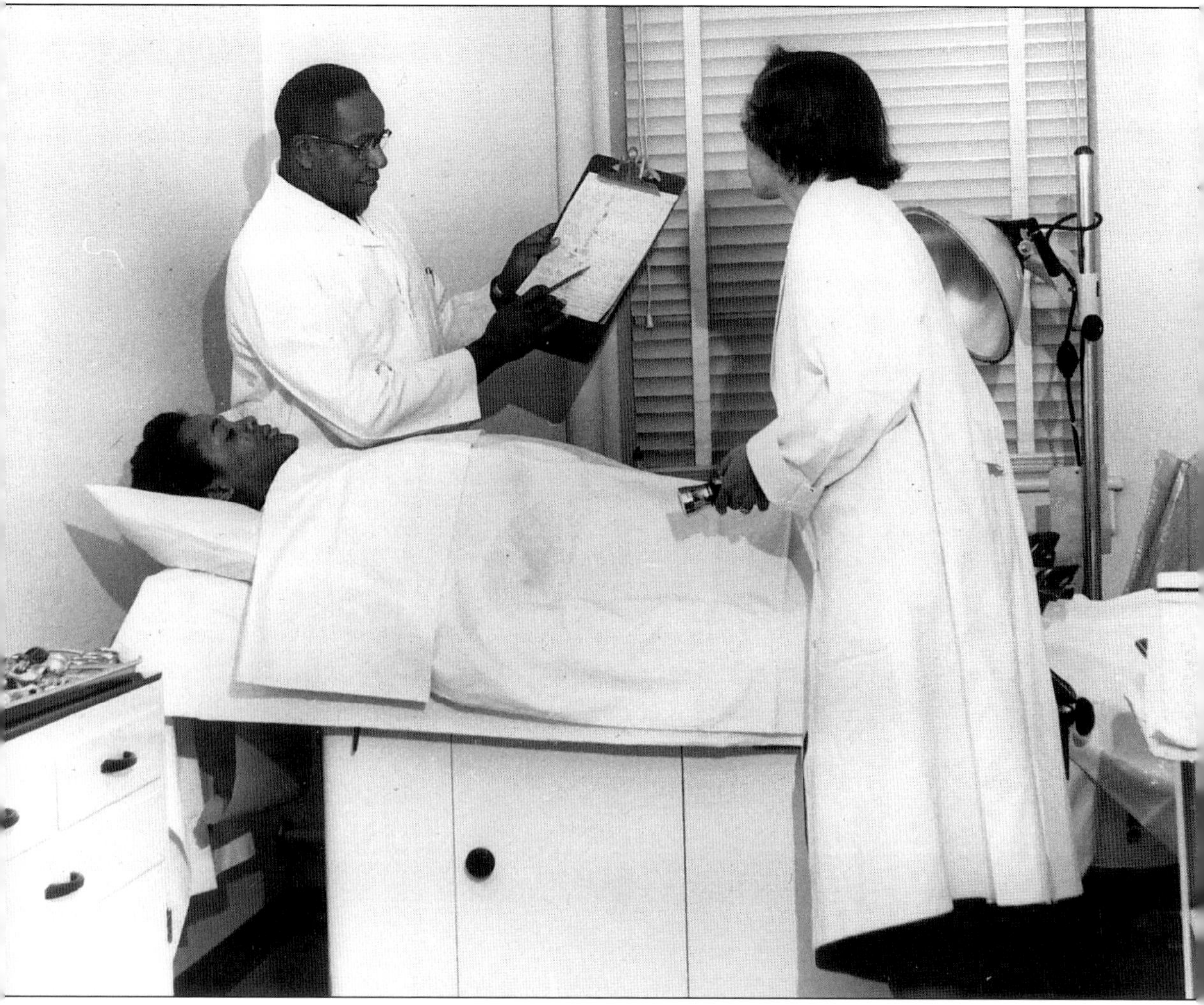

Dr. Leroy Swift completed his college and medical school education at Howard University and interned at Homer G. Phillips Hospital in St. Louis, Missouri. After residency in 1938, Dr. Swift completed training in ob-gyn under Dr. Eleanor Easley and Dr. Richard L. Pearce and became the first African-American resident at Lincoln Hospital to be board certified in ob-gyn. He was elected a fellow of the International College of Surgeons and a member of the American College of Abdominal Surgery. (Courtesy of Margaret Kennedy Goodwin.)

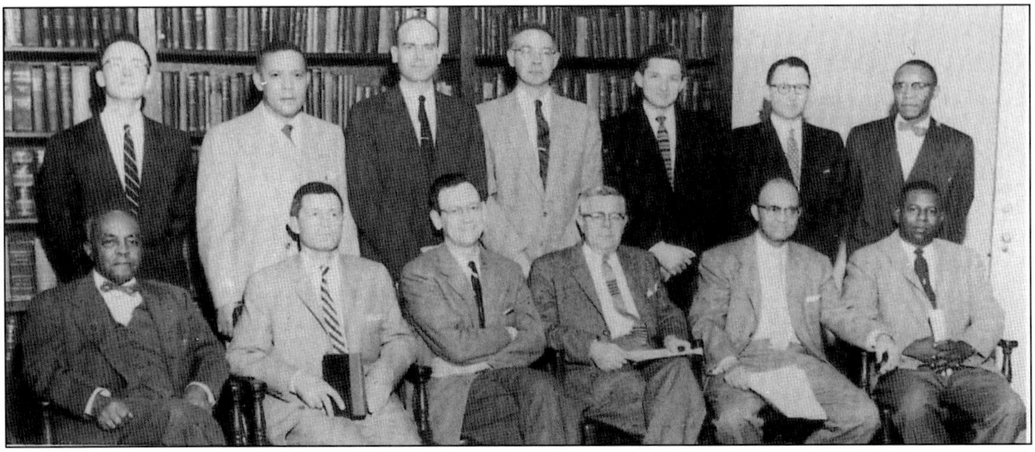

Lincoln Hospital had a bi-racial medical staff; members are pictured, from left to right, as follows: (standing) Drs. H.D. Lockhart, D.B. Cooke, R.W. Coonrad, E.I. Bugg, Jack Hughes, H.D. Cleaver, and W.A. Cleland; (seated) Drs. J.N. Mills, H.M. Schiebel, J.P. McCracken, I.E. Harris, R.P. Randolph, and R.E. Dawson. Those not pictured are Drs. J.W.V Cordice, C.D. Watts, C.D. Grandy, G.M. Carver, Louis Roberts, L.R. Swift, John Glasson, B.F. Fetter, R.J. Reeves, A.S. Hunter, J.E. Campbell, N. Cordice, and W.N. Ricketts. (Courtesy of *The Scalpel*, 1957.)

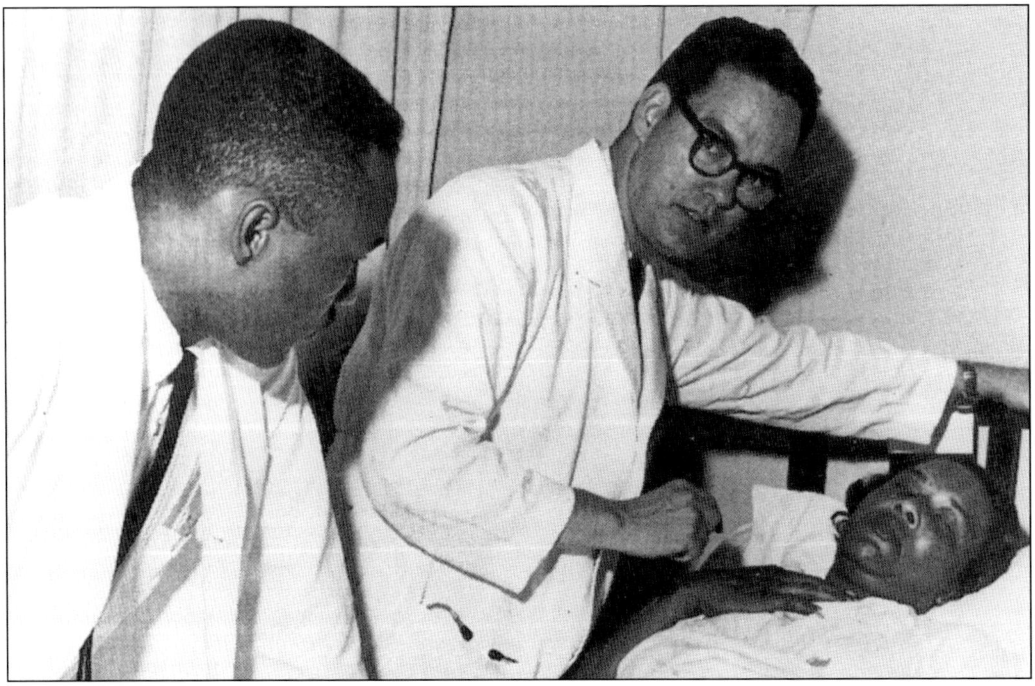

The medical and surgical staff of Lincoln Hospital spent time teaching the residents on daily ward rounds, in the operating room, and during conferences. In addition to bedside instruction, interns and residents were required to rotate through the radiology department and the laboratory department where they read x-rays and observed autopsies most often under the direction of physicians on staff at Watts and Duke Hospitals. (Courtesy of *The Scalpel*, 1963.)

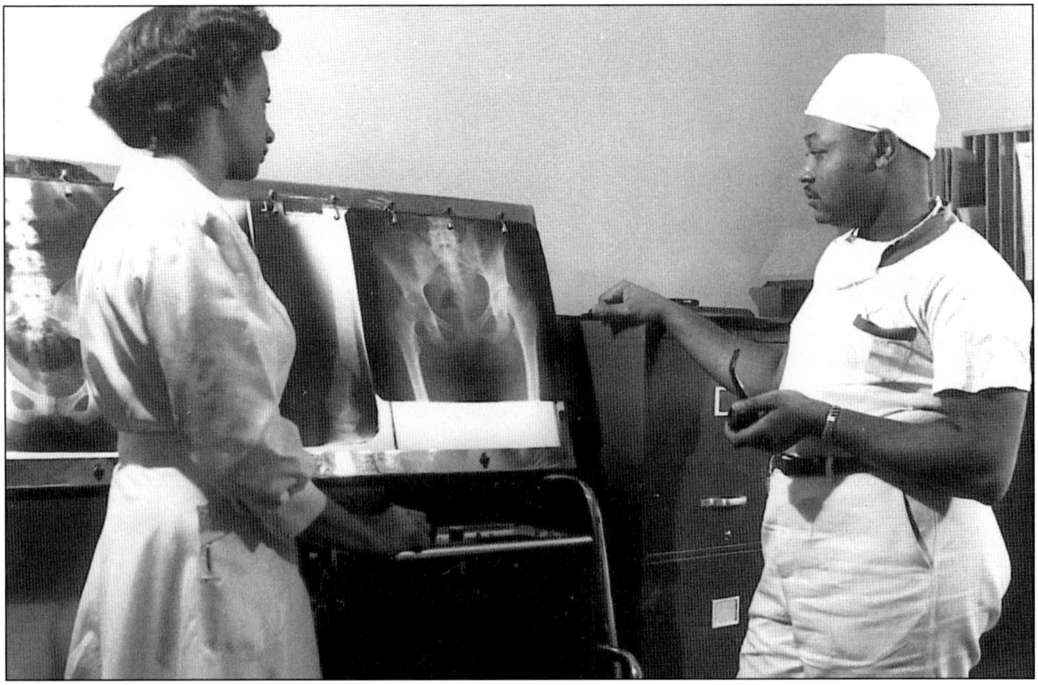

Similar to hospitals throughout the country, Lincoln Hospital's surgery residents often reviewed x-rays before the attending physician arrived since many had busy clinical practices away from the hospital. As head radiology technician, Mrs. Margaret Kennedy Goodwin took nearly all the x-rays of patients. From left to right are Mrs. Margaret Goodwin and Dr. Elroy Young. (Courtesy of Margaret Kennedy Goodwin.)

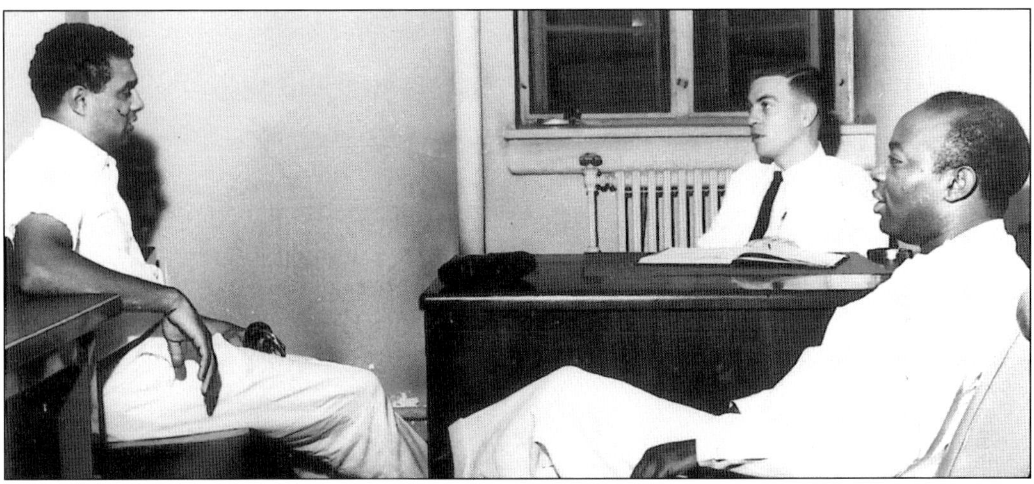

The Lincoln Hospital 3-Year Internal Medicine Residency Program was the idea of Dr. J.B. Johnson, chair of medicine at Howard University. Dr. Robert Dawson and Dr. Charles Watts, at Dr. Johnson's suggestion, asked Dr. Eugene Stead, chair of medicine at Duke medical school, to establish and oversee the new program. Dr. Stead approved the proposal and raised grant funds to cover the salaries of the residents and a full-time director of medical education. Pictured here are Duke and Lincoln Hospital residents discussing a patient's case. (Courtesy of Margaret Kennedy Goodwin.)

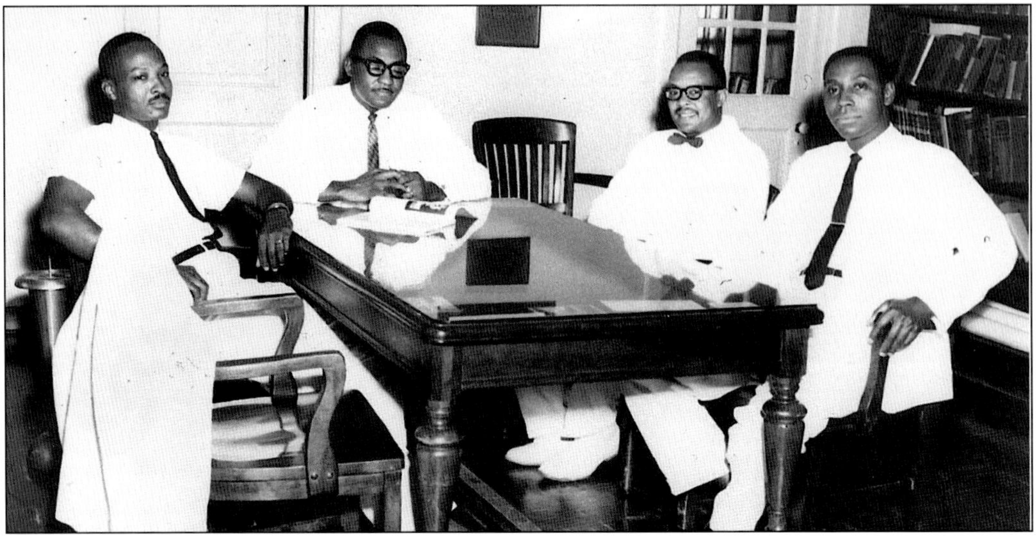

Seated in this *c.* 1964 photograph, from left to right, are Dr. Charles Johnson (medicine), Dr. Charles L. Curry (medicine), Dr. Clinton Battle (surgery), and Dr. Luther White Jr. (surgery). Dr. Curry and then Dr. Johnson, both graduates of Howard University School of Medicine, were the first two residents recruited into the Lincoln Hospital Internal Medicine Residency Program. (Courtesy of Margaret Kennedy Goodwin and photographer Claude Burthey.)

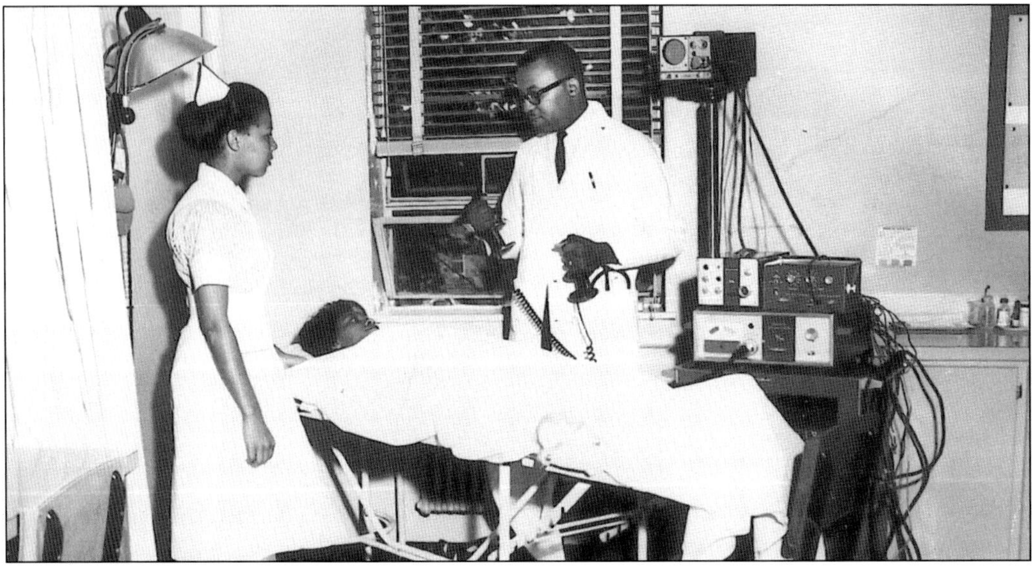

After finishing his residency in internal medicine at Lincoln Hospital, Dr. Charles Curry completed a fellowship in cardiology at the Duke–Veterans Administration Hospital. He returned to Lincoln as director of medical education where he oversaw the residency programs and practiced medicine. Shortly thereafter, he was recruited back to Howard as the J.B. Johnson professor of cardiology. In 1998, Dr. Curry was named the "Outstanding Physician of the Year" by the American Heart Association. Pictured here in this *c.* 1966 photo with Dr. Curry is student nurse Saundra Obie. (Courtesy of Margaret Kennedy Goodwin and photographer Claude Burthey.)

Donald T. Moore graduated from Morehouse College in 1954 and from Meharry Medical College with honors in 1958. After completing a general surgery residency, Dr. Moore concentrated on ob-gyn with further training at Meharry's Hubbard Hospital. In 1965 he completed a fellowship in gyn-endocrinology at Duke Hospital. From there Dr. Moore joined the staff of Lincoln Hospital. He maintained a busy clinical practice at Lincoln even after joining the Duke ob-gyn faculty in 1970. (Courtesy of Robert E. Dawson.)

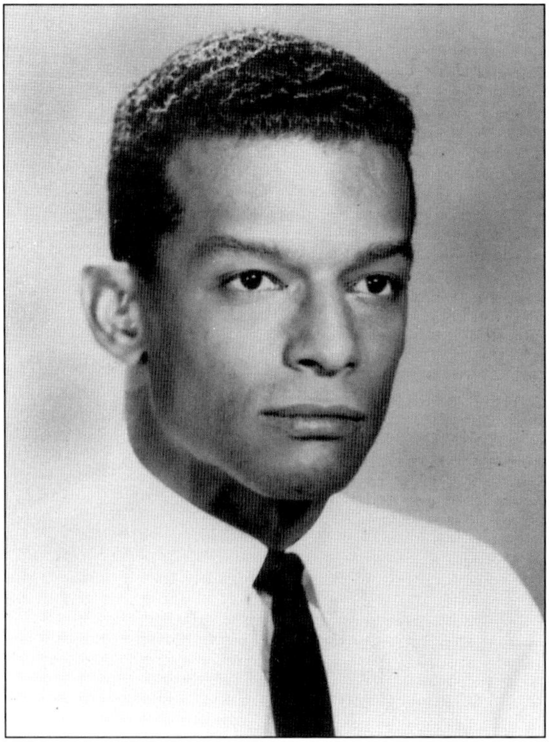

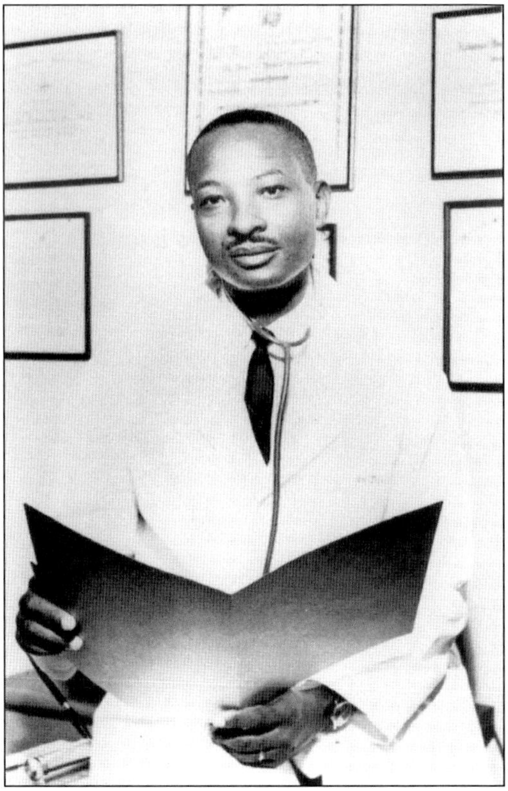

Dr. Charles Johnson was an honors graduate of Howard University and its medical school. After completing an endocrinology fellowship at Duke Hospital, he returned to Lincoln Hospital where he built a large clinical practice. In 1970 he became the first full-time, African-American faculty member in the Duke Department of Medicine. Over the years, he led efforts to diversify the faculty and student body. In 1999, he was awarded the Duke University "Medal of Distinction." (Courtesy of the Duke University Medical Center Archives.)

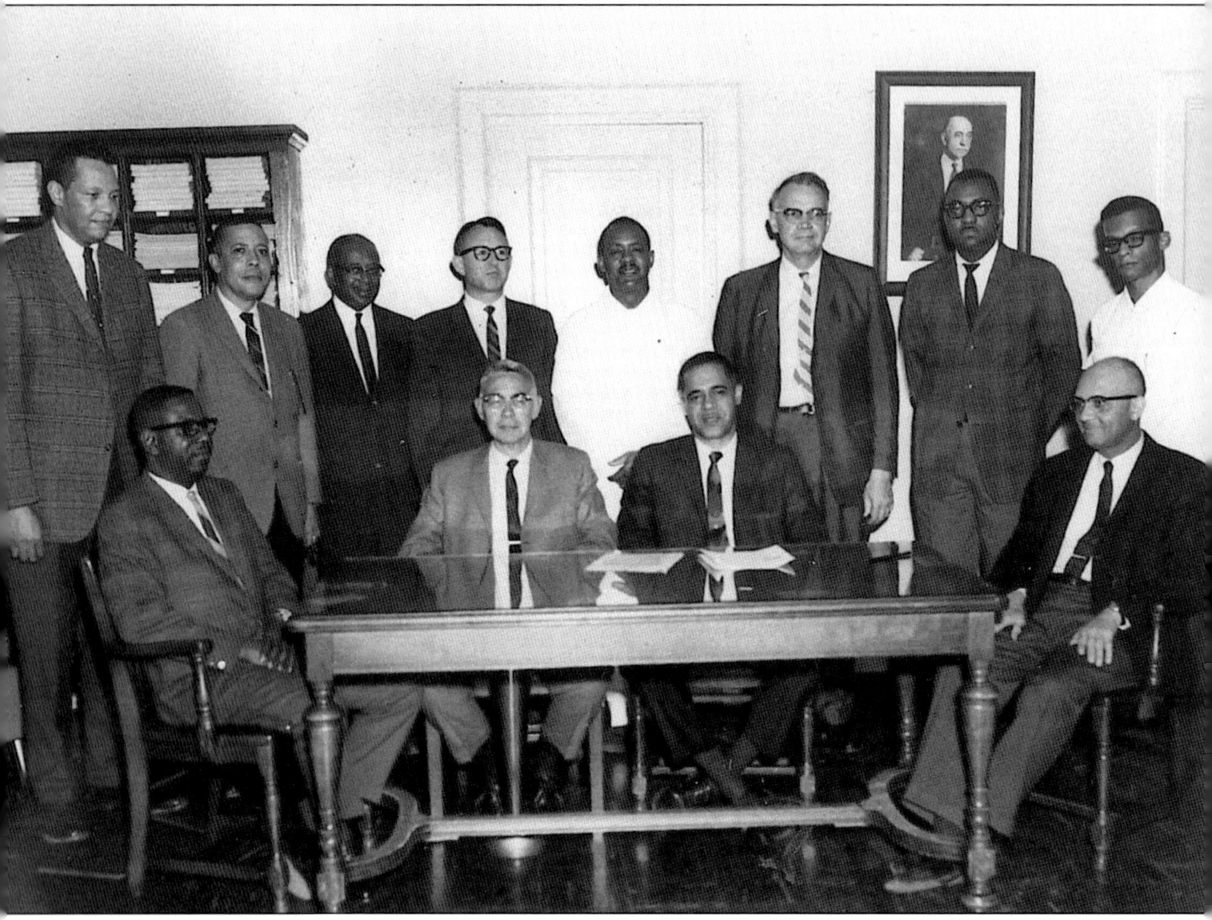

In 1965, Watts Hospital racially integrated its medical staff. Both white and African-American physicians continued to see patients at Lincoln Hospital, but increasingly patients of both races were admitted to other area hospitals. Pictured here, from left to right, are (seated) Drs. Robert Dawson, Everett Bugg, Charles Watts, and Robert Randolph; (standing) Drs. Robert King, David Cooke, Clemuel Grandy Sr., H.D. Cleaver, Clinton Battle, John Glasson, Charles Curry, and Donald Moore. (Courtesy of Margaret Kennedy Goodwin.)

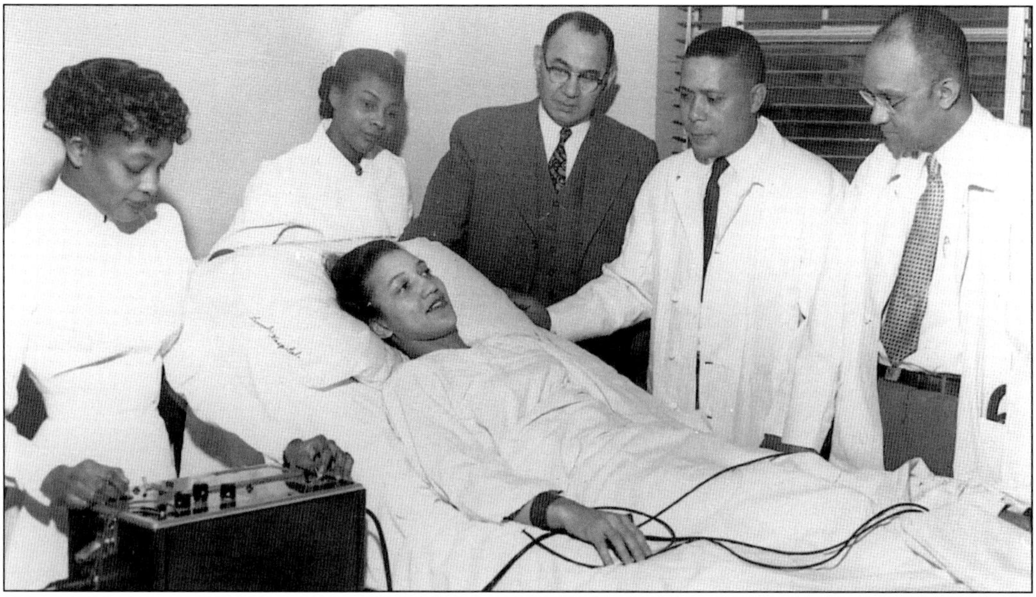

Lincoln Hospital retained on its staff Dr. Robert Randolph and Dr. David Cooke, both physicians who specialized in internal medicine. They had large practices in the African-American community and often cared for patients at Lincoln Hospital who were referred by white physicians at Watts Hospital. Pictured here, from left to right, are Mary Arnold, R.T., Geraldine Butler, R.N.; William Rich; Dr. David Cooke; and Dr. Robert Randolph. (Courtesy of Carolyn Henderson and photographer Charles H. Cooper.)

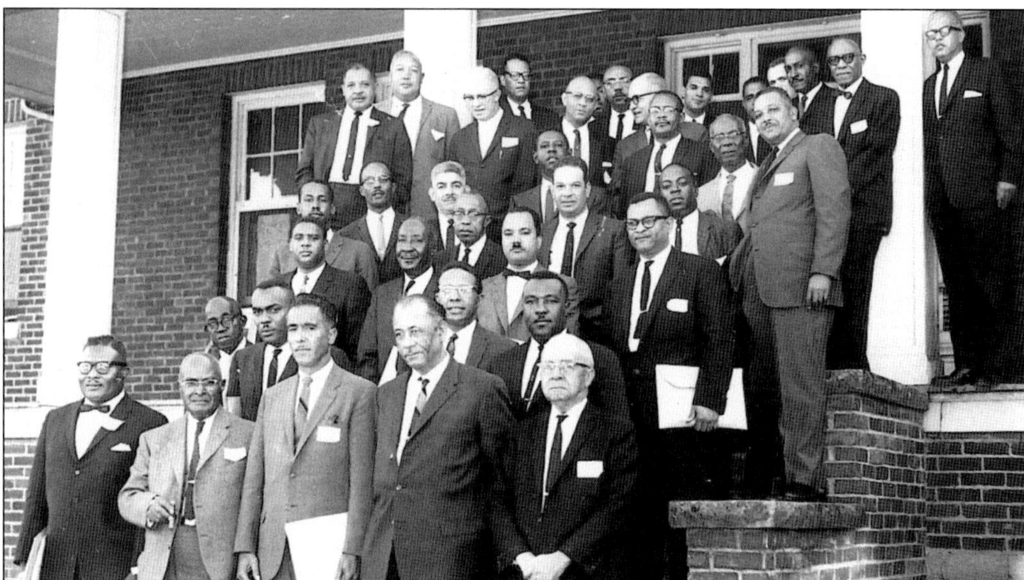

Lincoln Hospital continued to serve as a favorite meeting place for the Old North State Medical Society. In the era of Jim Crow, there were few hotel facilities available for African Americans, even for physicians. As a consequence, Lincoln Hospital was a favorite location for continuing education programs because of the dormitory facilities available at North Carolina College. (Courtesy of Margaret Kennedy Goodwin.)

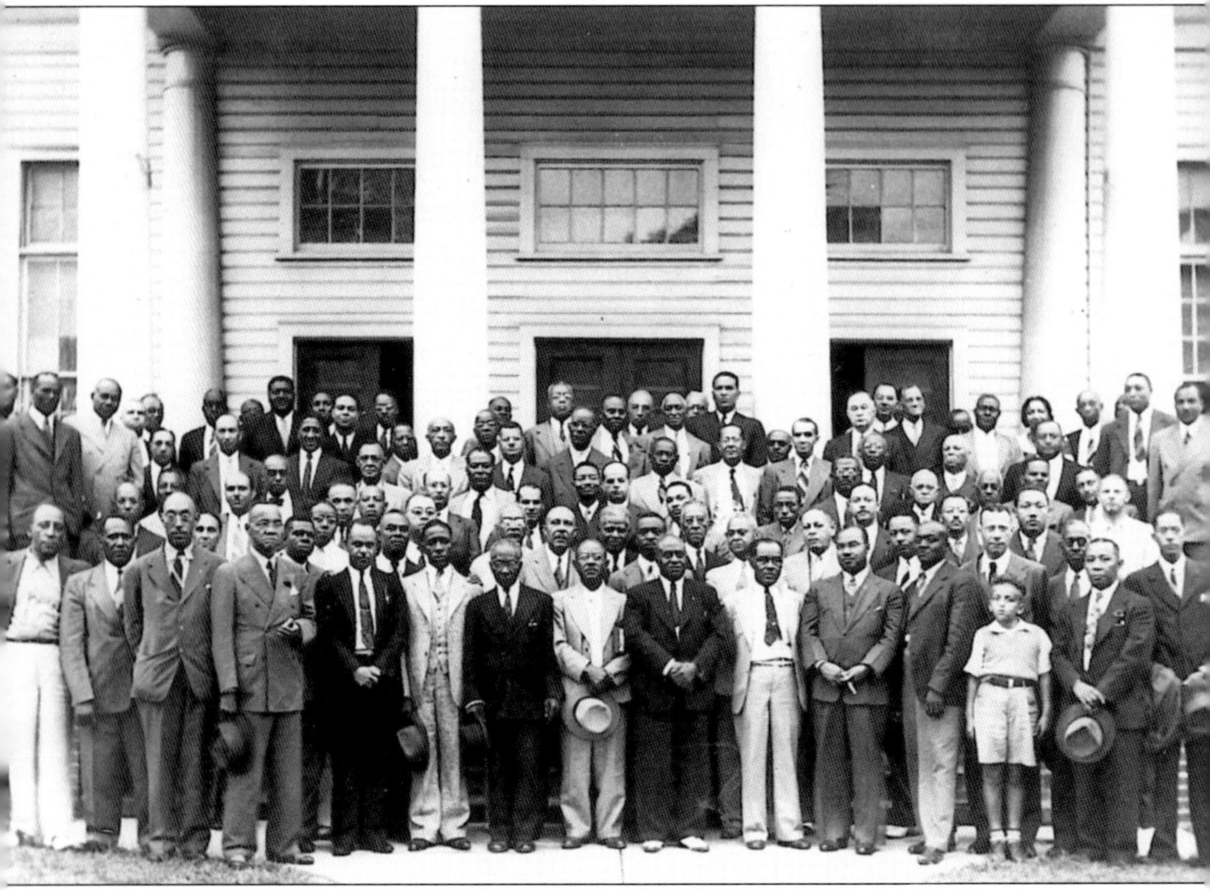

Periodically, Lincoln Hospital would open its post-graduate clinic to physicians from South Carolina and Virginia, as shown in this *c.* 1964 photograph. The clinic brought in speakers from Duke Hospital and the University of North Carolina to join the medical and surgical staff of Lincoln Hospital. The program provided a valuable opportunity to learn the most up-to-date medical information and surgical techniques. Except for a break during World War II, the Lincoln Hospital Post-Graduate Clinic ran continuously for nearly 30 years. (Courtesy of Margaret Kennedy Goodwin and photographer C.W. Richardson.)

Five

Education of Nurses and Allied Health Professionals

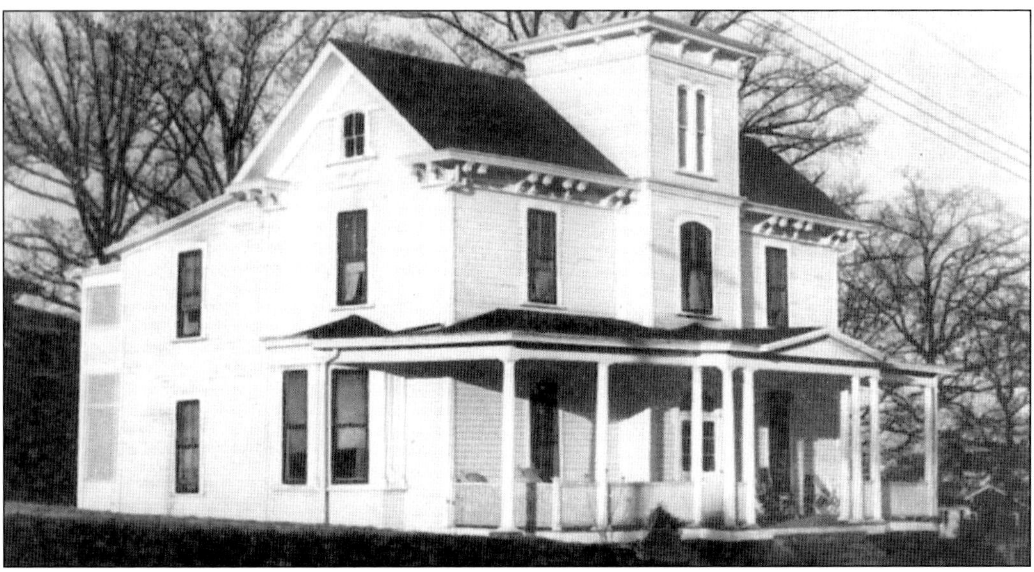

Stokes Home was the residence for the pre-clinical nursing students. When Dr. Aaron Moore died, he bequeathed to Lincoln Hospital three homes located on West Cozart Street, adjacent to the original hospital. Half of the income from this property was to aid worthy girls who were enrolled in the Lincoln Hospital School of Nursing. After 1971, when the School of Nursing closed, the Stokes Home provided accommodations to graduate nurses. (Courtesy of *The Scalpel*, 1946.)

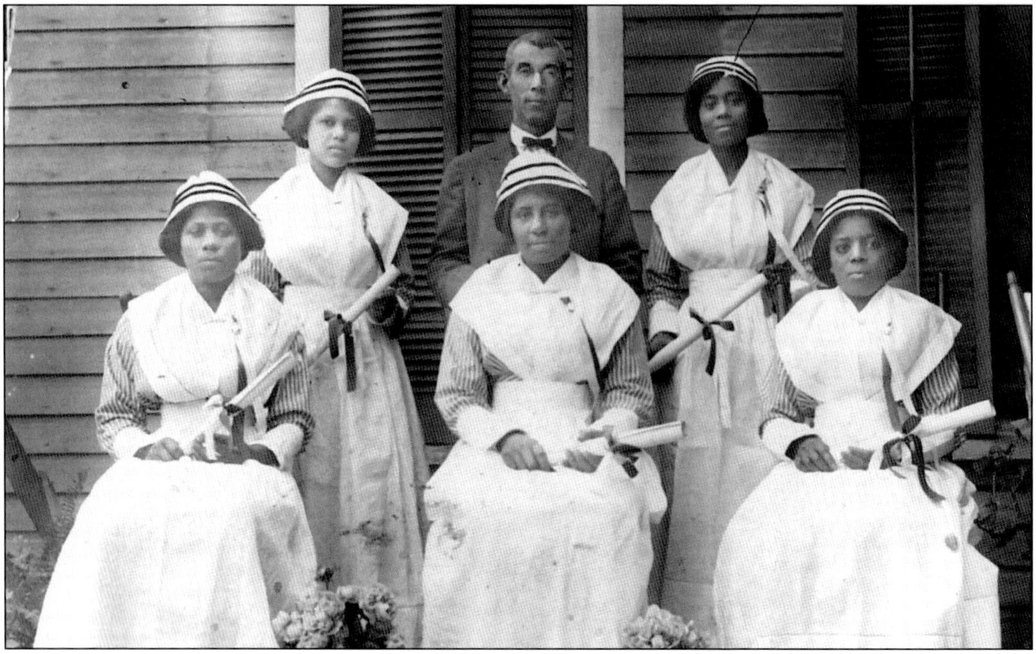

"Give the best to the world and the best will come back to you" was the motto of the Lincoln Hospital School of Nursing. The eighth annual commencement took place May 17–18, 1914. On Sunday the students participated in a baccalaureate sermon at Mt. Vernon Baptist Church and, on the following day, in graduation exercises at White Rock Baptist Church. Pictured here are Dr. Aaron Moore and the graduating class. (Courtesy of Ella W. Clarke.)

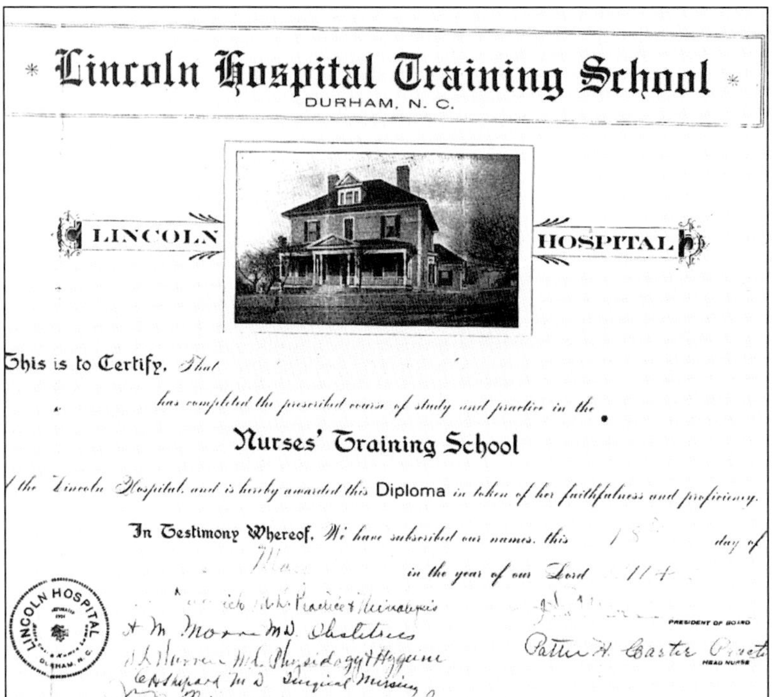

Lincoln Hospital Training School

DURHAM, N. C.

LINCOLN HOSPITAL

This is to Certify, That

has completed the prescribed course of study and practice in the

Nurses' Training School

of the Lincoln Hospital, and is hereby awarded this Diploma in token of her faithfulness and proficiency.

In Testimony Whereof, We have subscribed our names, this day of in the year of our Lord

PRESIDENT OF BOARD

HEAD NURSE

LINCOLN HOSPITAL DURHAM, N. C.

After awarding the diplomas in 1914, Dr. William Struckwick gave the prizes to the graduating seniors. All named for distinguished members of the Lincoln Hospital leadership, these prizes included the Merrick Prize, C.C. Spaulding Prize, J.E. Weaver Prize, Dr. A.M. Moore Prize, Dr. S.L. Warren Prize, Dr. J.N. Mills Prize, Dr. W.C. Struckwick Prize, and Miss Carter Prize. (Courtesy of Ella W. Clarke.)

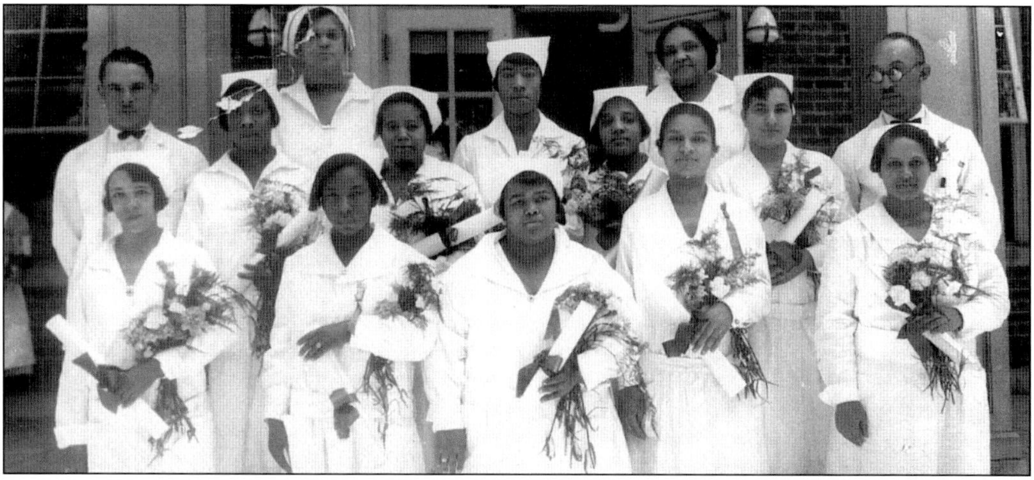

As the second nursing school in North Carolina, the Lincoln Hospital School of Nursing attracted applicants primarily from the Mid-Atlantic region. Instruction was provided in theory and clinical skills and combined lectures with bedside teaching. In 1910 the curriculum was lengthened to three years to meet increasing statewide standards for licensure. Miss Patty Carter, director of nursing, stands on the far right of the top row of this *c.* 1912 image, which also includes the graduating class. Miss Carter instilled into the students the tenets of "Ethics and Hospital Etiquette" which read, "Nurses must at all times observe the ethics of nursing, cultivate a professional spirit, which includes a cheerful, willing obedience to authority, as well as the trying of duties of the sick room. Dignity, decorum and quietness of manner must be observed. Unnecessary waste of time must be avoided. All communications with visiting doctors, interns, patients, orderlies or any other person shall be strictly professional." (Courtesy of Carolyn Henderson.)

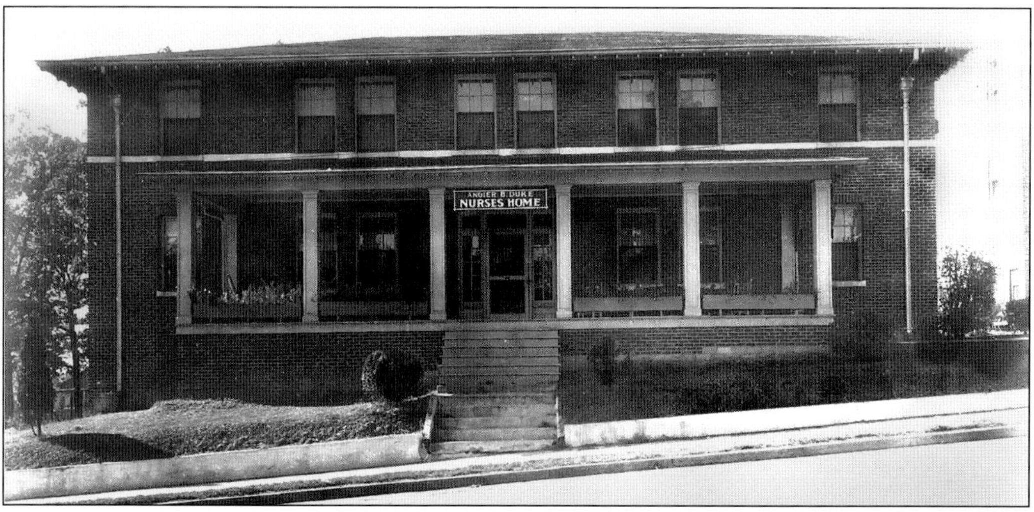

Benjamin N. Duke gave $35,000 in 1925 to construct a new home for the Lincoln Hospital nursing students. This money, combined with income from Dr. Moore's estate, furnished the nurses' home with beds and dressers for each room, couches and chairs for the recreation area, and modern equipment for the classrooms. Dr. Charles Shepard proposed naming it the Angier B. Duke Nurses Home in honor of Mr. Duke's son. (Courtesy of *The Scalpel*, 1946.)

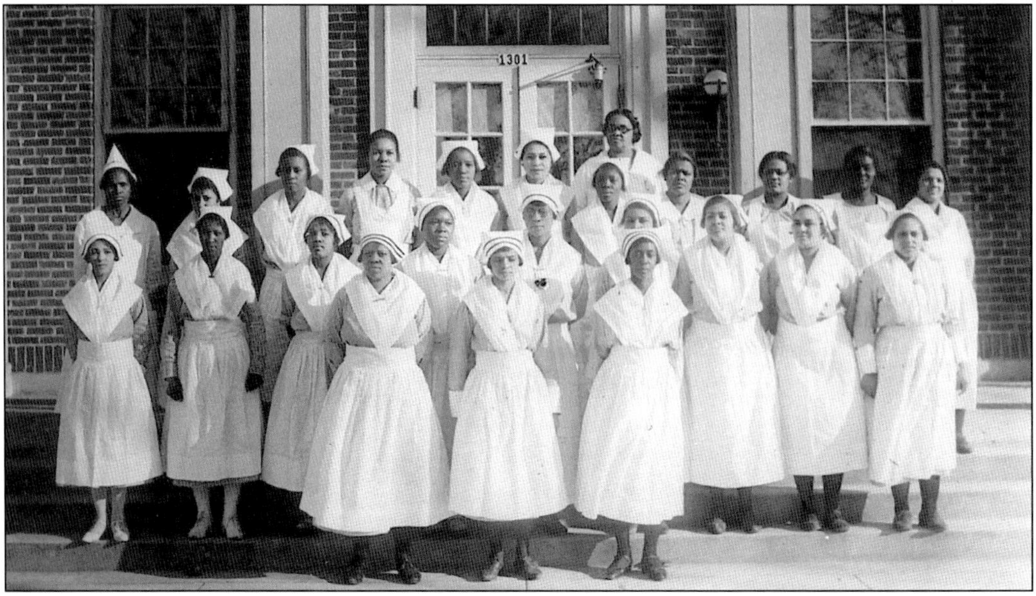

Lincoln Hospital was featured in *Modern Hospital* in 1926 as the first African-American hospital to be described in this national publication. The three classes of nursing students pictured here opened the story. Twenty-seven undergraduates were enrolled in the school of nursing with three planning to graduate at the end of the year. The Angier B. Duke Nurses Home provided accommodations for 40 nurses, giving ample room to house the students and graduate nurses. (Courtesy of *Modern Hospital*.)

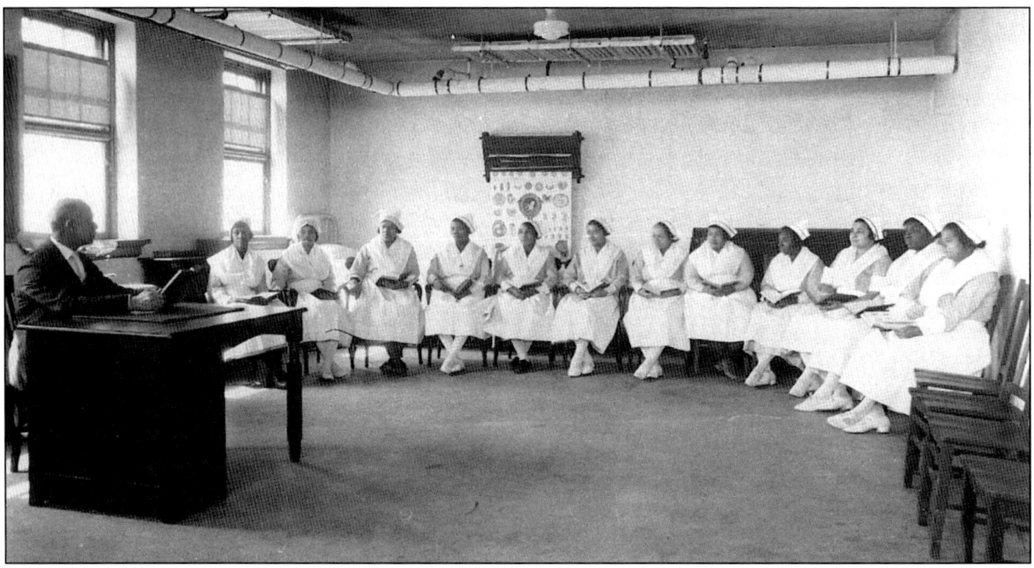

The physicians on staff at Lincoln Hospital were active in the teaching program of the Lincoln Hospital School of Nursing. The 1931 bulletin of the school of nursing lists 21 physicians responsible for various courses. In addition, three registered nurses, one dentist, and one psychologist contributed to the students' instruction. Pictured here is Dr. Stanford Warren, who taught nursing students the principles of physiology, hygiene, and later obstetrics every Wednesday afternoon. (Courtesy of Carolyn Henderson.)

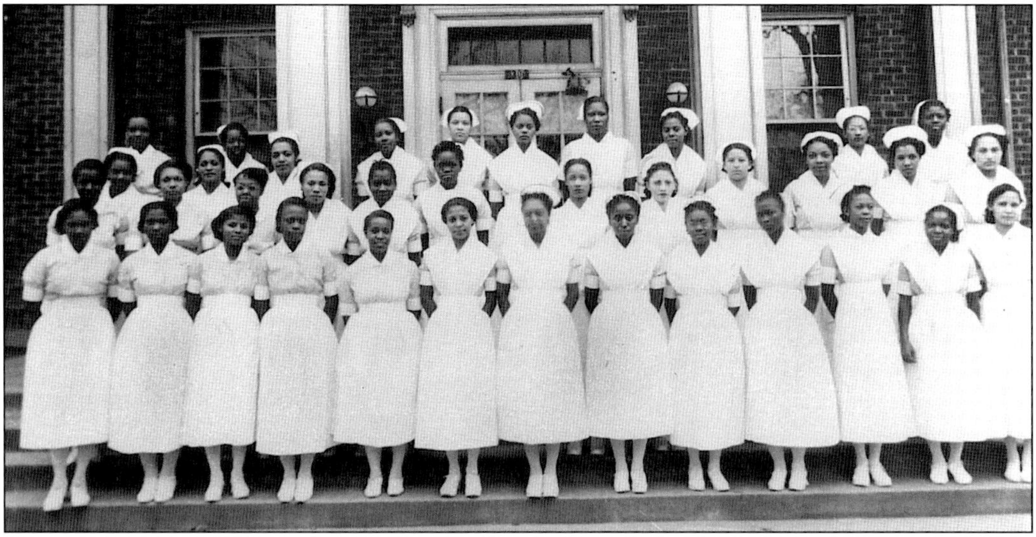

The Lincoln Hospital School of Nursing was fully approved by the Board of Nurse Examiners of the State of North Carolina. Students were graded on classroom instruction with a minimum 75 percent passing score, practical work, personal appearance, and their professional etiquette. After three years, students who successfully fulfilled graduation requirements would receive a diploma and then be eligible to take the state licensing examination. Only with passage of this examination could a nurse display her credentials as an R.N., or registered nurse. By 1938, over 180 graduates were working throughout the country in all branches of nursing. In addition, the Training School of the North Carolina State Sanatorium (Colored Division) was affiliated formally in that their students spent their third year of training in Durham. Pictured here are the nursing graduates in 1938. (Courtesy of Carolyn Henderson.)

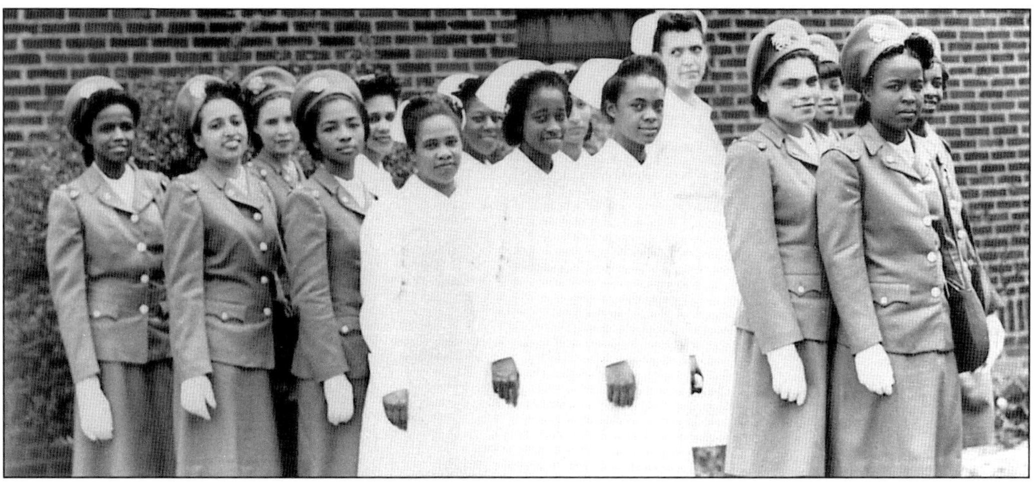

In 1943 both Lincoln Hospital and Watts Hospital entered into the U.S. Nurses Cadet Corps administered as a defense initiative by the Department of Defense. Each student enrolled as a U.S. Nurses Cadet received a salary while a student and, in return, spent the last six months of her training working in a federal hospital. Lincoln Hospital benefited through federal subsidies that paid the costs of textbooks, uniforms, and faculty salaries. (Courtesy of Carolyn Henderson.)

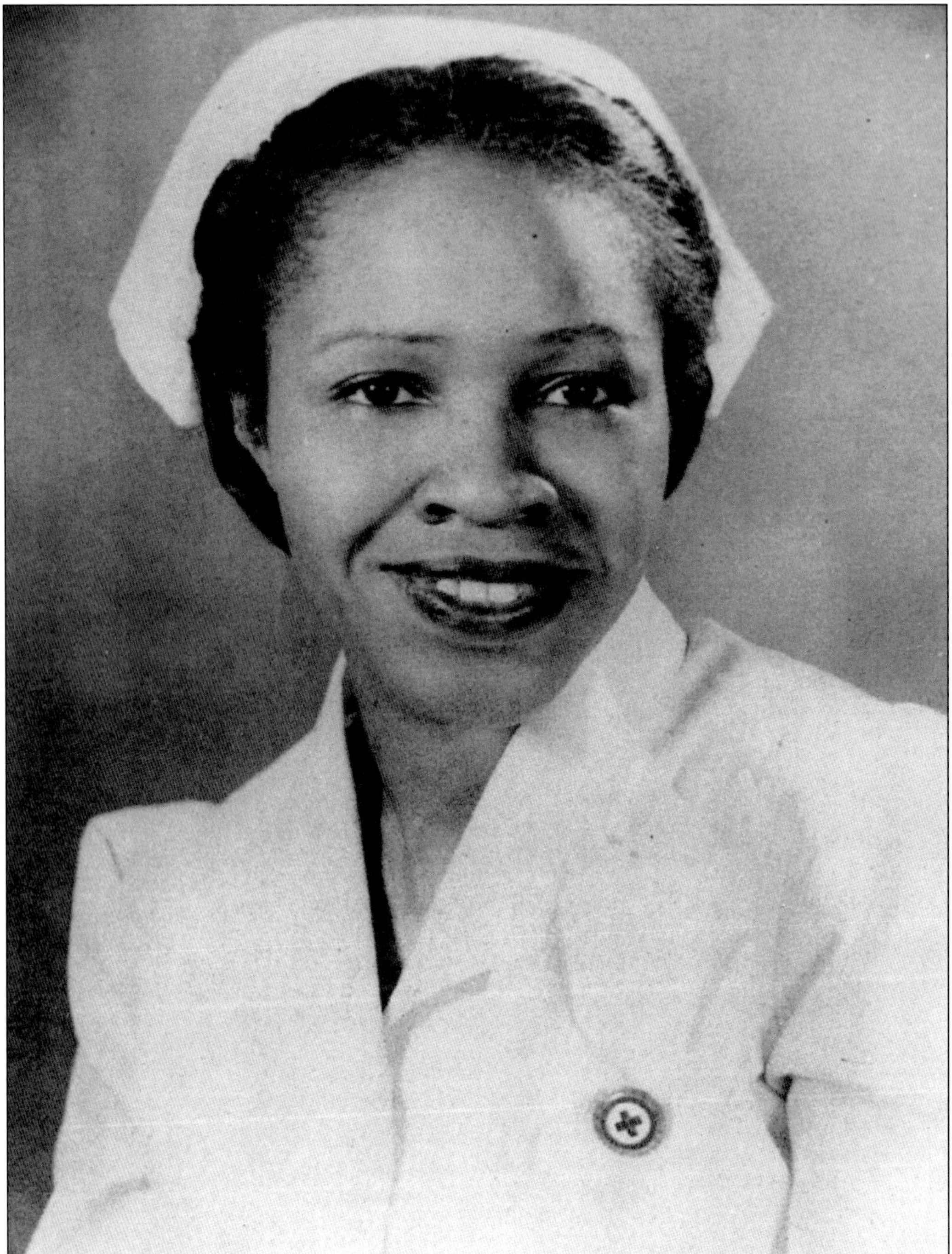

Mrs. Lucille Zimmerman Williams, R.N., a graduate of St. Agnes School of Nursing, joined the hospital in 1945. She assumed responsibility for the nurses training program and continued in that role until the school closed in 1971. Mrs. Williams maintained the traditions established by Miss Patty Carter with emphasis on professional attire, etiquette, and bedside manner. (Courtesy of *The Scalpel*, 1948.)

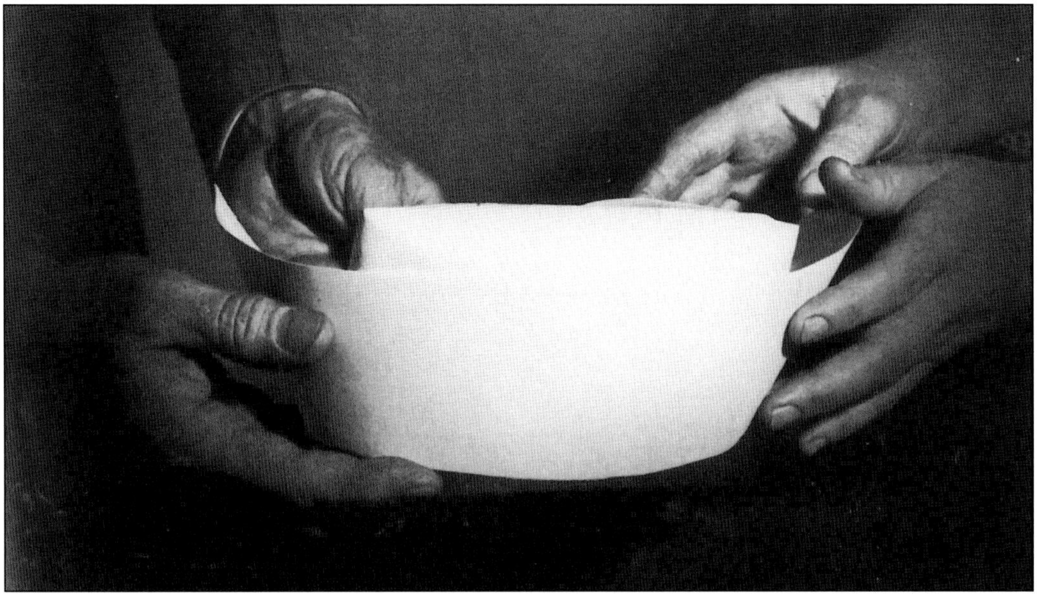

The cap given to each student prior to going onto the clinical wards had no stripes and was the freshman cap. The second year or junior cap had one stripe running vertically on each side of the front of the cap, while the third year or senior cap had two stripes on each side of the front of the cap. A Lincoln Hospital graduate R.N. wore a cap with one stripe running horizontally across the top. (Courtesy of *Nightingale*, 1959.)

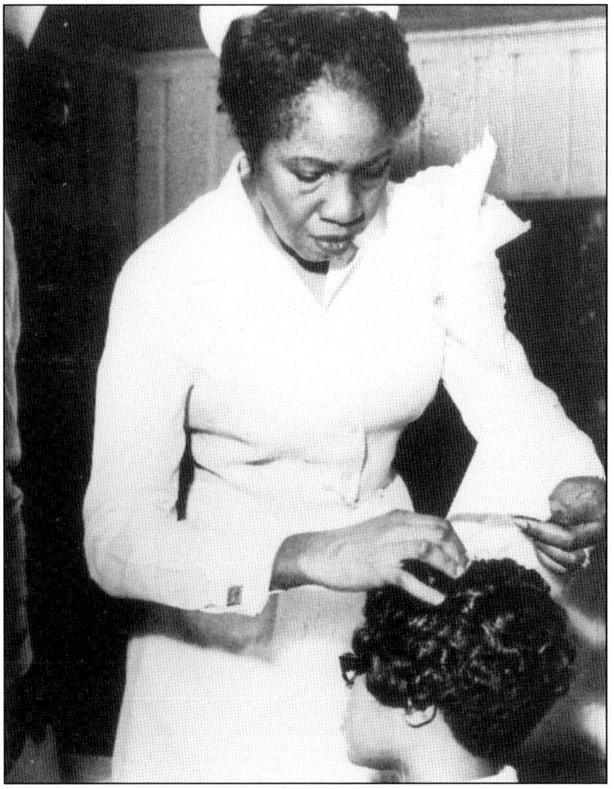

Lincoln Hospital School of Nursing celebrated its Capping Ceremony at the end of a student nurse's first or pre-clinical year. Pictured here is Mrs. Lucille Zimmerman Williams, R.N., who always wore a handkerchief in her pocket, as she pins the cap to the student's crown. (Courtesy of *The Scalpel*, 1962.)

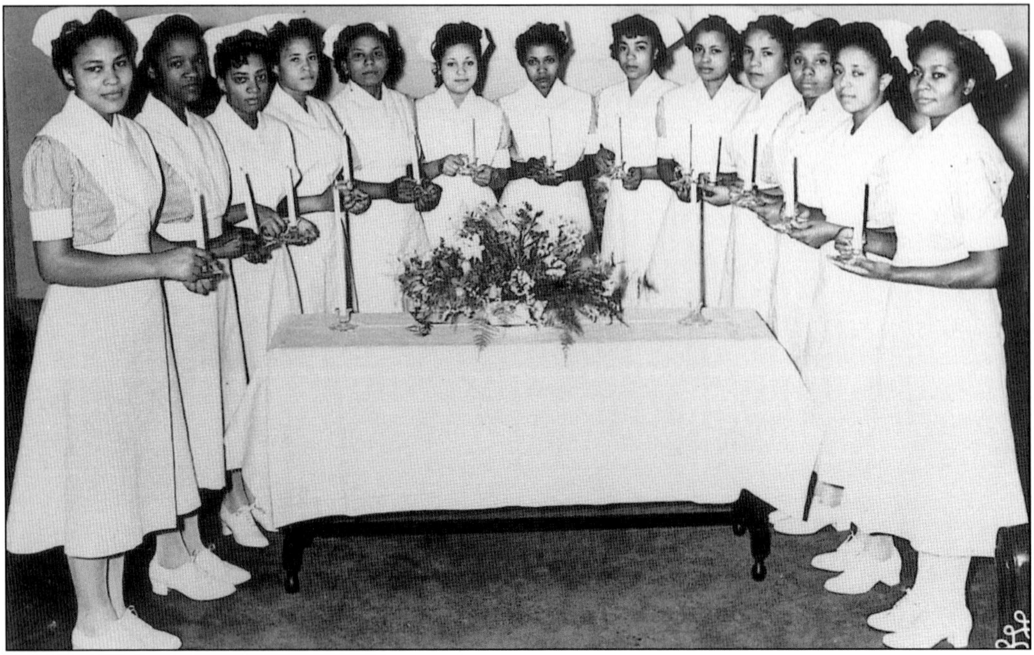

The Capping Ceremony was a serious occasion with candlelight and the recitation of the nurses' oath. Pictured *c.* 1945, from left to right, are Clara Miller, G. Flintall, E. Richardson, C. Baker, M. Watkins, D. Antis, D. Peters, M. Jones, G. Haricock, B. Walker, R. Parker, A. Greene, and C. Lancaster. (Courtesy of Carolyn Henderson.)

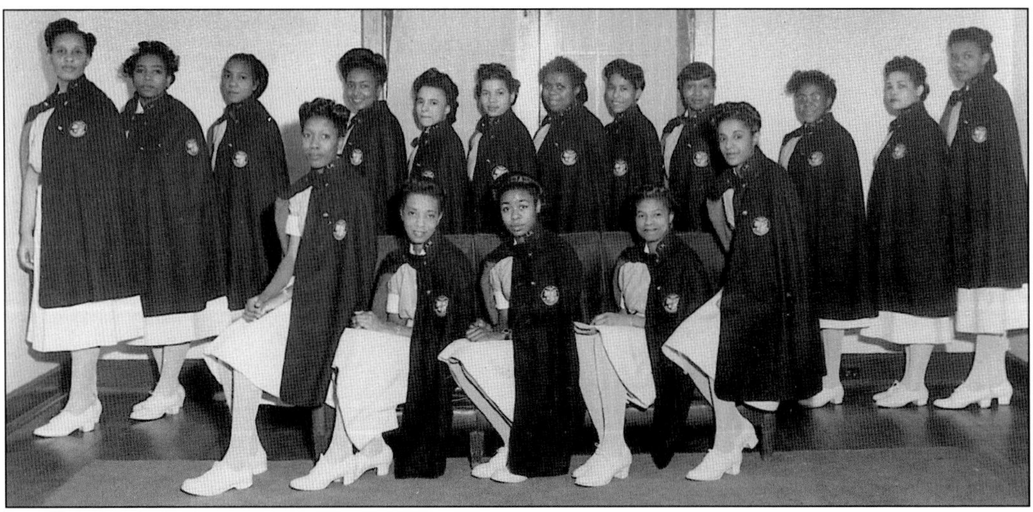

Each student who enrolled in the Lincoln Hospital School of Nursing was issued a set of clothing that included their white uniform and shirt, shoes, and a cape. They were expected to keep their white uniforms pressed and starched, shoes polished, and caps clean. The Lincoln Hospital nursing students in 1948, from left to right, are (seated) Lois Clements, Elizabeth Williams, Corona McClary, Muriel Harris, and Zella Peery; (standing) Dorothy Farley, Theresa Clark, Margaret Davis, Georgia Major, Rosebud Roderick, Fannie Choates, Othello Cave, Katherine Carter, Helen Black, Alice Williams, Lillian Brown, and Annie Coley. (Courtesy of *The Scalpel*, 1946.)

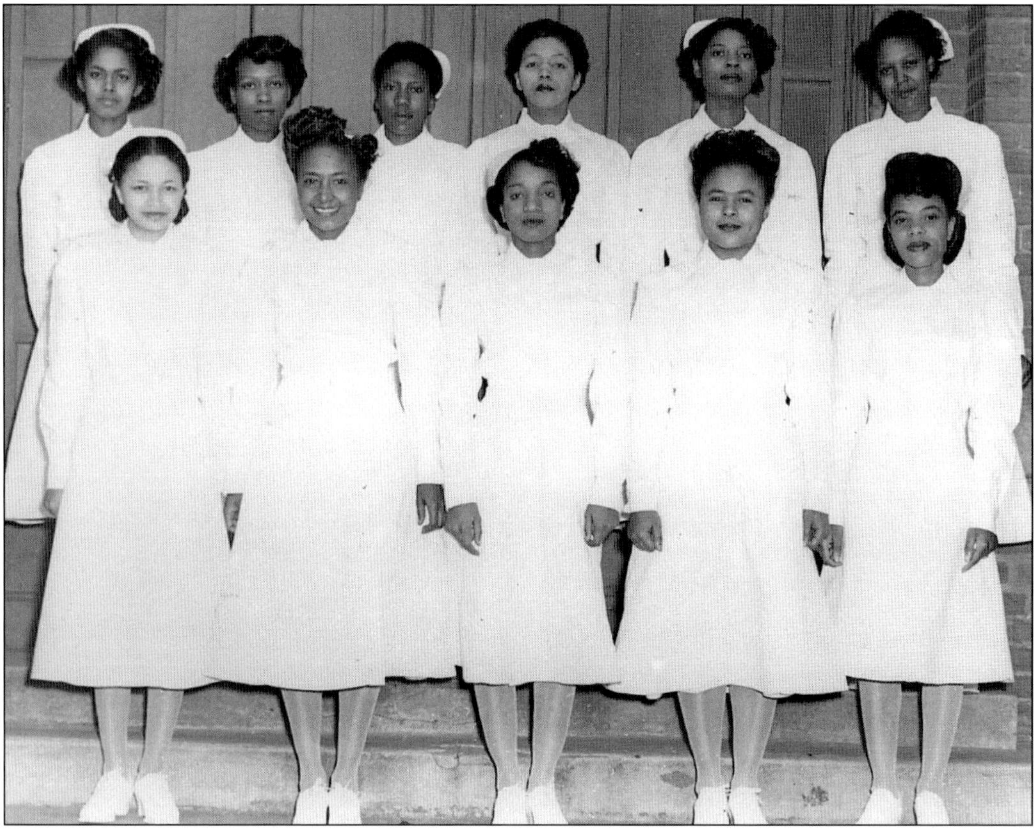

These 1949 nursing graduates are, from left to right, are Evelana Saunders, Georgia Major, Eloise McKeitha, Lucille Hart, Emma Crow, Madeline Gardner, Edith Tan Kersley, Eleanor Malthewson, Alease Wood, and Annie Evans. (Courtesy of Carolyn Henderson.)

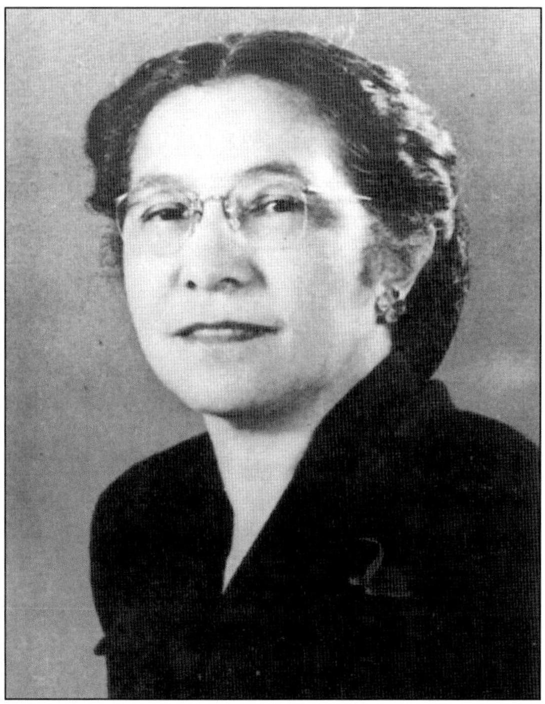

The nursing students had a 24-hour chaperone, Miss Albertine Mason, whose title was "House Directress." Miss Mason was a mother to many of the girls because of her devotion to oversee their needs. If a student wanted to leave the premises, she had to secure permission first from Miss Mason, who kept a tight watch on curfews. (Courtesy of *The Scalpel*, 1948.)

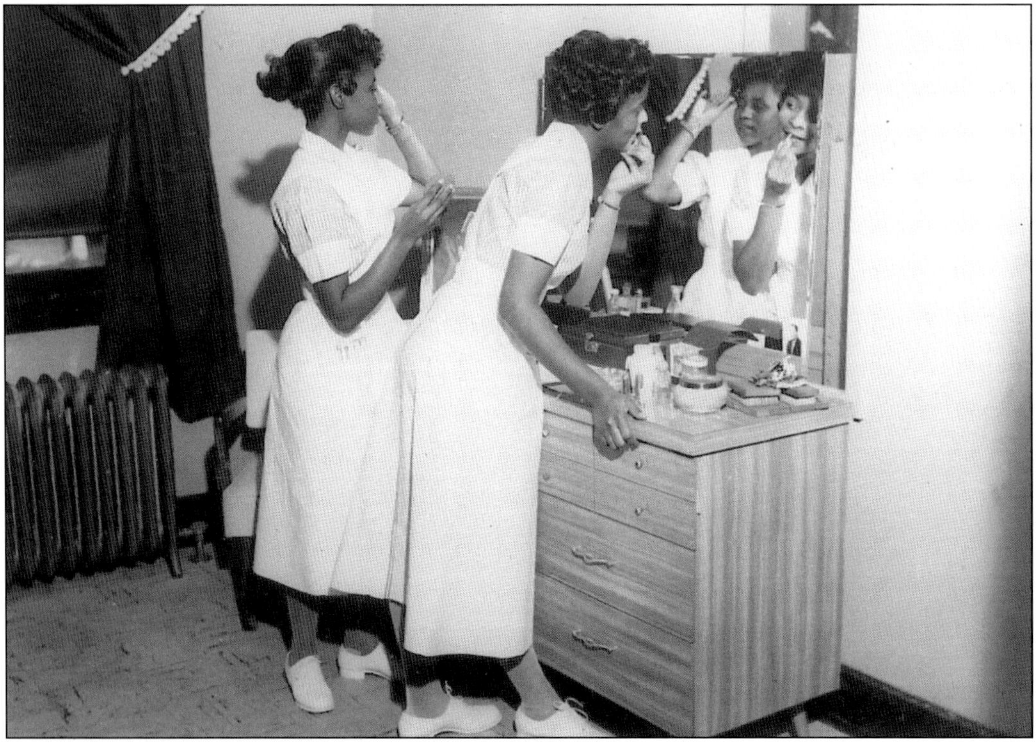

Pictured here are two nursing students, Rosa Outerbridge and Edwina Sellers, in their room making final preparations for a day of learning and work. (Courtesy of Carolyn Henderson.)

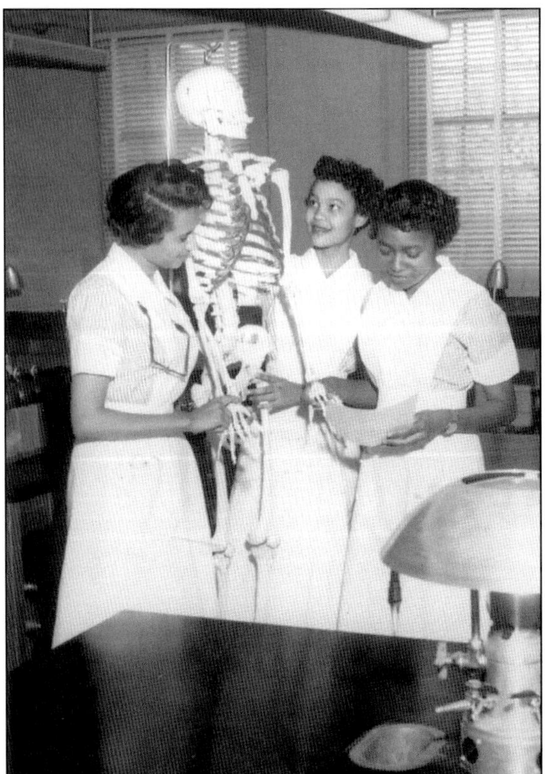

The first year of the Lincoln Hospital School of Nursing curriculum was devoted to the basic sciences of nursing. Students took anatomy, chemistry, bacteriology, nutrition, and other relevant subjects. Many of these courses were taught in the clinical laboratory located in the Angier B. Duke Nurses Home. (Courtesy of *The Scalpel*, 1957.)

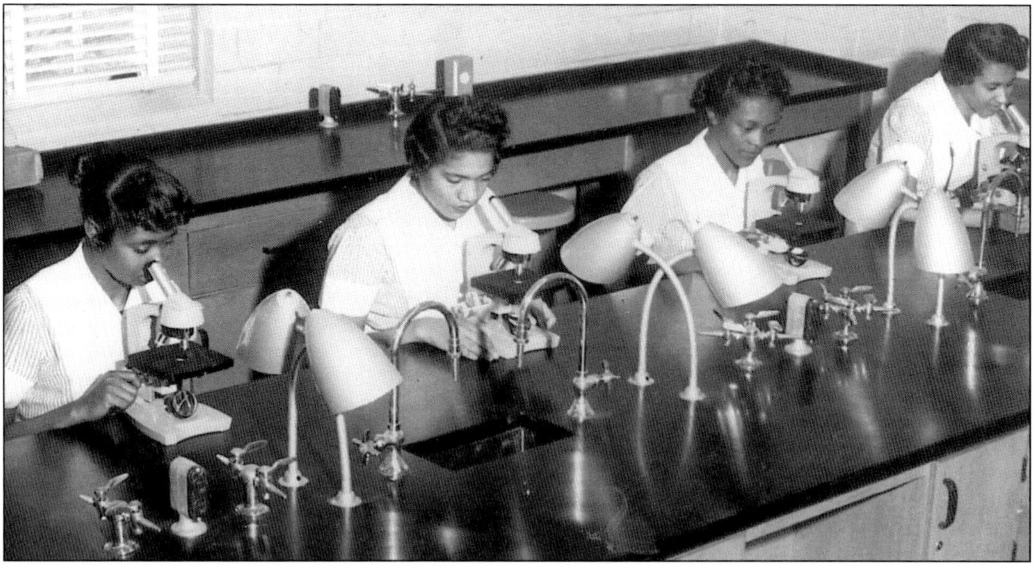

Lincoln Hospital established formal ties with North Carolina College for Negroes in 1930. Faculty of the college taught the students psychology, psychiatry, chemistry, and bacteriology. The college library and gymnasium were available also to the Lincoln Hospital nursing students. The close proximity of North Carolina College to Lincoln Hospital enabled the students to walk back and forth to class and the hospital and nurses home, where they ate their meals and often spent the evening studying. These close affiliations continued until the nursing school closed in 1971. They also enabled some students with additional coursework to receive a bachelor of science in addition to their R.N. (Courtesy of Margaret Kennedy Goodwin.)

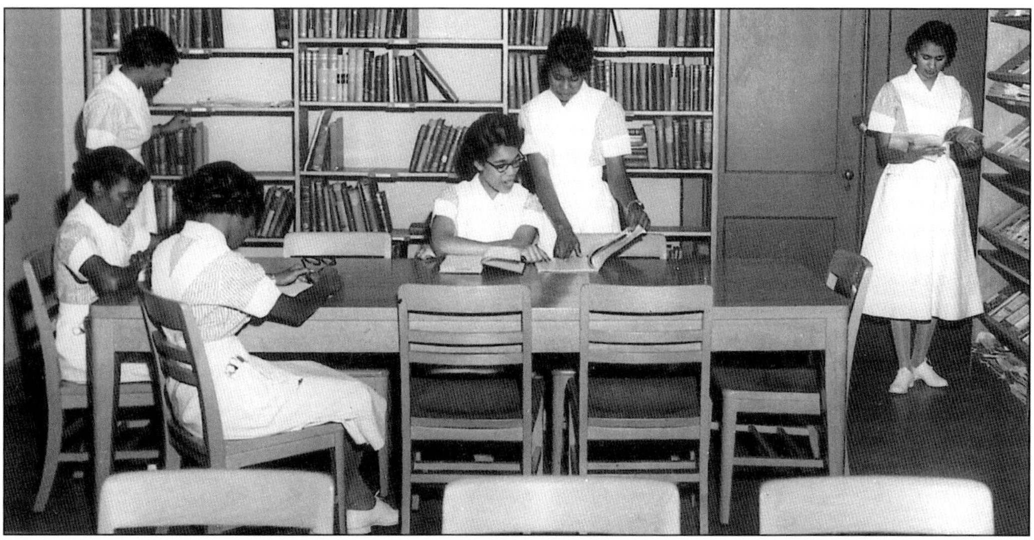

The nursing student library was small but contained all the major textbooks. Students who were able to purchase their own textbooks often studied in the evening in their rooms. Others found the facilities at North Carolina College more conducive to preparation for exams. Pictured here are Mary Pointer, Grace Green, Maurice Otelia Blount, Margaret Wilson, Rosa Outerbridge, and Bobbie Hightower. (Courtesy of Carolyn Henderson.)

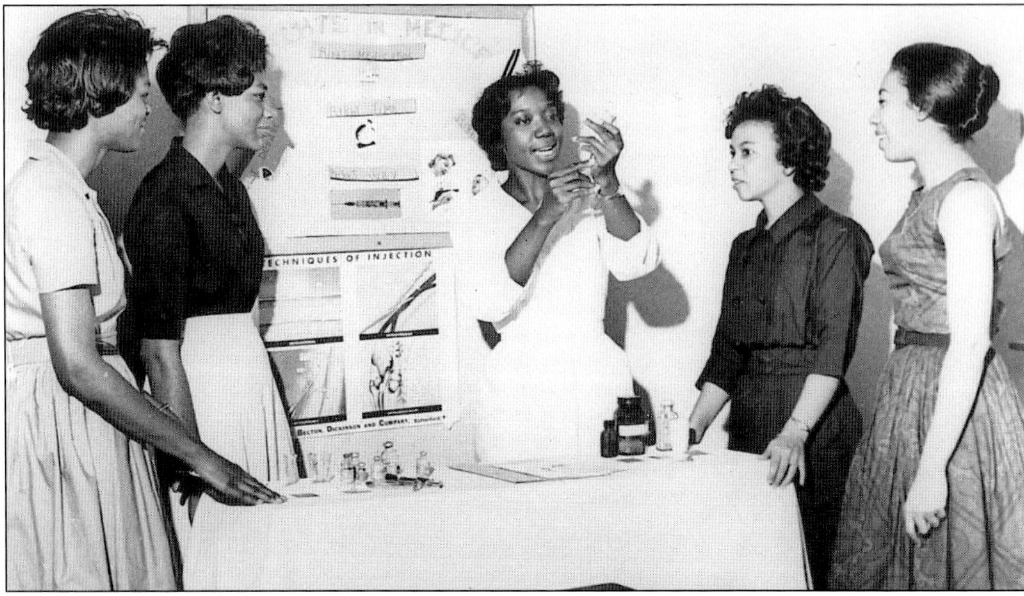

The Lincoln Hospital School of Nursing maintained full accreditation from the North Carolina Board of Nurse Examiners until the mid-1960s when the loss of patients at Lincoln Hospital compromised the school's clinical program. Sylvia Overton was one of the faculty members responsible for teaching the students skills in clinical nursing, such as how to give an injection. She is pictured here demonstrating how to draw up fluid into a syringe. (Courtesy of *The Scalpel*, 1962.)

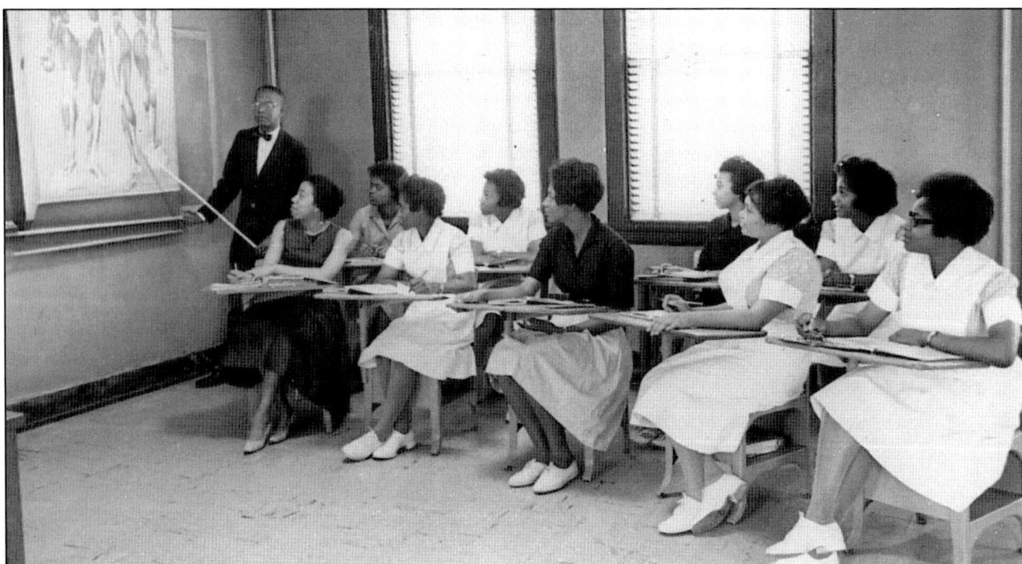

The medical staff of Lincoln Hospital continued to serve as faculty for the nursing school. Students attended classes in the Angier B. Duke Nurses Home often reviewing clinical topics given by physicians who were specialists in those fields. This provided them an opportunity to obtain didactic and practical instruction in areas such as ophthalmology, diseases of children, and surgical anatomy. (Courtesy of *The Scalpel*, 1962.)

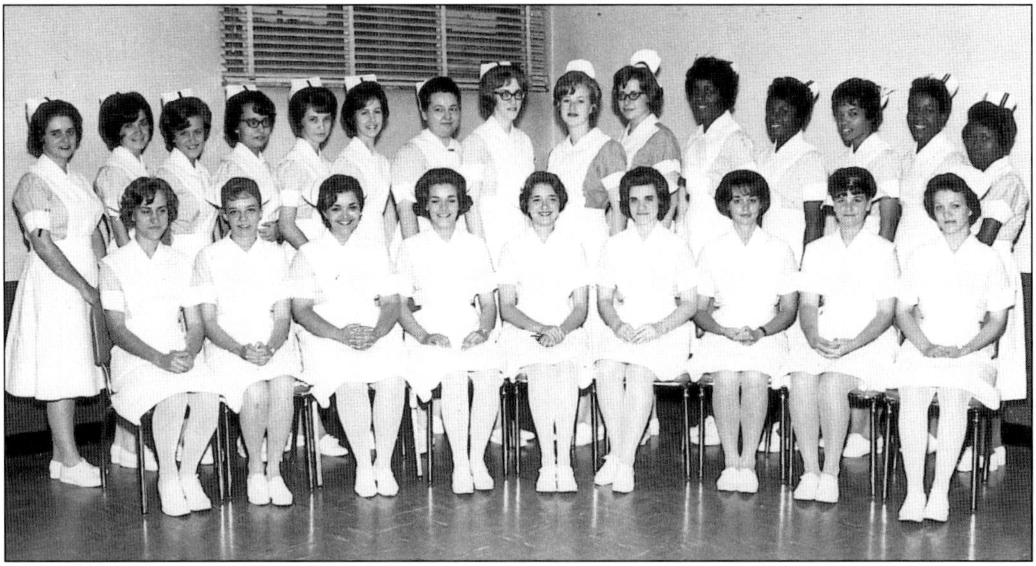

To meet accreditation requirements, the Lincoln Hospital School of Nursing established affiliations with hospitals available for the training of African-American students. These affiliations included the University of Cincinnati and Freedmen's Hospital for pediatrics; and John Umstead State Hospital in North Carolina and Eastern State Hospital in Lexington, Kentucky, for psychiatry. Pictured here are the students from several programs who rotated through Eastern State Hospital in 1965. (Courtesy of Carolyn Henderson.)

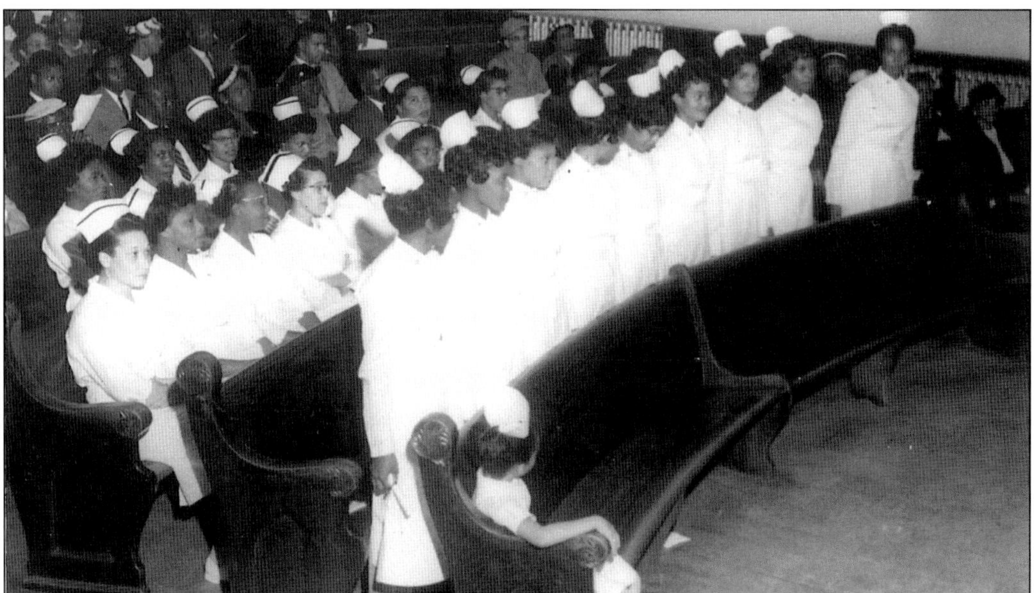

Graduation exercises for the Lincoln Hospital School of Nursing, shown here *c.* 1959, rotated annually from their location on the front lawn of the hospital to the pews of Durham's African-American churches. Nearly every church in the African-American community hosted some part of the celebration, whether it was baccalaureate or graduation itself, at some point in its history. (Courtesy of Carolyn Henderson.)

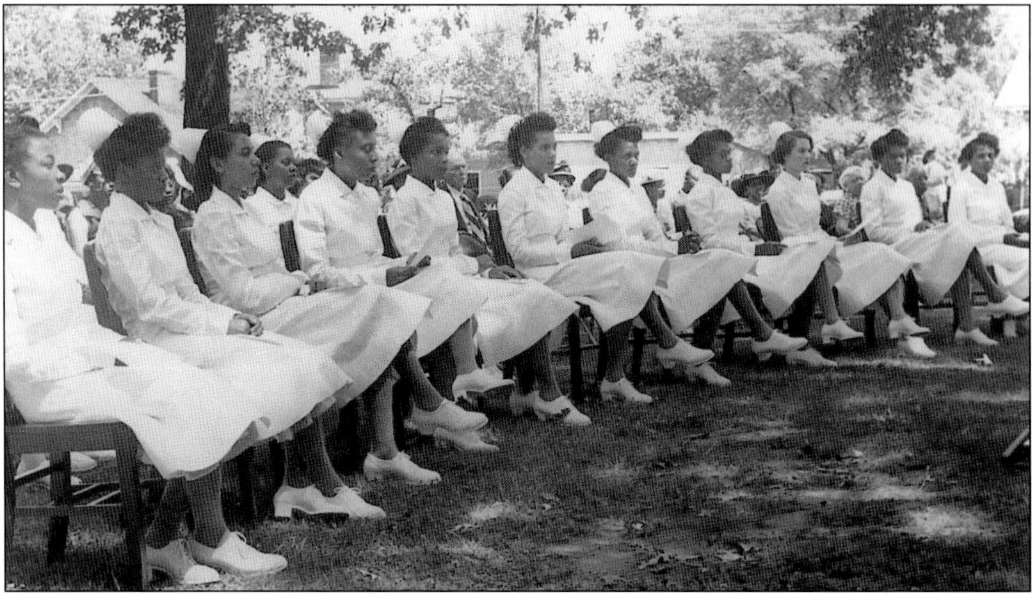

In the later years, after prayer, singing, speeches, and presentation of the diplomas, awards were given to the graduating nurses. These included prizes for "Excelling in Theory and Practice in the Operating Room," "Highest Scholastic Average," "Most Technically Competent," "Neatest," "Most Courteous to Patients," and "Excelled in Leadership Ability." Dr. Clyde and Martha Donnell also gave to each graduating nurse an individual prize. This is a *c.* 1954 photograph of graduation exercises. (Courtesy of Carolyn Henderson.)

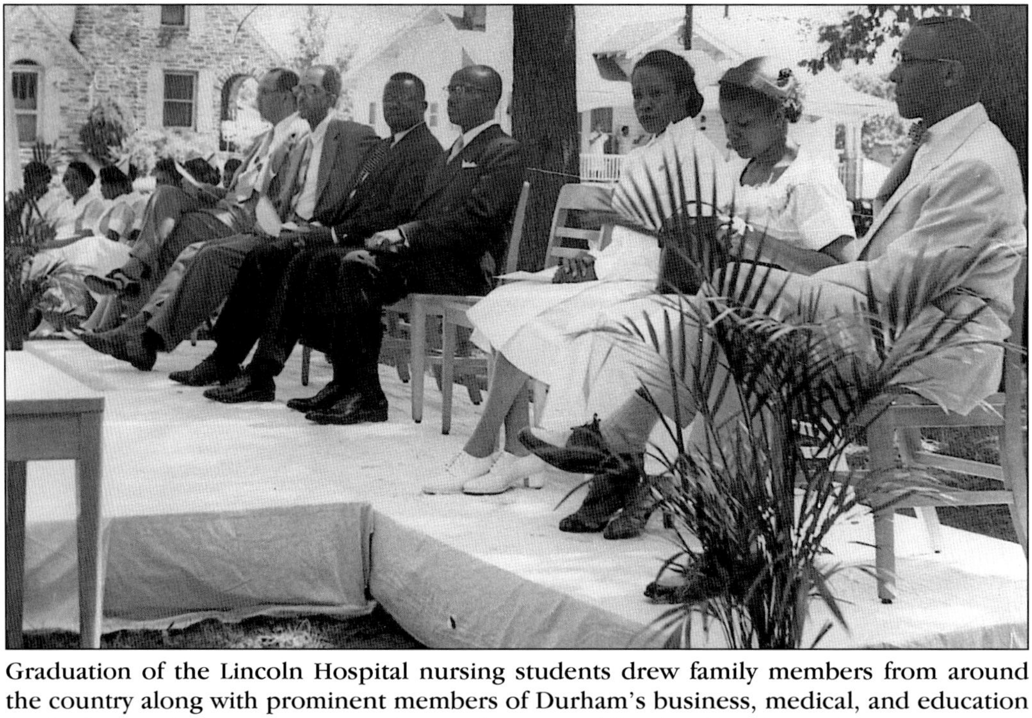

Graduation of the Lincoln Hospital nursing students drew family members from around the country along with prominent members of Durham's business, medical, and education institutions and the community-at-large. (Courtesy of Carolyn Henderson.)

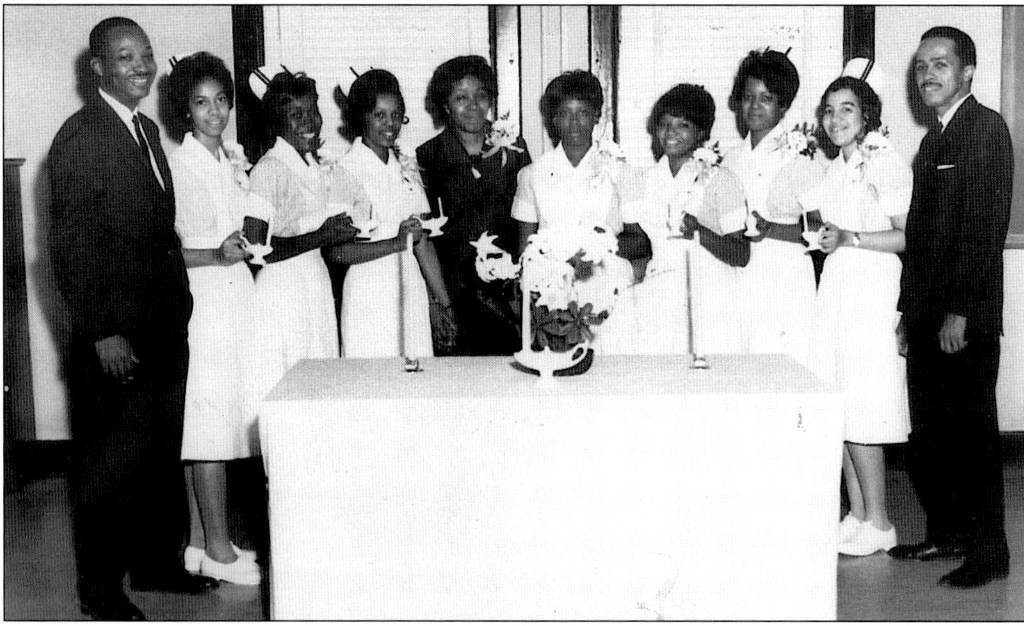

The Santa Filamena was the honor society for the nursing students. Honorees had to achieve at least a 3.0 grade point average and were selected in their junior year by the faculty. Senior students attended the induction ceremony for the new honorees. Pictured on the far left, *c.* 1966, is Dr. Charles Johnson and on the far right is Rev. Miles Mark Fisher IV, son of the pastor of White Rock Baptist Church. Mrs. Lucille Zimmerman Williams, R.N., stands in the middle. (Courtesy of Carolyn Henderson and photographer Claude Burthey.)

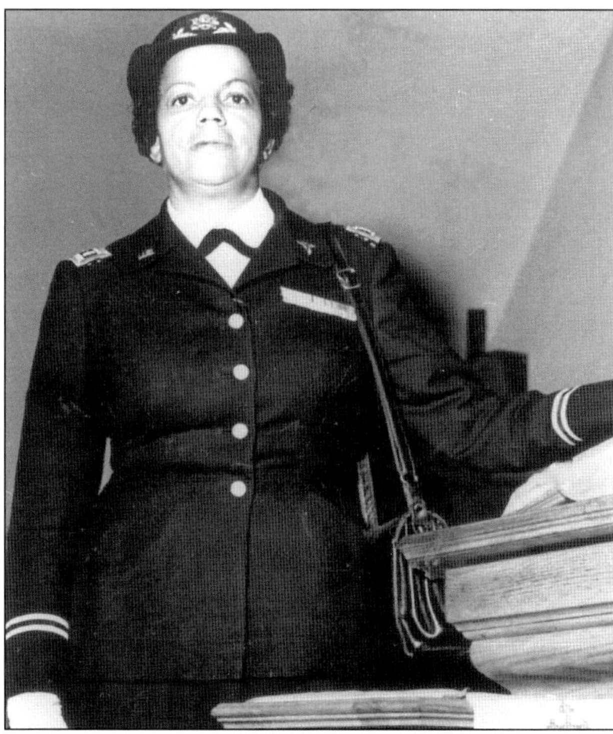

Most of the graduates of the Lincoln Hospital School of Nursing became registered nurses and worked in hospitals or in a doctor's office. Della Rainey Jackson was one of the school's most distinguished graduates. She was the first African-American nurse to answer the call for nurses in World War II. She entered service at Fort Bragg in April 1941 and was later transferred to the Tuskegee Army Flying School in March 1942. Lieutenant Raney was the first African-American nurse to be promoted to the rank of chief nurse and the first to be in charge of an army hospital. She later received her doctorate from Columbia University. (Courtesy of Carolyn Henderson.)

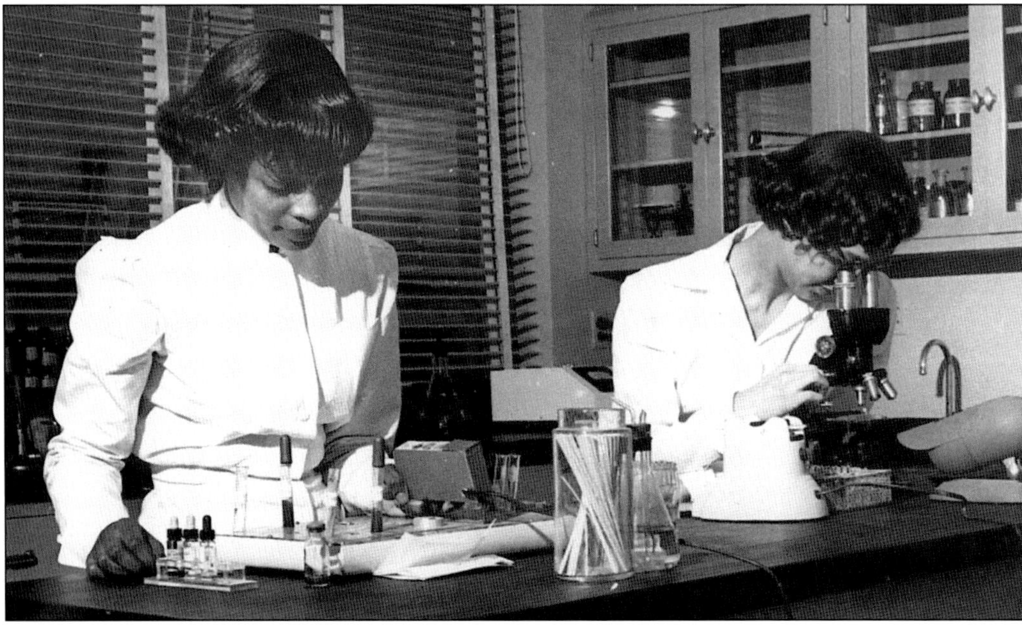

Lincoln Hospital offered training for laboratory and radiology technologists beginning in the late 1930s. After World War II, the program was formalized with a two-year curriculum. Mrs. Margaret Kennedy Goodwin directed the program in collaboration with faculty from Duke University School of Medicine. The students obtained their basic science coursework at Duke and their practical experience at Lincoln Hospital. Two graduates of the Lincoln Hospital School of Medicine and X-ray Technology, shown from left to right, are Mary Arnold and Patricia Tyler. (Courtesy of Margaret Kennedy Goodwin.)

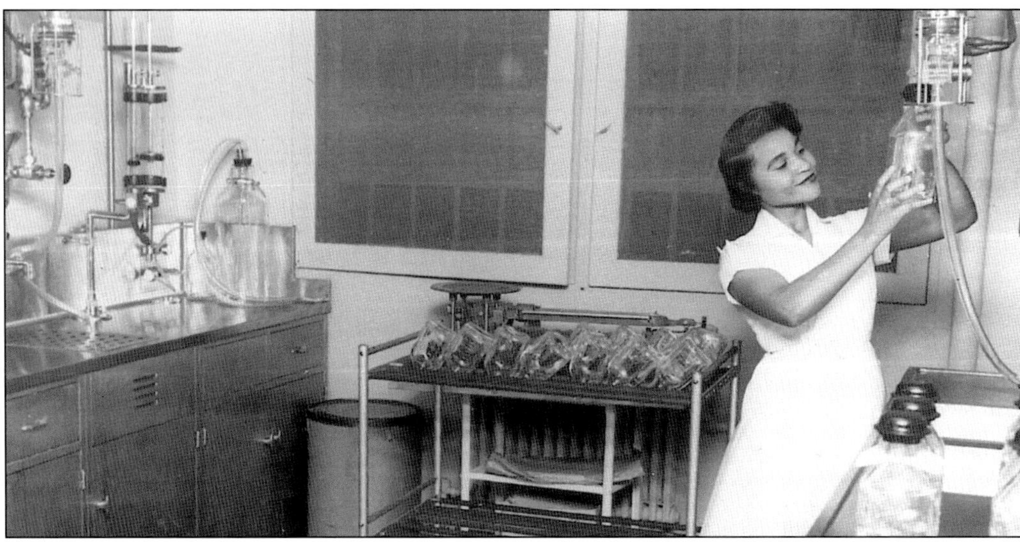

Not only were medical technician students required to master skills in preparing hematology slides and running urinalysis and chemistry examinations, but student nurses rotating through the lab also had to learn them, as seen here *c.* 1958. Most importantly, Mrs. Goodwin expected all students to keep their work area free from bacteria and other contaminants of patient specimens. (Courtesy of Carolyn Henderson.)

Six

Social Life

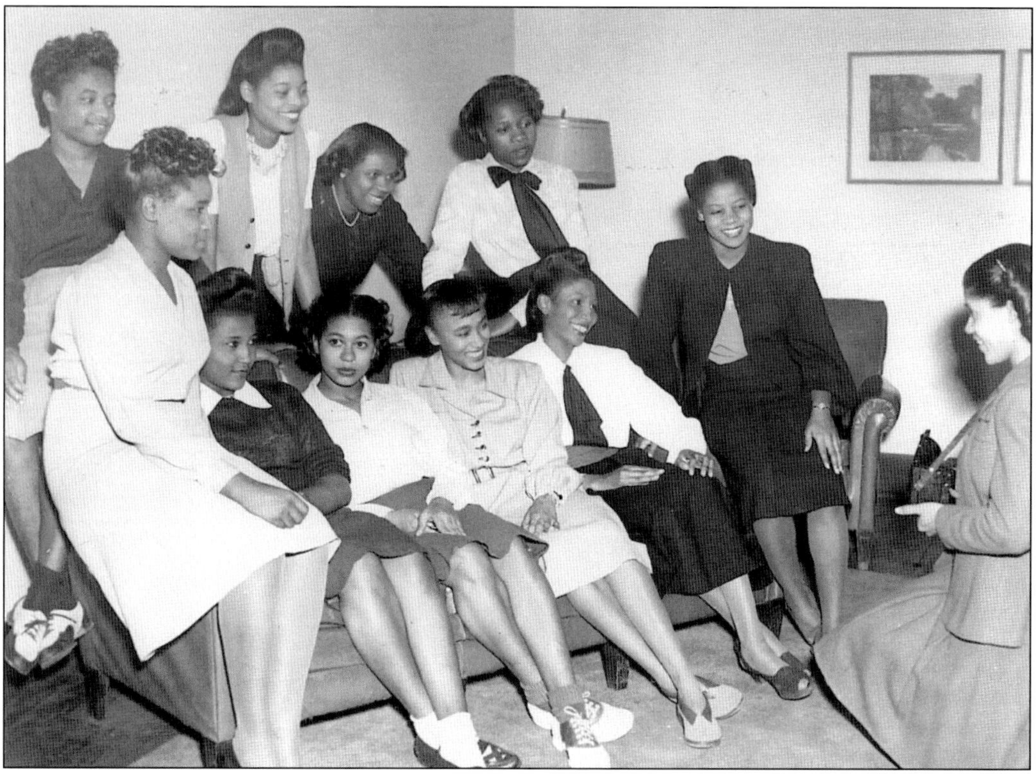

The Lincoln Hospital School of Nursing students organized a photography club that was active for many years. The students took photographs of their own activities as well as scenes inside the hospital. They often developed their own film and practiced on themselves, learning how to pose and center groups of people. (Courtesy of Margaret Kennedy Goodwin.)

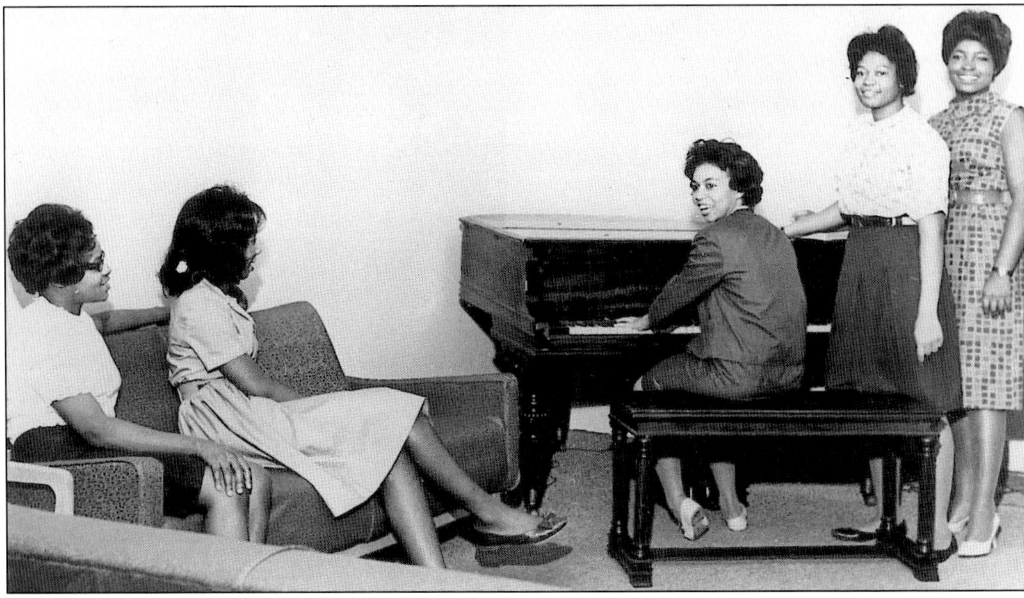

The Angier B. Duke Nurses Home housed a grand piano that often became the center of music and sing-alongs. Pictured here, *c.* 1962, from left to right, are Margaret Kindred, Evelyn Booker (Wicker), Carolyn Lewister, Jenine L. Adams, and Geraldine Richardson. (Courtesy of Carolyn Henderson.)

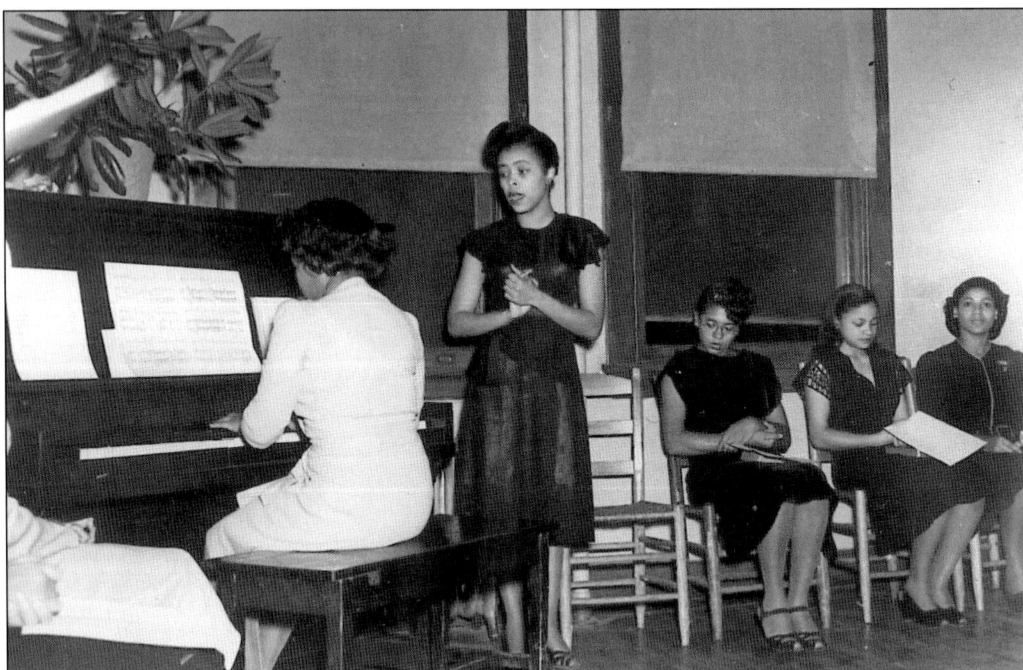

The nursing students performed in various programs from theatrical plays to music productions. They also sang at graduation ceremonies. Mrs. Lucille Zimmerman Williams plays the piano, *c.* 1948, as she was often known to do, accompanying students during rehearsal and performances. (Courtesy of Carolyn Henderson.)

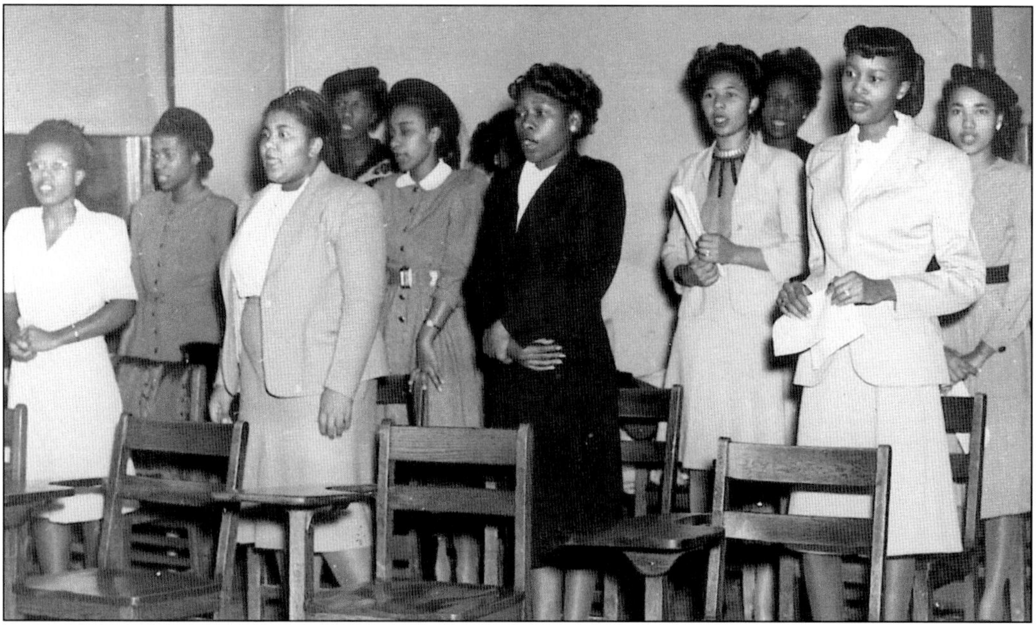

The Lincoln Hospital School of Nursing had a choir comprised mostly of students and a few graduate nurses and hospital staff. They practiced weekly and performed at events at Lincoln Hospital and throughout the community. One of the first steps toward racial integration between Watts Hospital, Duke Hospital, and Lincoln Hospital came from these vocal musicians when they performed as one choir for the Christmas season every year from 1958 and through 1967. (Courtesy of Carolyn Henderson.)

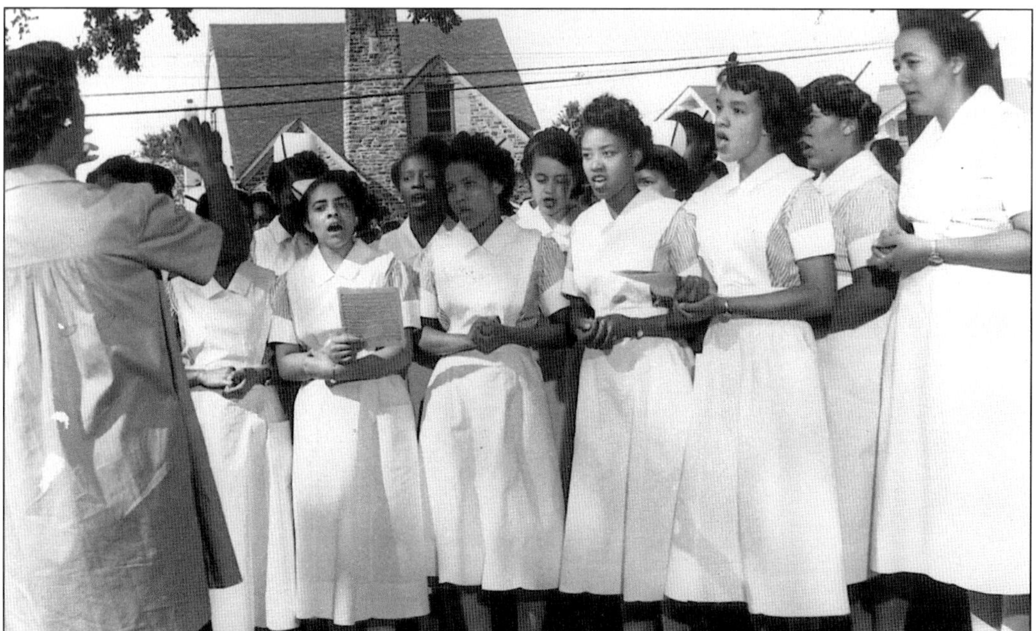

Pictured here is the Lincoln Hospital School of Nursing Choir performing at graduation on the lawn of Lincoln Hospital. (Courtesy of Margaret Kennedy Goodwin.)

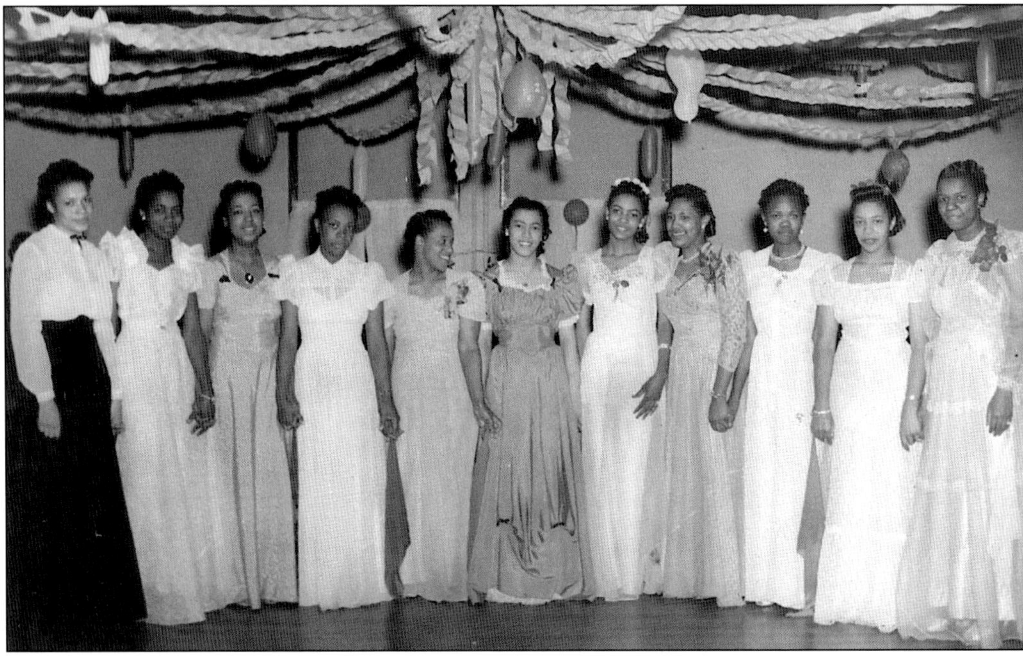

The junior class of nursing students hosted an annual ball for the graduating class. The evening was filled with dancing and socializing with the young African-American men in Durham, many of whom were students at North Carolina College. Pictured here is the 1941 senior class adorned in their evening gowns. With few places in Durham available to purchase evening attire, most of the girls made their own dresses. (Courtesy of Margaret Kennedy Goodwin.)

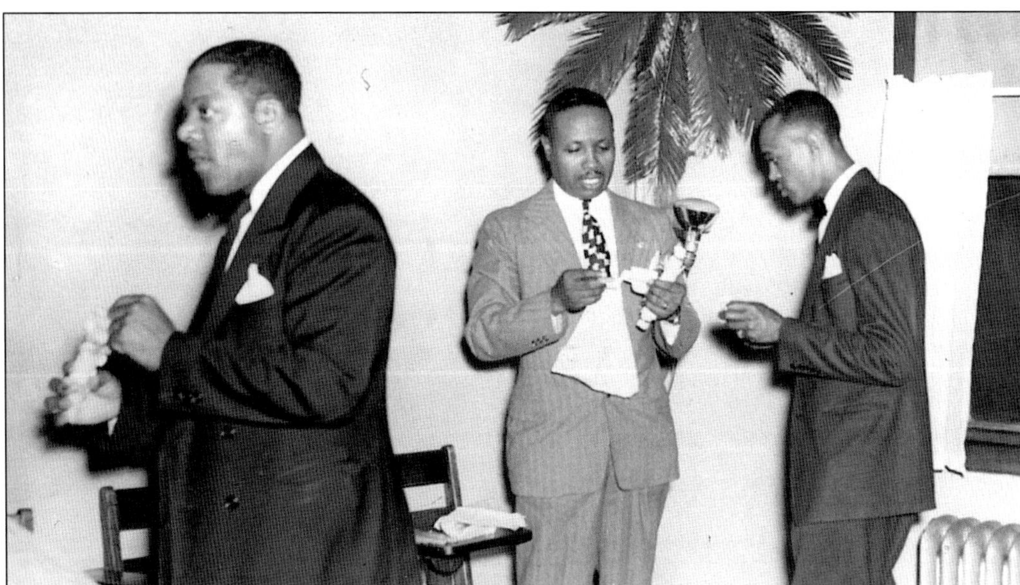

Invitations to the annual Nursing Student Ball went to people throughout the community, making the evening a memorable affair in many ways. Pictured, from left to right, are Louis Jones, Johnny Betts, and William P. Flintall. (Courtesy of Margaret Kennedy Goodwin.)

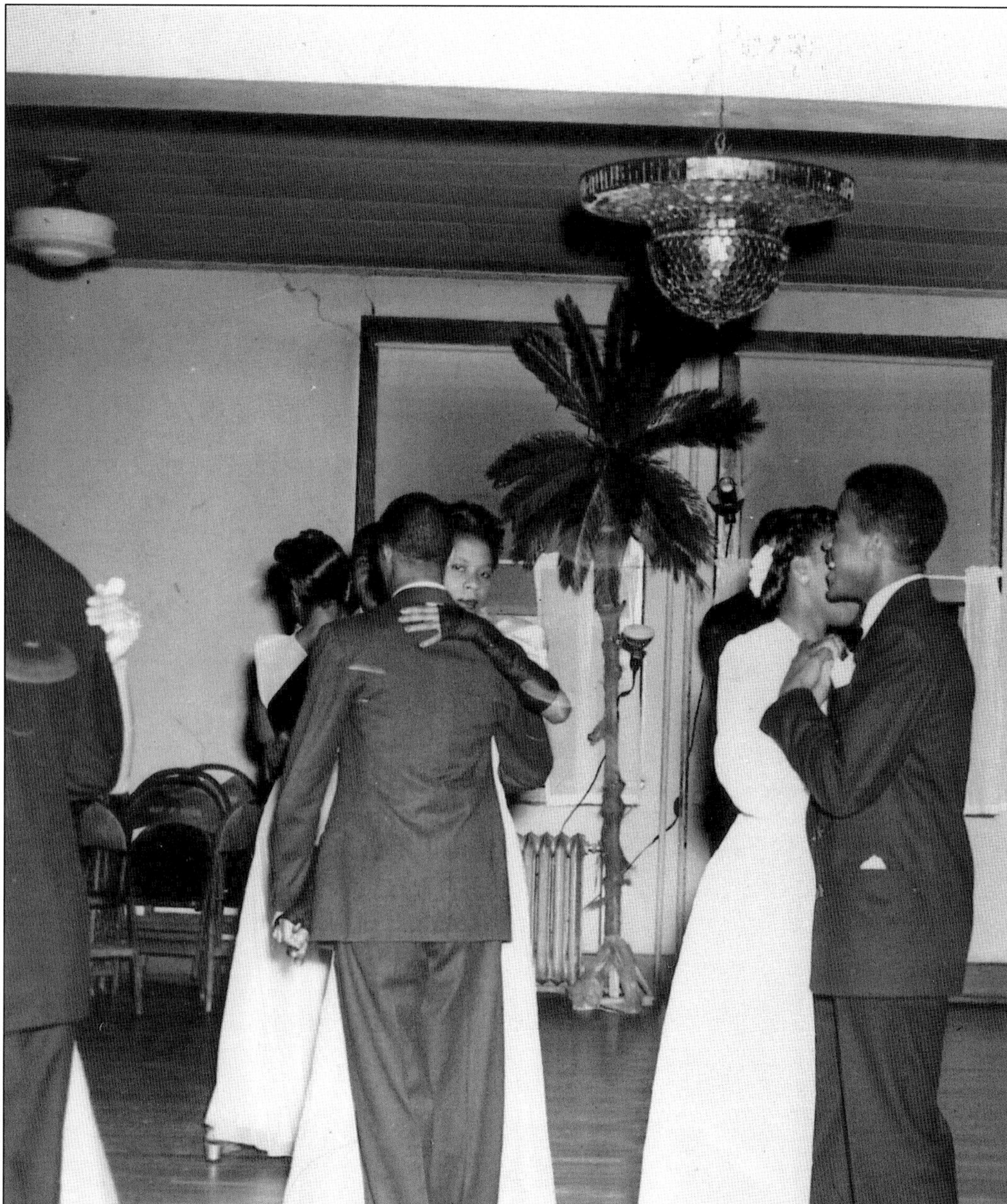

The Lincoln Hospital School of Nursing students were not permitted to marry while in school, so opportunities to socialize were enjoyed by all. (Courtesy of Margaret Kennedy Goodwin.)

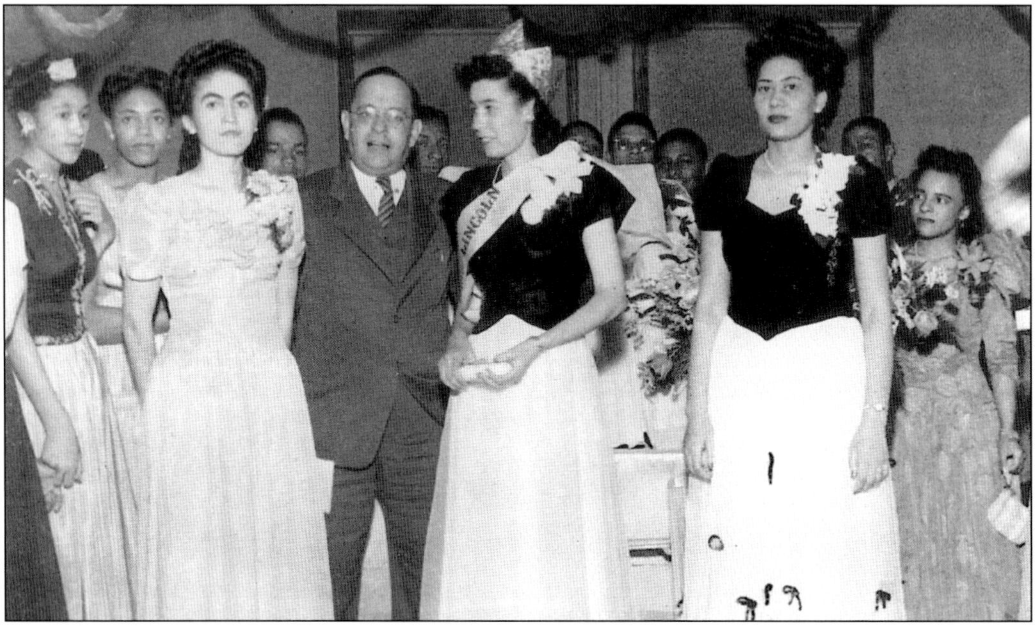

The highlight of the Nursing Student Ball was the crowning of "Miss Lincoln" awarded by popular vote to a member of the junior class. Pictured here is Miss Lois Smith who was crowned "Miss Lincoln" in 1946. Mr. Rencher Harris, president of Bankers Fire Insurance Company, is shown making the presentation to Miss Smith. (Courtesy of *The Scalpel*, 1946.)

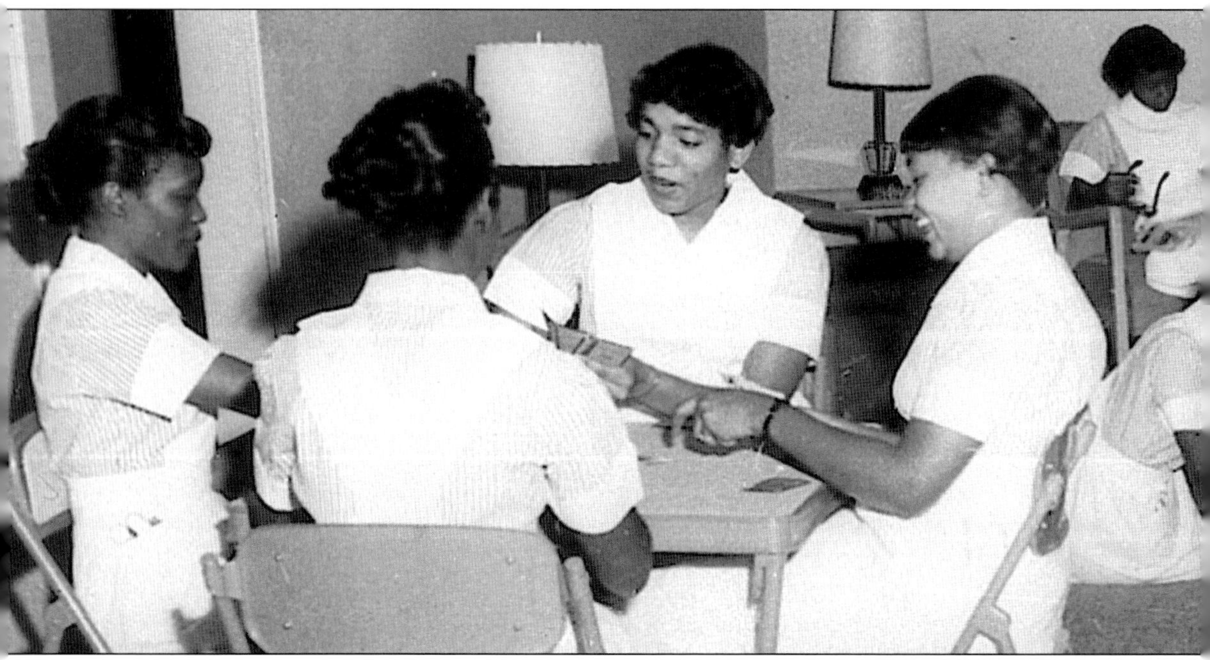

The Angier B. Duke Nurses Home was the residence for all the student nurses at Lincoln Hospital. The recreation room located on the first floor was occupied often on weekend evenings by students playing card games and board games or simply reading and socializing among themselves. Pictured here, from left to right, are (at table) Cleo Marie Dunn, Mary

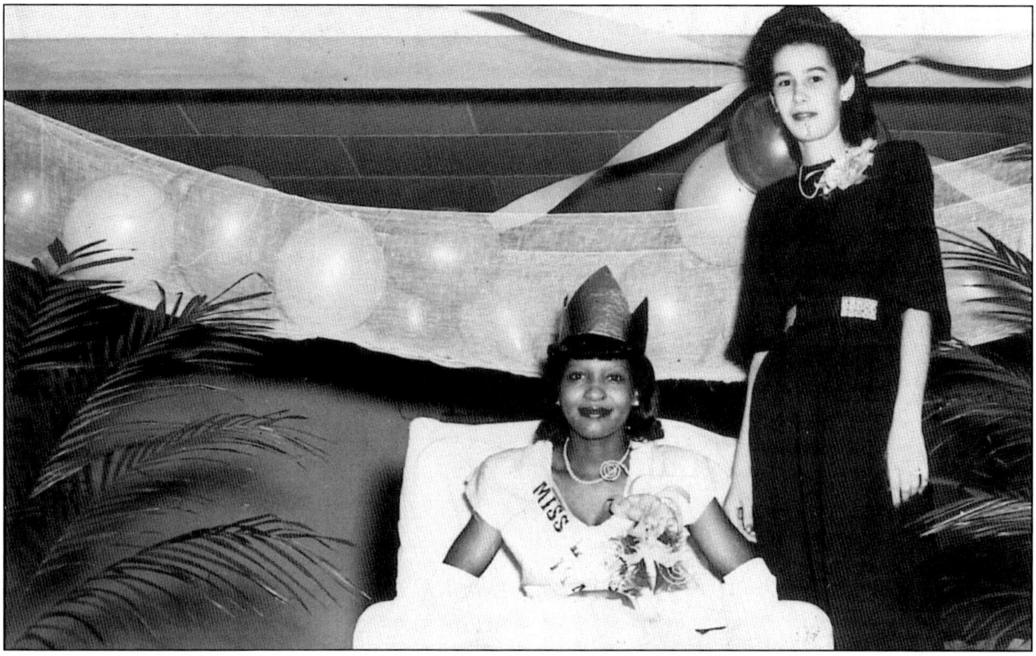

As a senior nursing student, Miss Smith was responsible for placing the crown on the next young woman voted "Miss Lincoln." Seated at the left is Miss Helen Black; standing at the right is Miss Lois Smith. (Courtesy of Carolyn Henderson.)

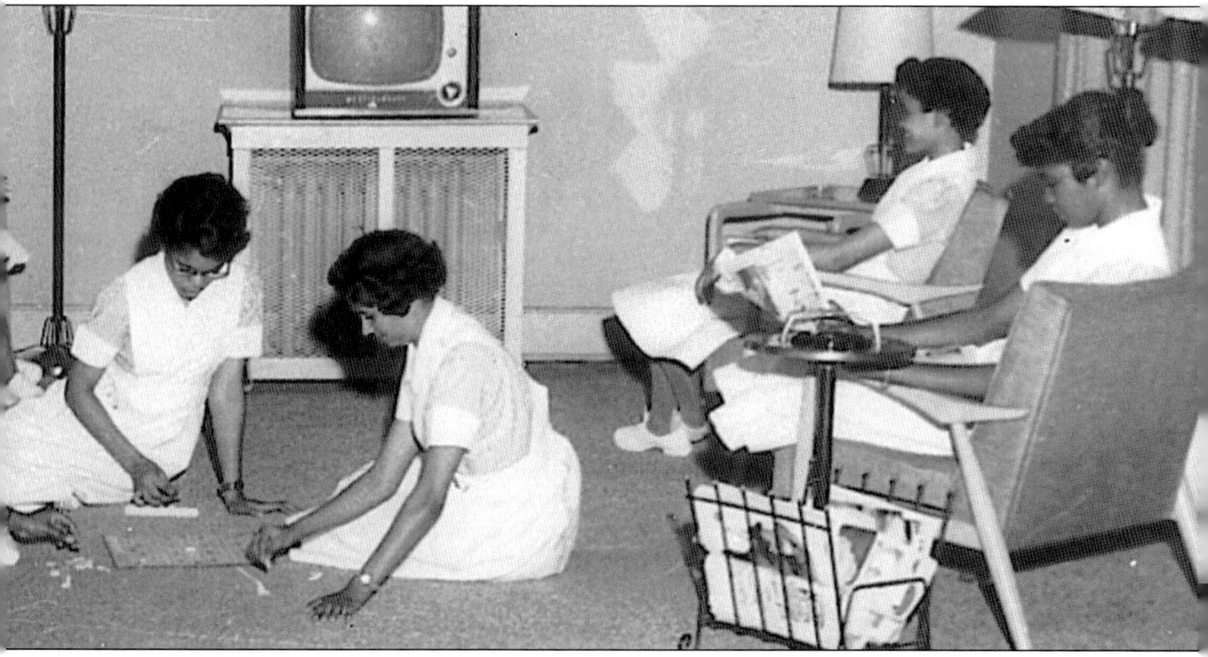

Pointer, Grace Green, and Rosa Outerbridge; (on floor) Edwina Sellers, Margaret Wilson, and Bobbie Jean Hightower; (in chairs) Valretta Roberts, Ruby Bell Barder, and Maurice Otelia Blount. (Courtesy of Carolyn Henderson.)

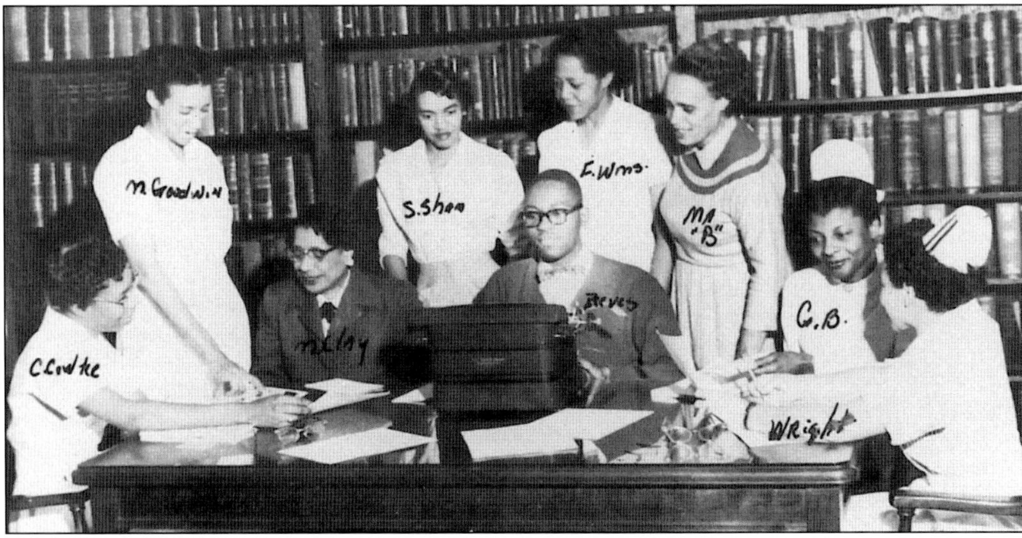

The student nurses periodically published a yearbook. The photography club supplied many of the photographs along with professional photographers from the community. These photographers included Claudie Coleman Burthey of Burthey's Photographic Lab, Nat Purefoy of Purefoy's Lab, Charles Stanback, Bob Lawson, and Carlton Graham. In addition, Mrs. Margaret Goodwin and other staff of the hospital spent countless hours laying out the pages and raising money in the community to cover publication costs. (Courtesy of Margaret Kennedy Goodwin.)

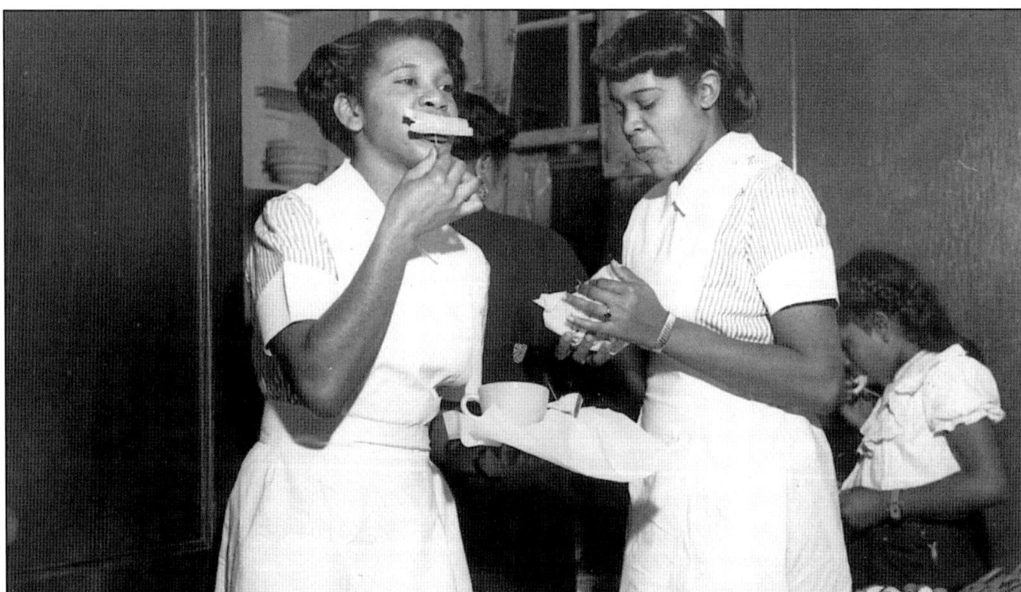

Throughout the year receptions were organized as a way to express appreciation for the many hours of service provided by the volunteers and Women's Auxiliary. In addition, receptions were held to celebrate graduation from one stage of a nursing student's education to the next level. Seen here standing are nursing students Laura Halsey on the left and Elizabeth Kearney on the right.(Courtesy of Margaret Kennedy Goodwin.)

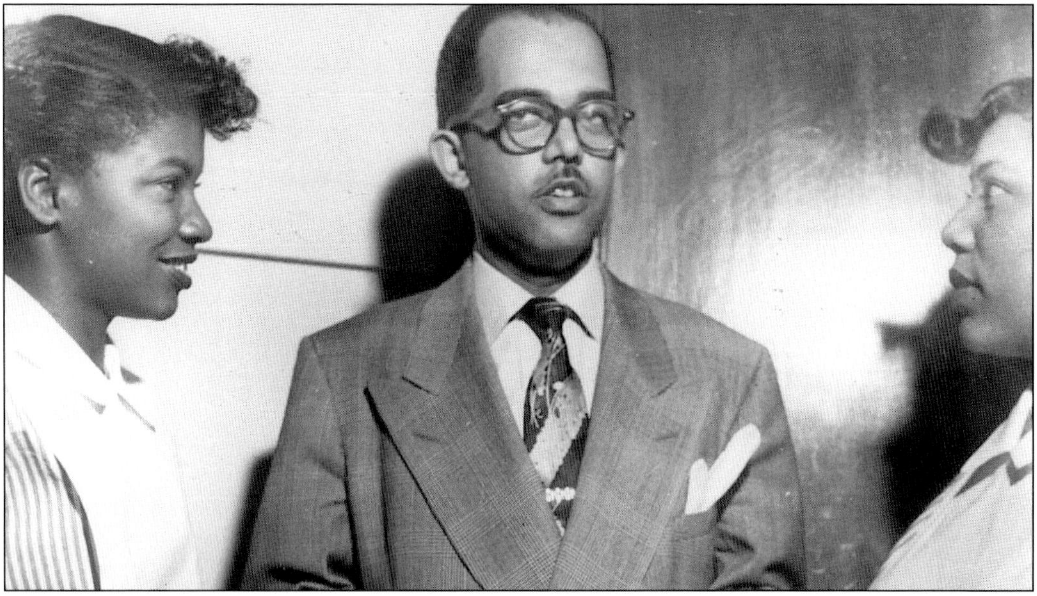

Superintendent Frank Scott is pictured here at a reception for the student nurses talking with Mary Royster on the left and Marion Glenn on the right. (Courtesy of Margaret Kennedy Goodwin.)

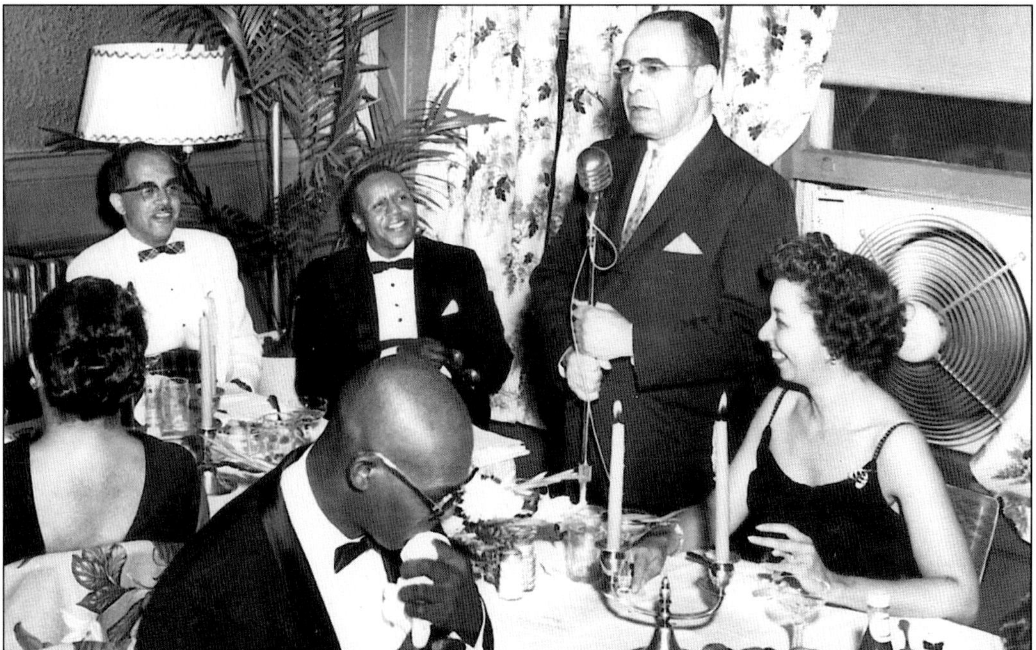

Lincoln Hospital hosted visiting lecturers and special events for the physicians and hospital staff. Dr. Montague Cobb, professor of anatomy and anthropology at Howard University and editor of the *Journal of the National Medical Association*, was the guest speaker one year. Pictured clockwise from Dr. W. Montague Cobb (standing) are Dr. Leroy Swift, Mr. Frank Scott, Mrs. Laura Bruce, Mr. Franklin Shanks, and Mrs. Charlie Swift. (Courtesy of Margaret Kennedy Goodwin.)

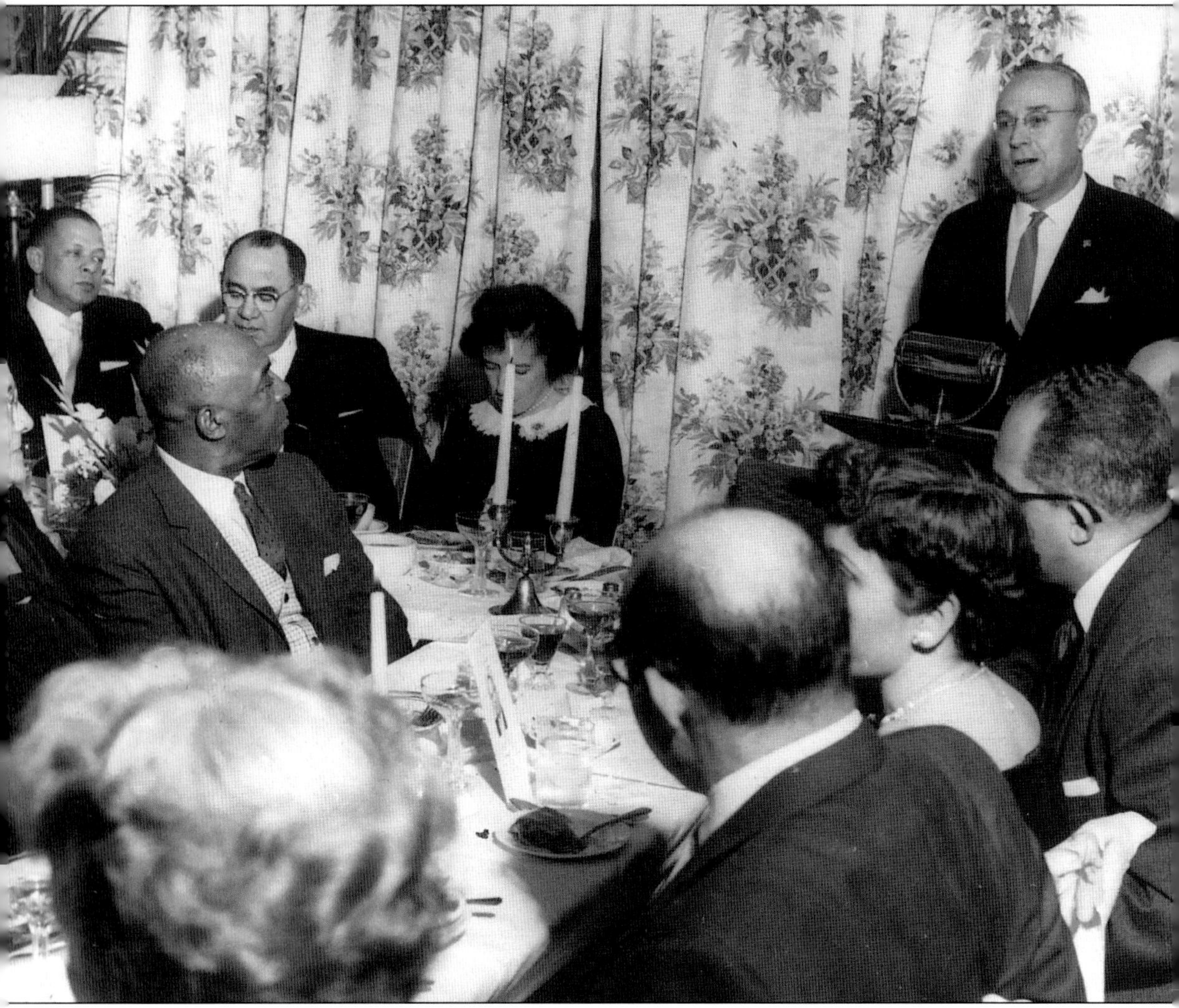

Awards banquets also were held at Lincoln Hospital. Pictured here are Mrs. Mary Semans, William Rich, John Wheeler, Rev. William Fuller, Mrs. Veda Hinson, Dr. and Mrs. Kyle, Mr. and Mrs. Frank Scott. (Courtesy of Margaret Kennedy Goodwin.)

Seven

Preparing the Day's Work

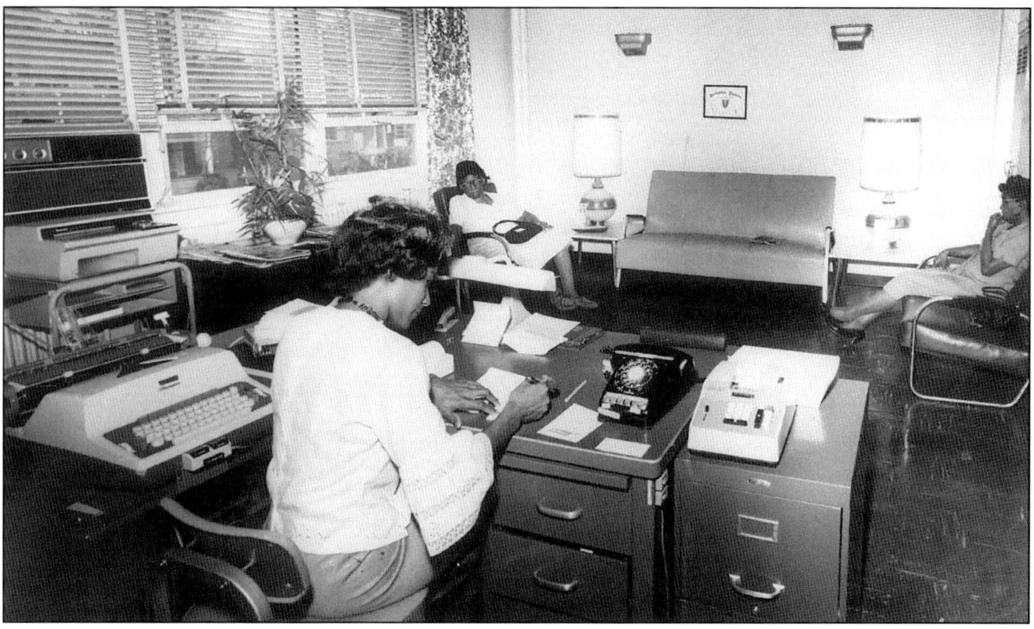

The admitting office of Lincoln Hospital was the first stopping point for patients who entered the hospital for elective procedures. As much information as possible was obtained in order to determine their financial resources. Those patients who were indigent were provided care without charge, but those with even modest resources were asked to pay the full costs of their hospital bill. Lincoln Hospital obtained some funds from the Duke Endowment and the Durham City and County governments to help meet the expenses of care to non-paying patients. (Courtesy of Margaret Kennedy Goodwin.)

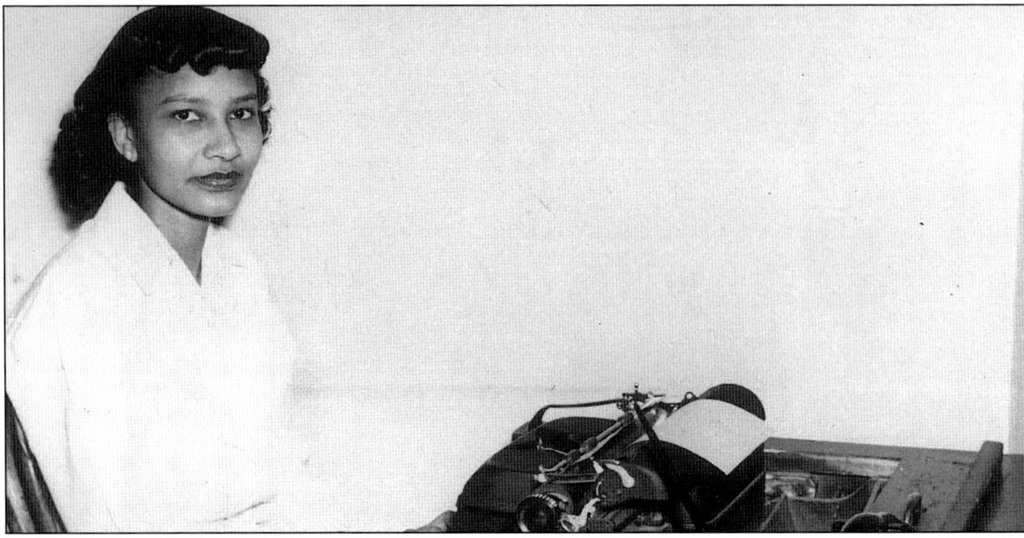

Pictured above is Miss Julia L. Tapp, billing clerk, *c.* 1948. When William Rich joined the staff of Lincoln Hospital in 1934, he instituted a system of accounting and billing. Annually, Lincoln Hospital hosted a meeting sponsored by the Duke Endowment to help African-American hospitals in the Carolinas capture data, especially with regard to indigent days of care. These days were reimbursed by the endowment at a rate of $1 per day of care to each indigent patient. By receiving payment on outstanding hospital bills, Miss Julia Tapp enabled Lincoln Hospital to lower the number of non-paying patients and recover its costs of providing hospital care. (Courtesy of Margaret Kennedy Goodwin.)

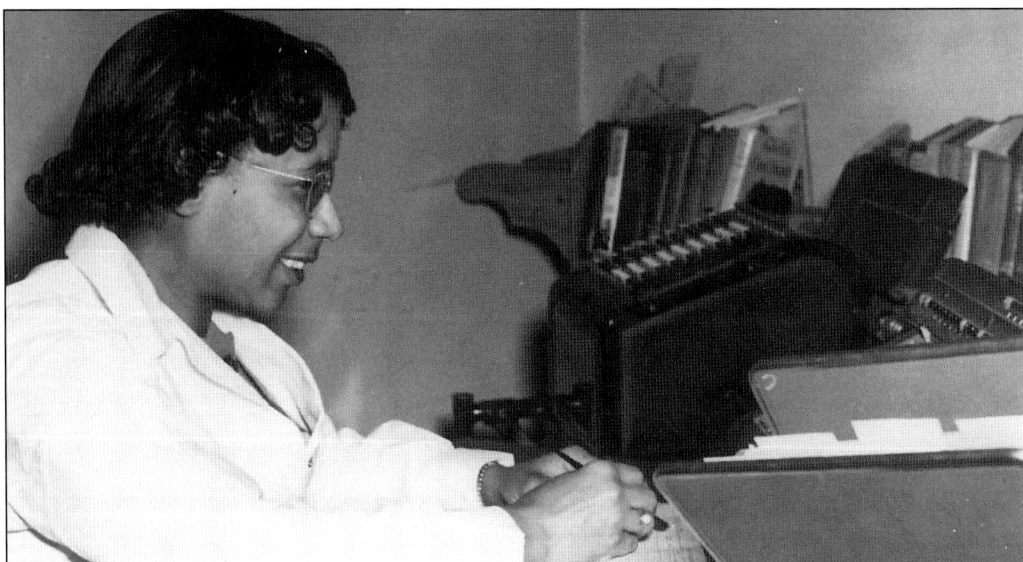

Seated in the picture is Mrs. Mary K. Clay, *c.* 1948. Mrs. Clay was the sister of Mr. William Jesse Kennedy Jr., president of the North Carolina Mutual Life Insurance Company. She worked at Lincoln Hospital in accounting for many years and kept the financial records up to date and ready for review by auditors, the Durham City and County governments, and the Duke Endowment. (Courtesy of Margaret Kennedy Goodwin.)

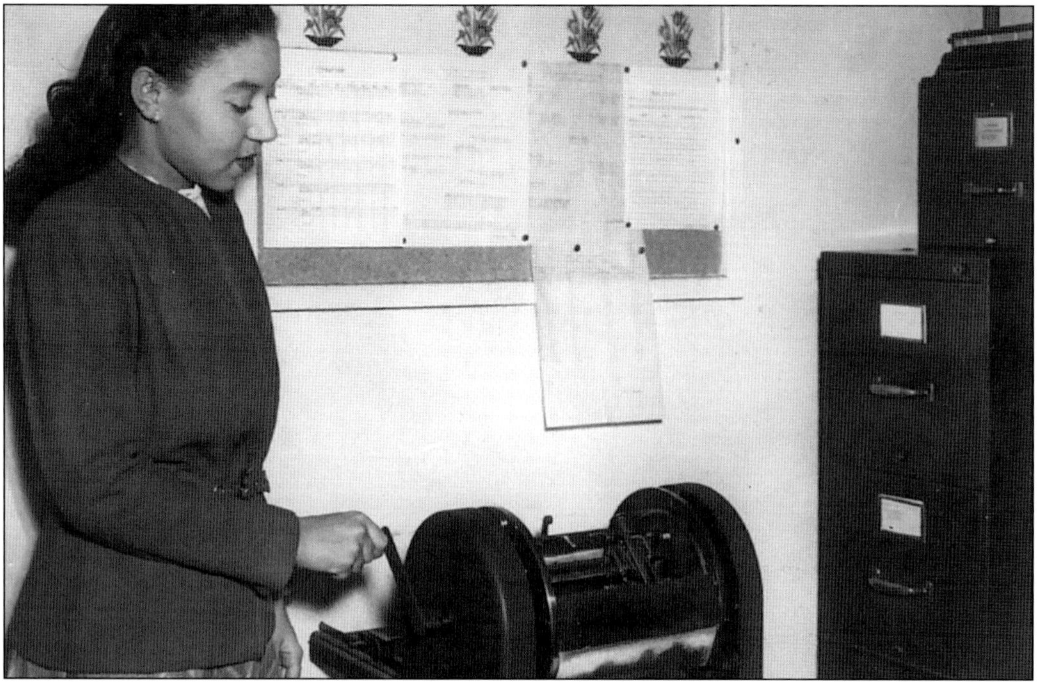

Administrative staff worked in areas throughout the hospital such as the admitting office, medical records, billing and accounting, and the nursing school. Each nursing student had on file her application and letters of recommendation as well as her grades and comments of instructors and the director of nursing. In addition, the office of the school of nursing kept up with alumni by sending out invitations to graduations and social events. Pictured here is a member of the staff using an early version of a mimeograph machine. (Courtesy of Margaret Kennedy Goodwin.)

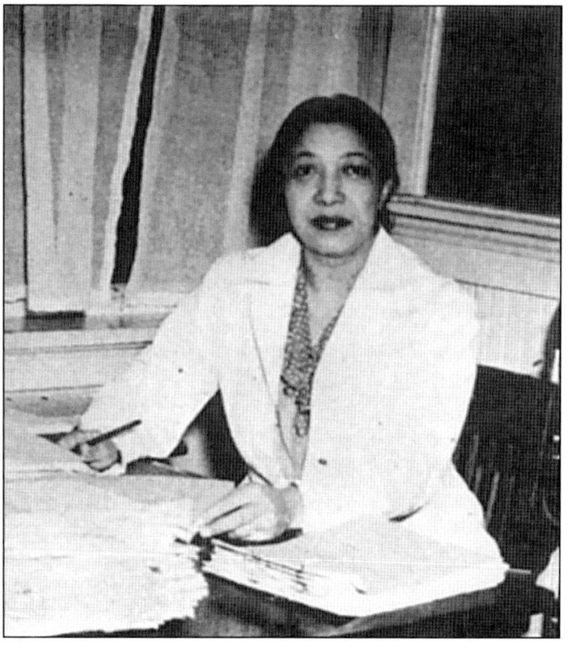

Mrs. Laura Bruce was the first full-time medical records librarian at Lincoln Hospital, a position she held for 39 years. Mrs. Bruce was awarded a Julius Rosenwald Fund fellowship in 1941 to do further study in library and hospital recording at the Provident Hospital in Chicago. The hospital standardization movement created greater demands for accurate and complete medical records. Mrs. Bruce worked with the residents and physicians to achieve these higher standards, but also with the Duke Endowment staff to capture all the clinical data necessary for annual reporting on the quality of patient care. (Courtesy of *The Scalpel*, 1948.)

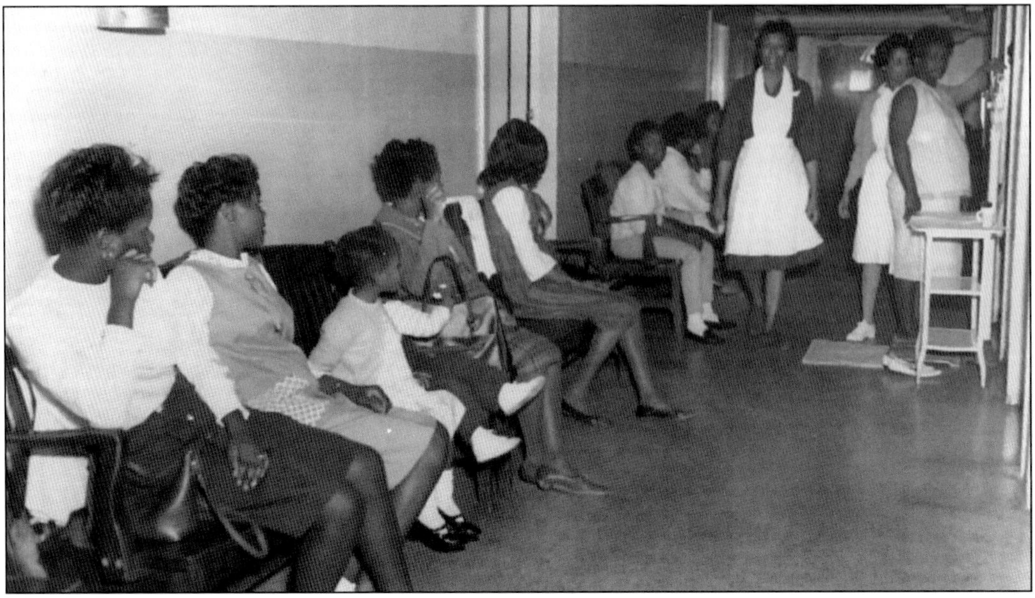

Pictured here walking down the hall is Mrs. Ruth Flintall Betts, R.N., a 1935 graduate of Lincoln Hospital School of Nursing. She received a B.S. in Nursing from North Carolina Central University in 1966 and also held a certificate in Public Health Nursing from St. Phillips Medical College in Richmond, Virginia. Mrs. Betts assumed multiple responsibilities in Durham's health care community, working for the Durham County Health Department where she organized public education programs, ran the outpatient clinics, and assisted Dr. William A. Cleland in the well-baby clinics. (Courtesy of *The Scalpel*, 1948.)

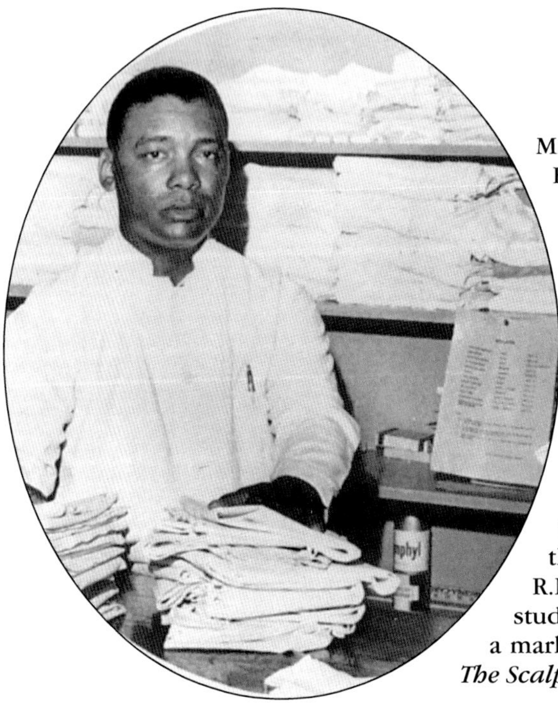

Mr. John Chambers directed the Lincoln Hospital laundry. It was a tremendously busy operation because of the daily demand for clean sheets and towels for patients and uniforms and surgical scrubs for residents, physicians, and nurses. In the early years of Lincoln Hospital, the nurses' uniforms were cleaned, pressed, and starched by the laundry personnel. In later years, nurses would pay for their uniforms to be cleaned and pressed while students learned the skills as part of their professional training. Miss Patty Carter, R.N., and then Mrs. Lucille Zimmerman Williams, R.N., directors of nursing, demanded the students' uniforms be clean and starched as a mark of their professional roles. (Courtesy of *The Scalpel*, 1962.)

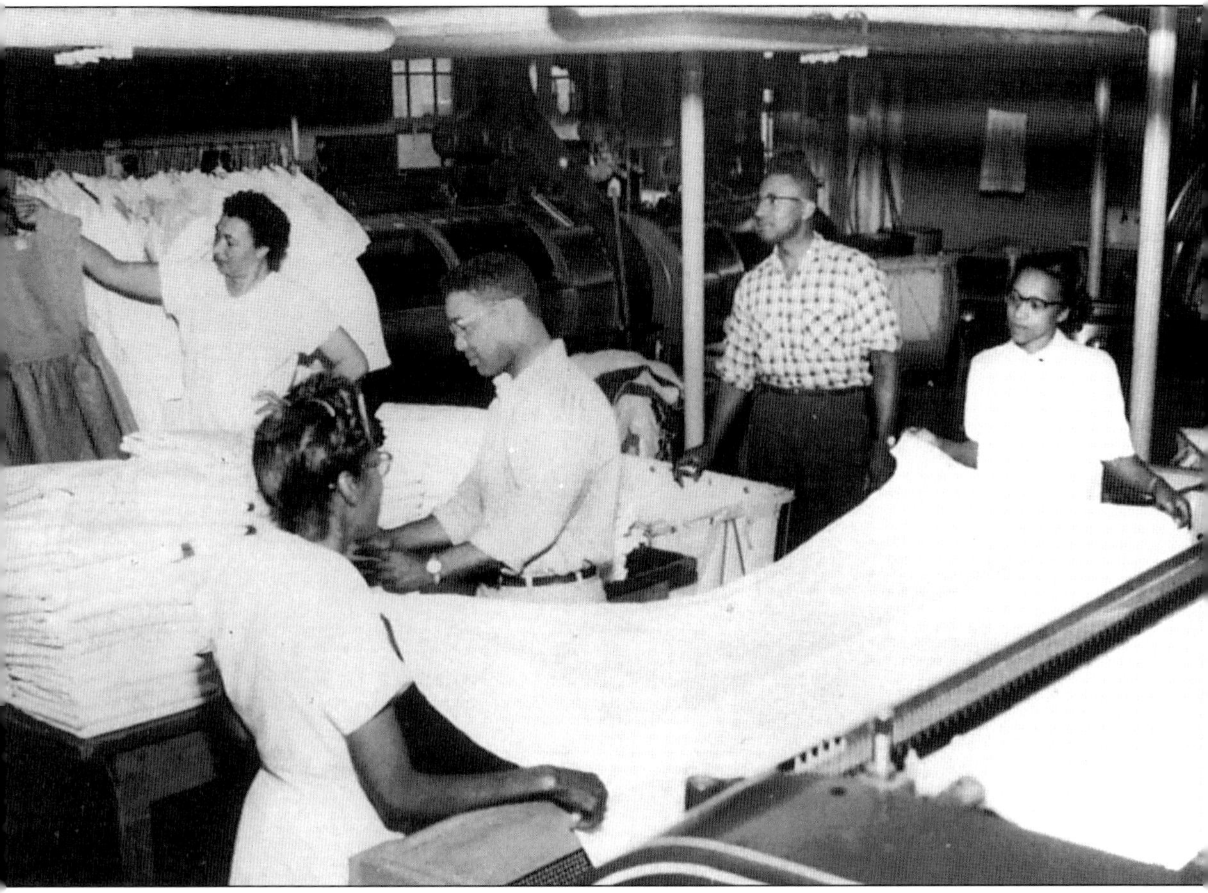

"And they keep us clean" was the motto for the Lincoln Hospital laundry. Laundry staff members pictured here are Mrs. Cates, Mrs. Hamilton, Mr. Chambers, Mr. Kearney, and Mrs. Pippins. (Courtesy of *The Scalpel*, 1957.)

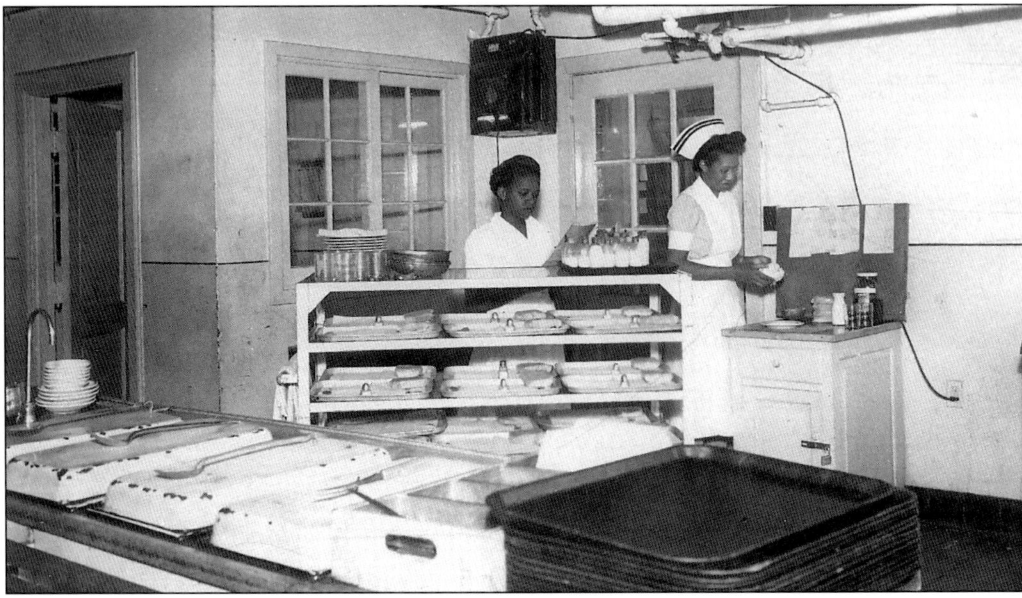

The kitchen personnel included a full-time dietician as well as cooks and student nurses. Meals were prepared for patients for breakfast, lunch, and dinner, along with food for physicians, nurses, and other hospital staff. The hospital purchased its food supplies from local vendors and farmers, balancing freshness against cost. Pictured above are dietician Miss Christine Hall (right) and student nurse Helen Neal (left). (Courtesy of Margaret Kennedy Goodwin.)

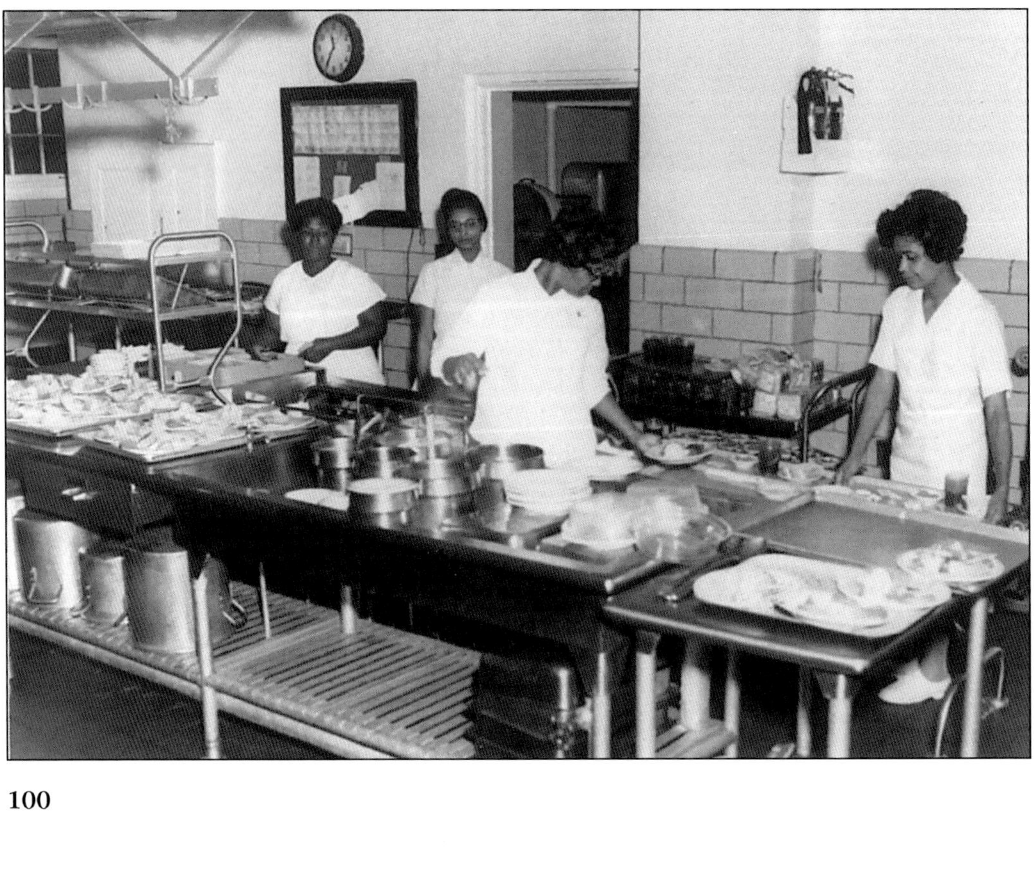

Mr. Everlee Jones was an essential member of the culinary team and worked as the chef to prepare seasoned and nutritious dishes. (Courtesy of *The Scalpel*, 1962.)

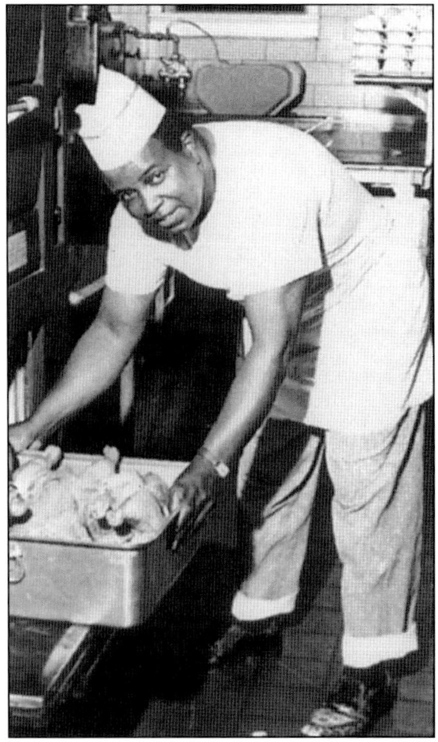

Unlike many hospitals throughout the country, the physicians at Lincoln Hospital did not eat in a separate dining room from the nurses and staff. This created a sense of family among all who worked in the hospital and increased opportunities for professional interaction. (Courtesy of Margaret Kennedy Goodwin.)

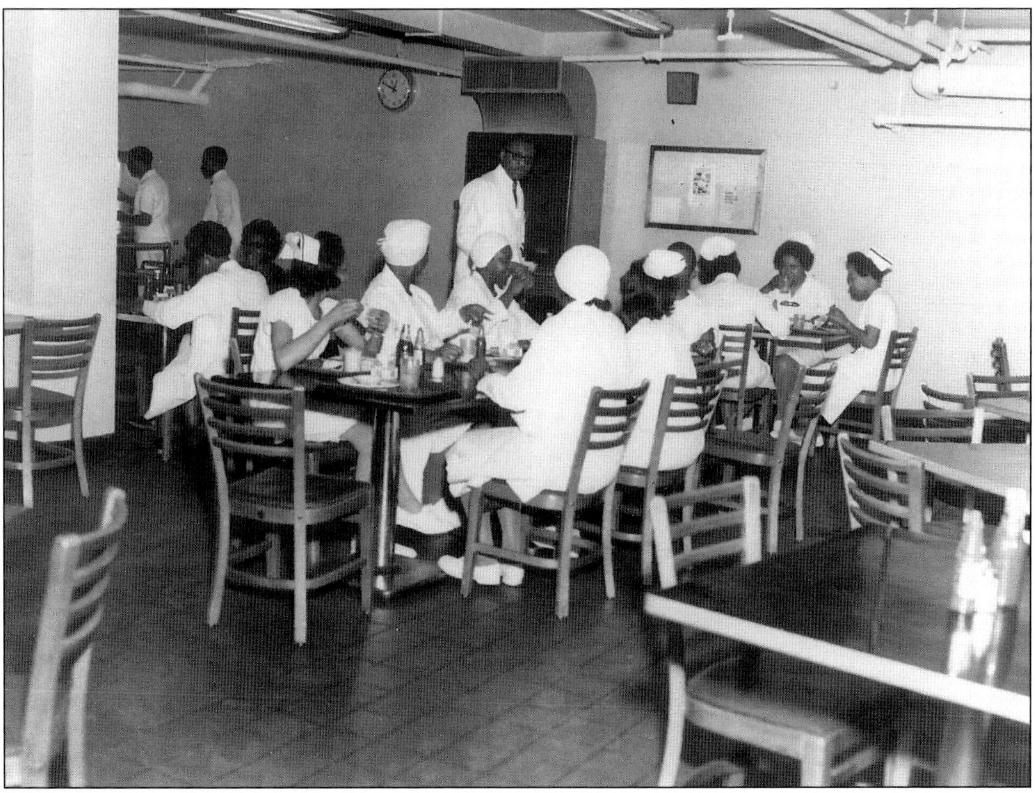

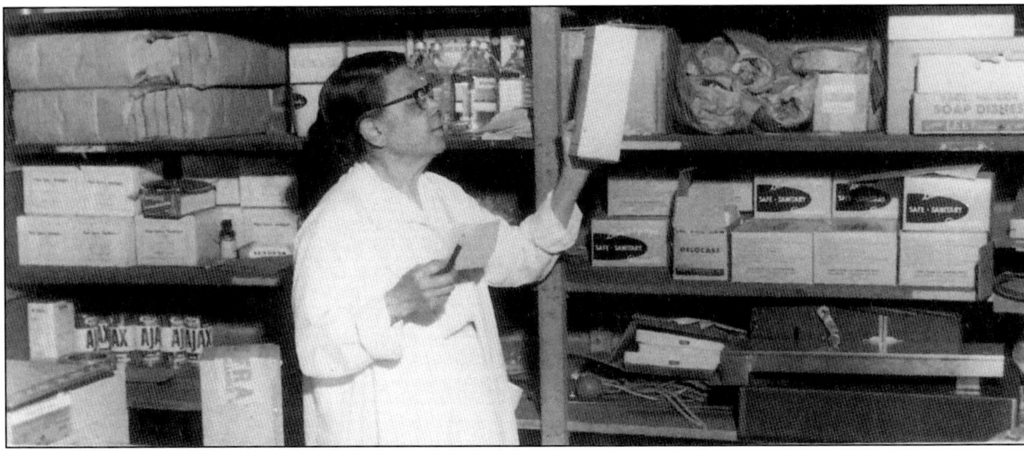

The housekeeping department was responsible for keeping the hospital floors, patient wards, operating suites, nurses quarters, clinics, and laboratories swept, mopped, and clean. In addition, the personnel had to stock bathrooms with Kleenex, paper towels, toilet paper, and soap, and the kitchen with cleanser. There were endless details to keeping the hospital clean not only for patients, nurses, and physicians, but also for national hospital and local health department inspectors. (Courtesy of *Nightingale*, 1959.)

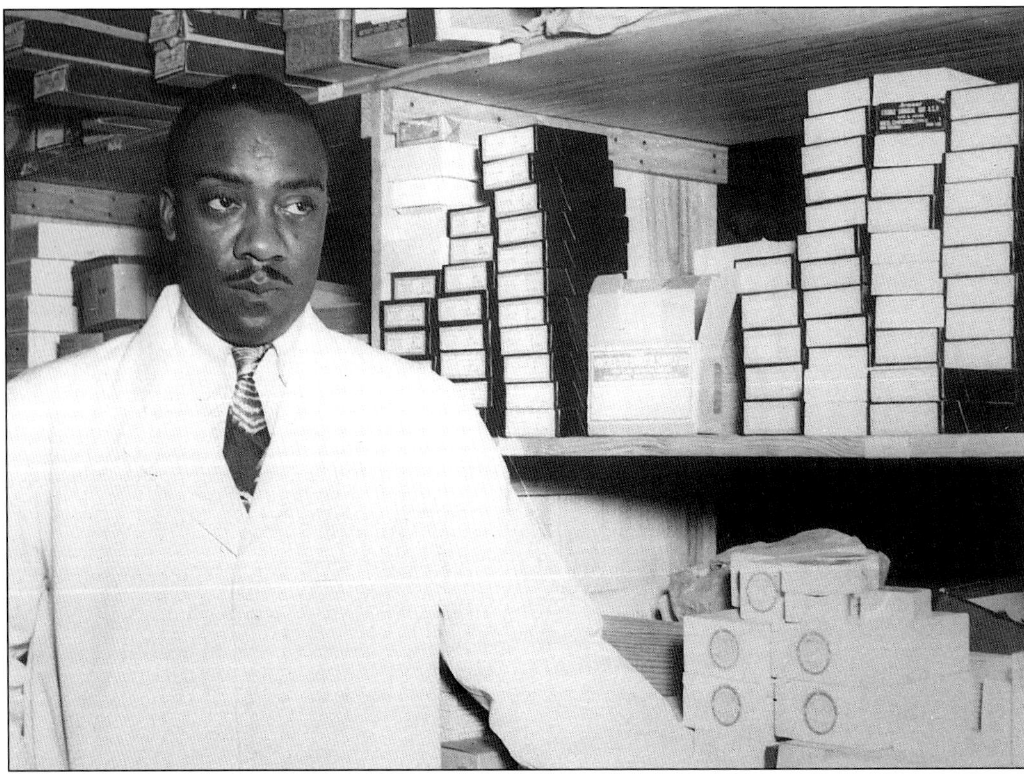

Lincoln Hospital's central supply was like any other hospital. It had to have adequate bandages, splints, and plaster for mending broken bones and sprained ankles as well as syringes, needles, and tubing for dispensing of medications on the hospital floors. Pictured here is Haskell Hudson, director of central supply. (Courtesy of *The Scalpel*, 1948.)

Mr. Fred Wilson was recruited to Lincoln Hospital as director of the medical laboratory. The laboratory was responsible for running all blood hematology and chemistry studies, urinalyses, and examinations to investigate the presence of infectious organisms. He also oversaw the blood bank (which had been established by Dr. Max Schiebel, chief of surgery) and preparation of blood for surgery and transfusions. (Courtesy of *Nightingale*, 1959.)

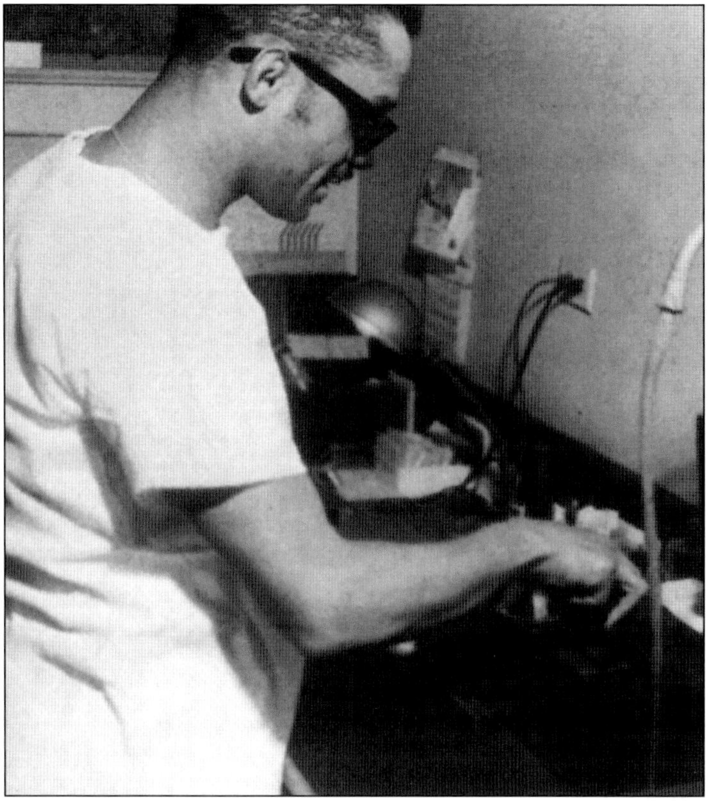

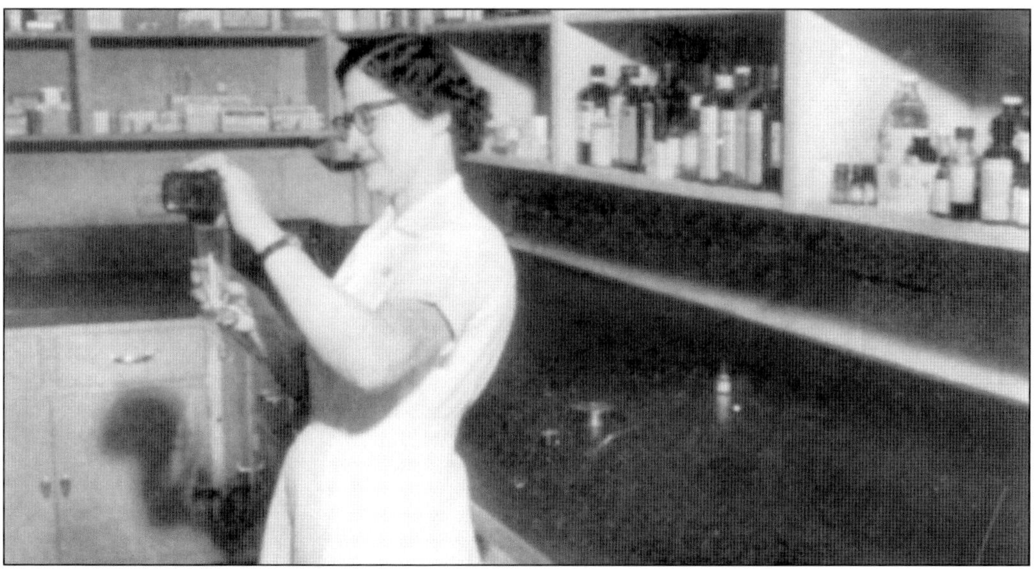

The original Board of Trustees of Lincoln Hospital included James E. Shepard who graduated from Shaw University School of Pharmacy. Dispensing of medications was an important task and the Lincoln Hospital pharmacy supplied both the in-hospital patients as well as ambulatory patients with prescriptions from their physicians. (Courtesy of *Nightingale*, 1958.)

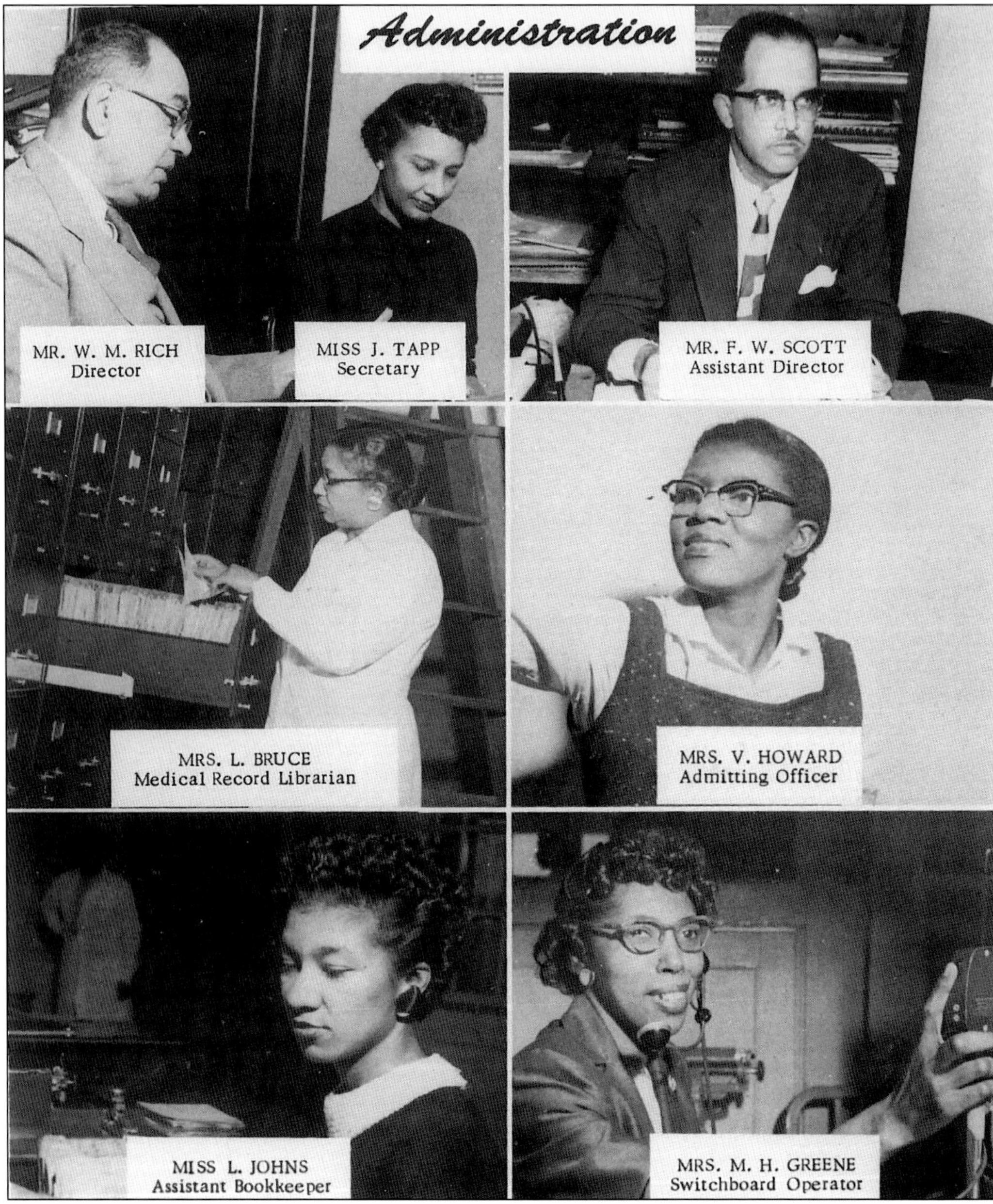

By the mid-1950s, Lincoln Hospital administration had grown to include Mr. Frank Scott as assistant director and Miss L. Johns as assistant bookkeeper. All of these individuals kept the busy hospital operating smoothly and at the same time served as leaders in the Durham community. (Courtesy of *The Scalpel*, 1956.)

Eight

Community Support and Public Service

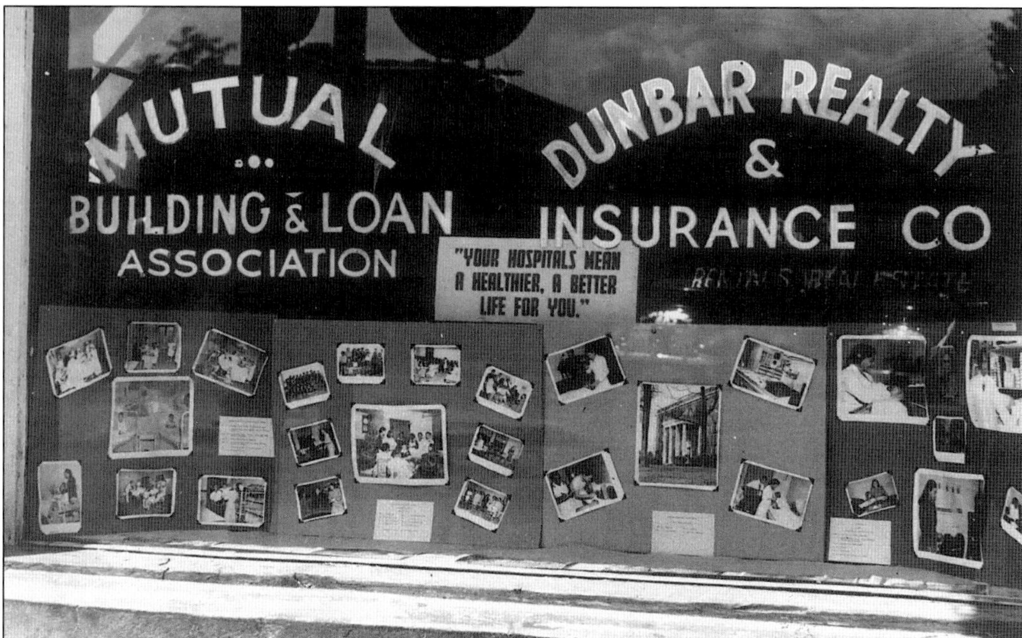

Celebration of Hospital Day each year on May 12th occurred throughout country. The day was set aside by President Warren G. Harding to commemorate the life and service of Florence Nightingale. In Durham, Hospital Day was designed to bring Lincoln Hospital closer to the African-American citizens. Posters describing many services and clinics offered at Lincoln Hospital rested in the front windows of the main businesses located along Fayetteville Street. (Courtesy of Margaret Kennedy Goodwin.)

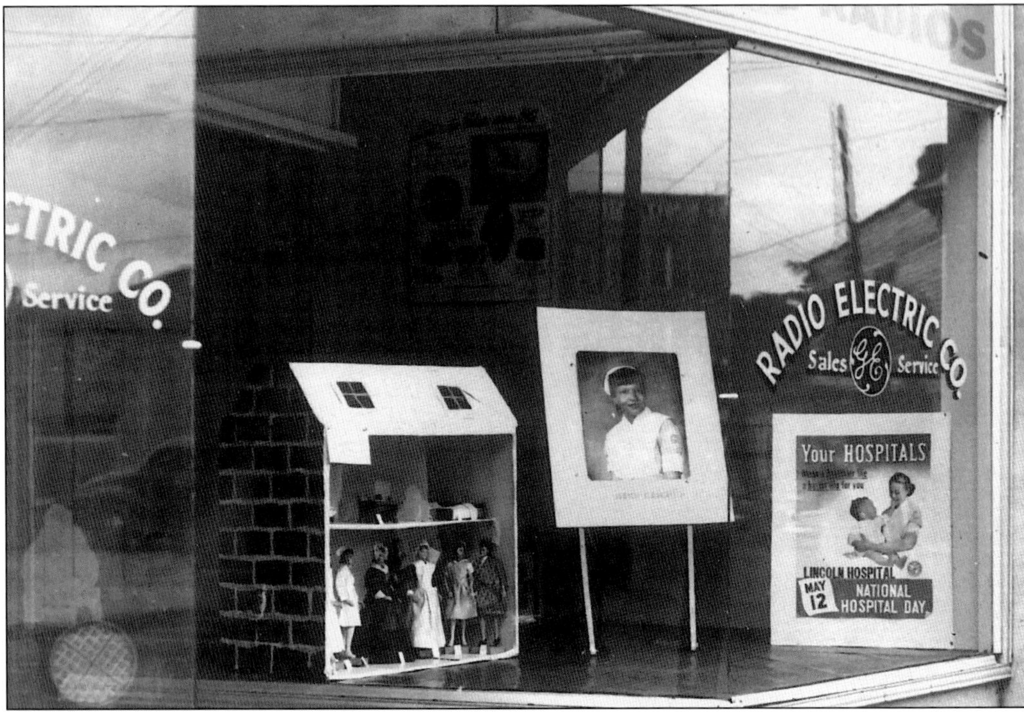

Lincoln Hospital organized tours and other events to encourage people to visit the hospital and to educate them about ways to prevent illness. These events were publicized in the *Carolina Times*, the local African-American newspaper. At the close of Hospital Day in 1938, Lincoln Hospital sponsored a lecture for the community at North Carolina College drawing close to 500 people. (Courtesy of Margaret Kennedy Goodwin.)

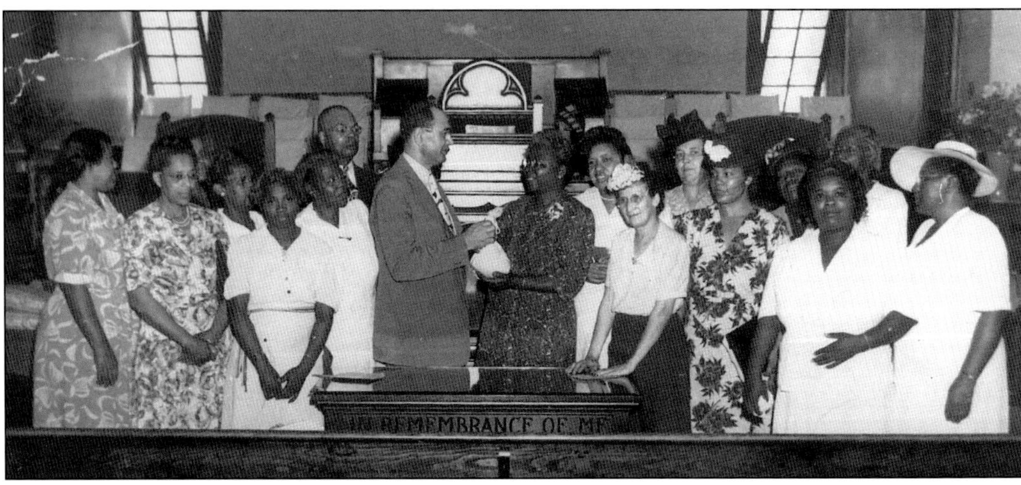

William Rich, superintendent from 1934 to 1959, worked with the church leadership to raise money and supplies for Lincoln Hospital. Annually, churches throughout Durham gathered bed linens, robes, and clothing for use by the hospital and its patients. The women of the churches often raised additional funds through special drives and events. Pictured here is the inside of Mt. Zion Baptist Church. The minister's wife, Mrs. Dovie Grady, is wearing a hat and standing across from William Rich. (Courtesy of Carolyn Henderson.)

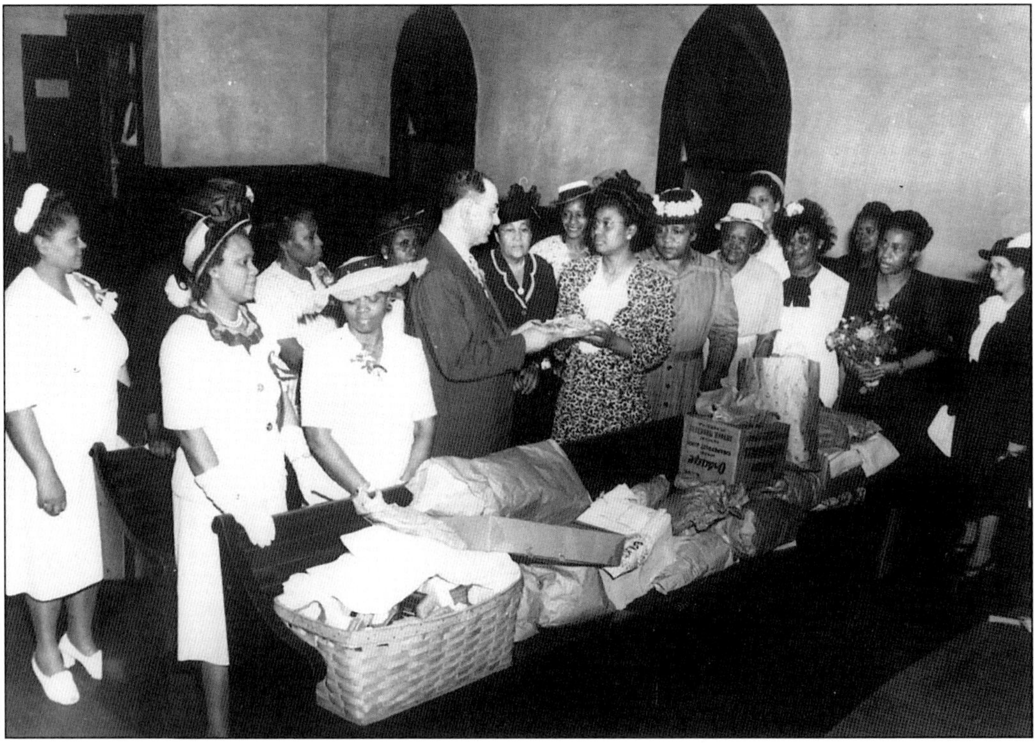

Lincoln Hospital developed a broad base of support throughout the community by working through the churches. Through special church offerings everyone came to understand the financial struggles of operating a hospital with a heavy charity load. Ultimately, Lincoln Hospital became cemented in the hearts of the African-American citizens because everyone felt invested in maintaining its presence as a place of healing and hope. Pictured above is the inside of Mt. Zion Baptist Church. (Courtesy of Margaret Kennedy Goodwin.)

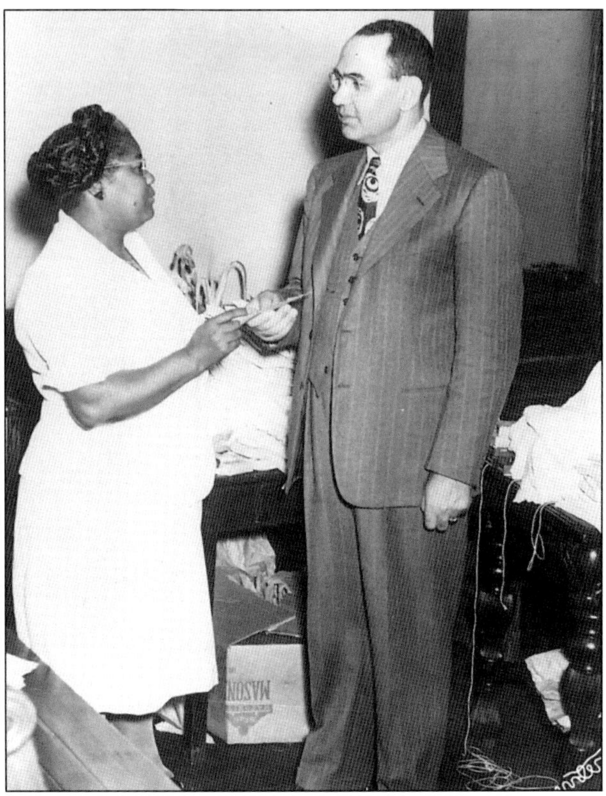

William Rich receives a donation of money and linen. (Courtesy of Margaret Kennedy Goodwin.)

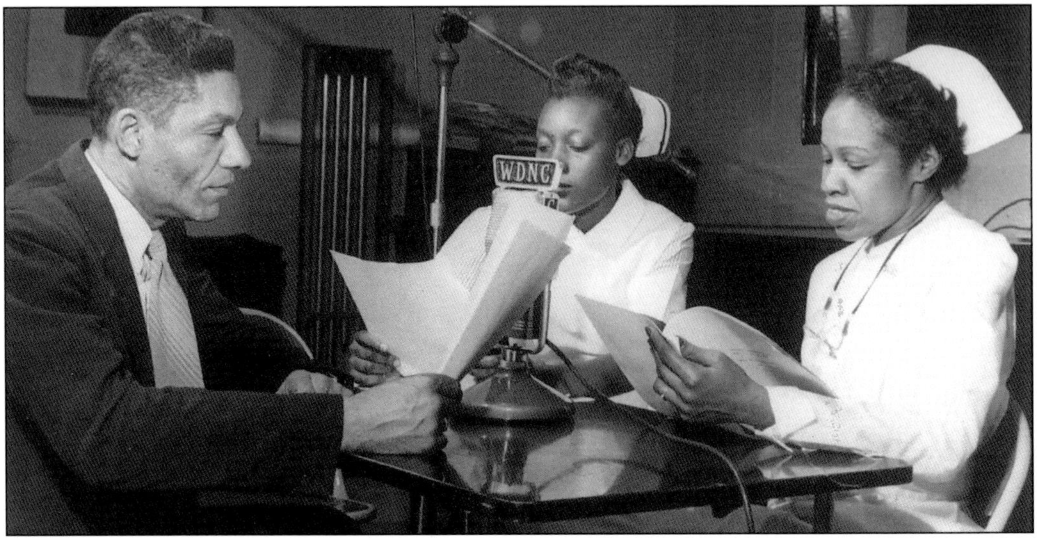

The Lincoln Hospital nursing students were required to contribute to voluntary programs in the community. One favorite activity was health education over the airwaves. Every other week, Mrs. Lucille Zimmerman Williams, R.N., director of the Lincoln Hospital School of Nursing, would broadcast a health education program with one of the students. Pictured here is Norfleet Whitted, the first African-American radio broadcaster in Durham preparing to air the program on WDNC with student nurse, Eursala O'neil and Mrs. Lucille Zimmerman Williams, RN. (Courtesy of Carolyn Henderson.)

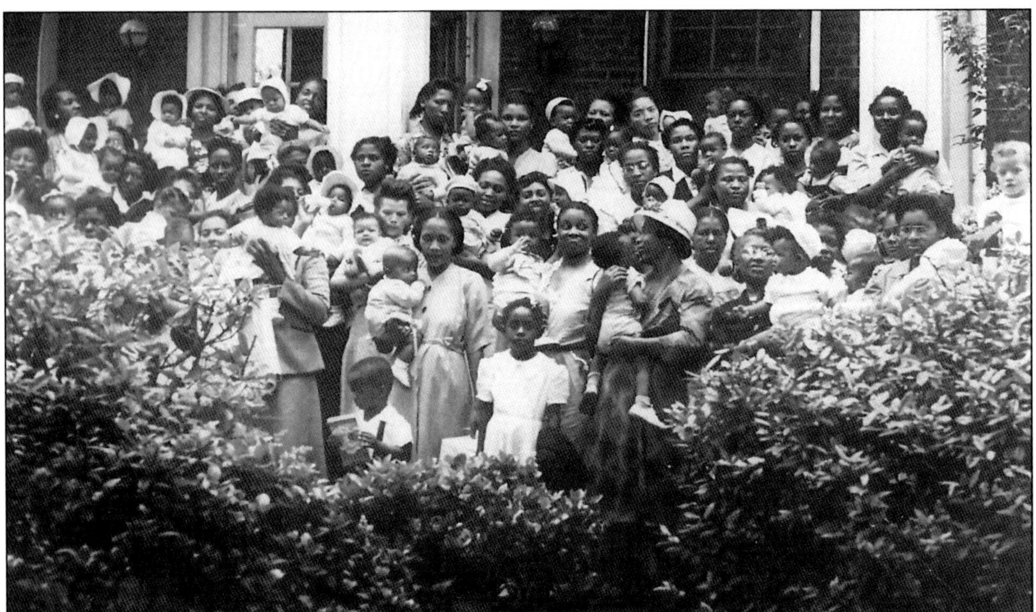

Beginning in 1938, the Lincoln Hospital Women's Auxiliary organized "Baby Reunion Day" every other year, shown here *c.* 1947. Every woman who had delivered a baby at Lincoln Hospital was invited. Through "Baby Reunion Day," Lincoln Hospital stayed in touch with mothers and provided information about the well-baby clinic. Each baby received a gift donated from local businesses. (Courtesy of Margaret Kennedy Goodwin.)

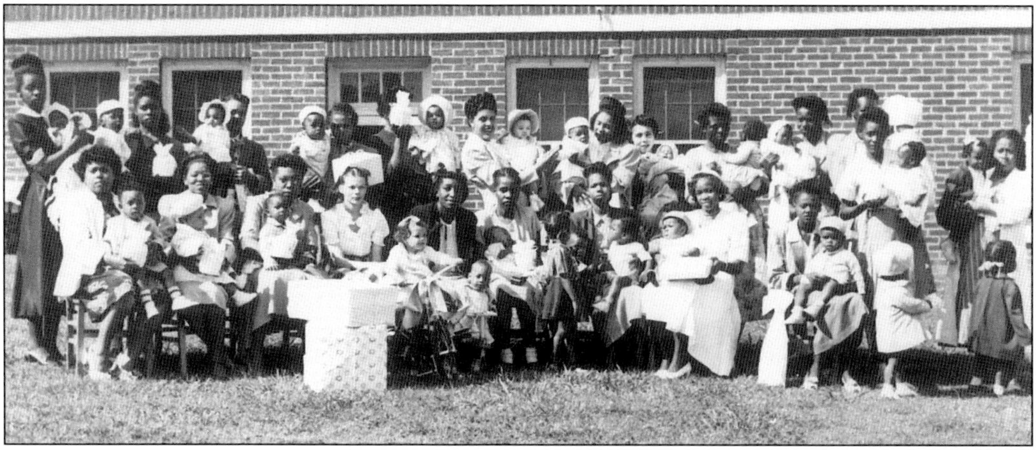

This photograph shows Lincoln Hospital's "Baby Reunion Day," *c.* 1949. (Courtesy of Margaret Kennedy Goodwin.)

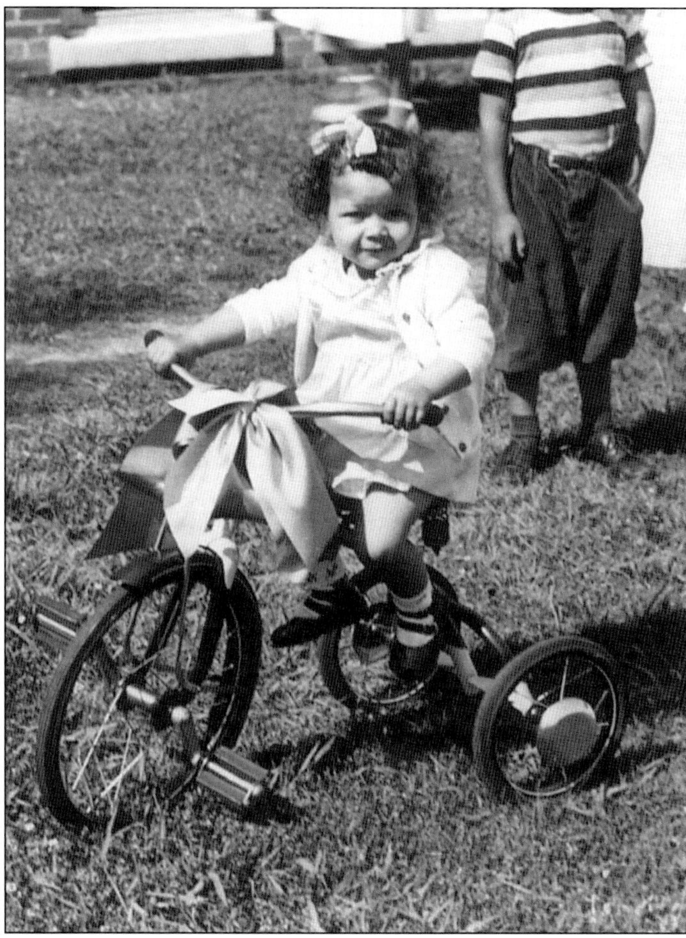

The capstone of the reunion day's events was the crowning of "Baby Lincoln," with prizes given to the winners and their mothers. Pictured here is "Baby Lincoln," *c.* 1949. (Courtesy of Margaret Kennedy Goodwin.)

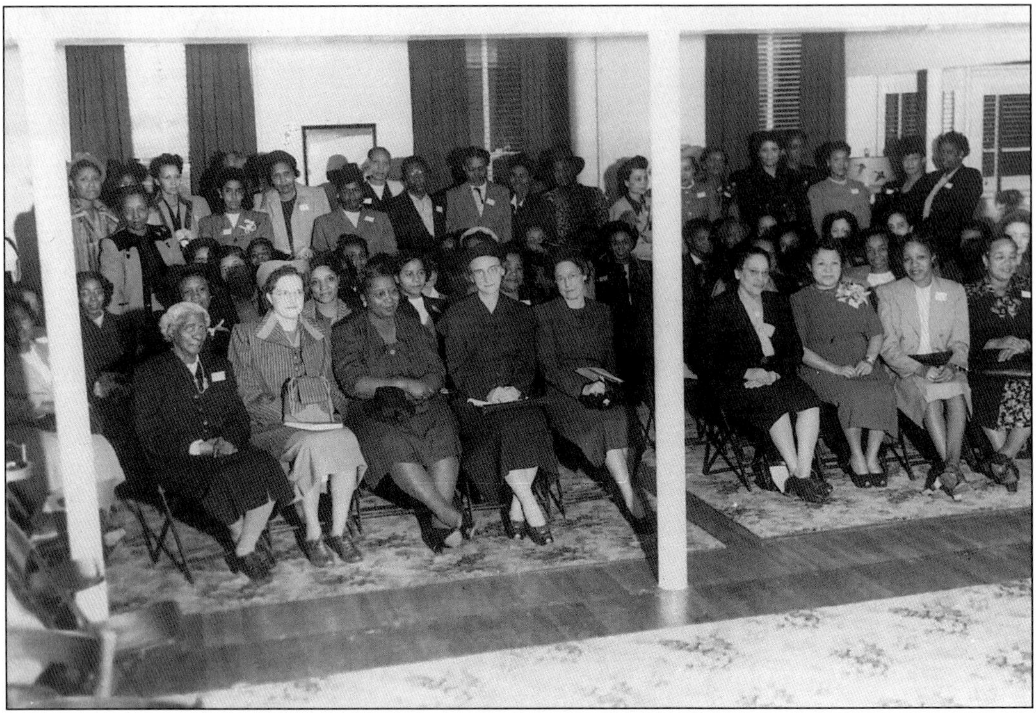

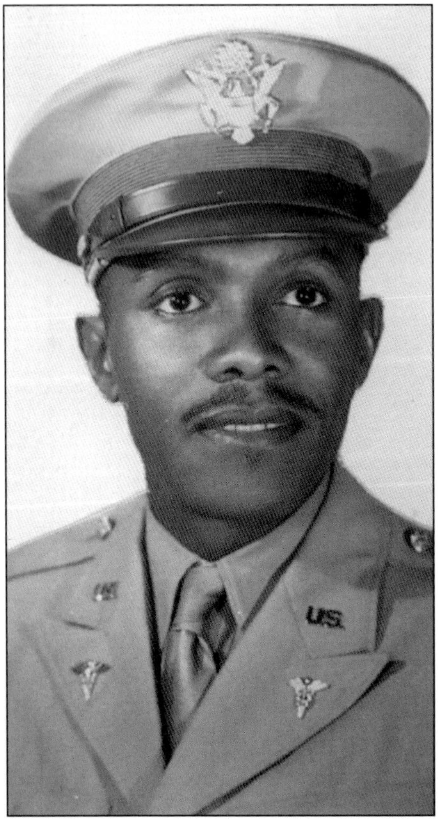

The Women's Auxiliary was comprised of prominent African-American women in Durham along with some of the nurses. They sold candy and sodas to patients and lent books provided by the public library. With money raised through these activities, they purchased needed equipment for the hospital. In addition, they organized a candy-stripers program for young volunteers. (Courtesy of Margaret Kennedy Goodwin.)

Dr. William A. Cleland, Durham's only African-American pediatrician, was determined to be expendable by the World War II Draft Board and required to report for army duty in 1942. He was drafted as a first lieutenant. With his advanced training, the army sent him to serve at the 25th Station Hospital in Liberia, Africa. The 25th Station Hospital was designed as an experiment to test whether or not a racially integrated medical and surgical staff could work together. They did just fine. Dr. Cleland returned to Durham in 1945 and once again faced the task of building his clinical practice as the lone African-American pediatrician. Dr. Robert Randolph and his wife, Emma, also served in World War II. (Courtesy of William A. Cleland.)

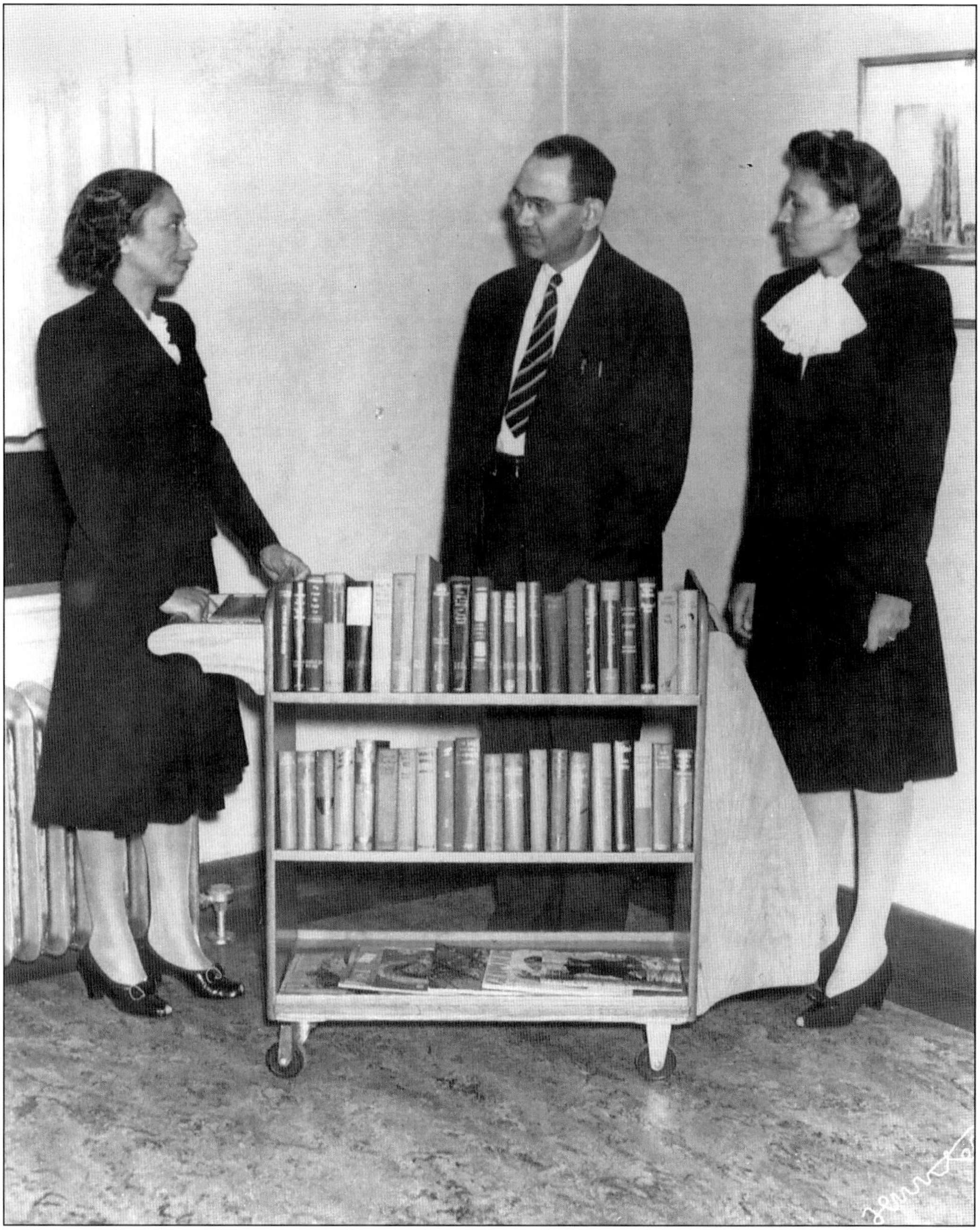

Selena Warren Wheeler, pictured on the left *c.* 1940, is the daughter of Dr. Stanford Warren. She assumed responsibility as head librarian of the Stanford Warren Public Library in 1934. Under her leadership the library developed mobile units that extended the reach of the library to neighborhoods throughout Durham County. She also established the hospital's lending library and provided books from the public library on a rotating basis. Mr. William Rich is standing in the middle and Gladys Hawkins, a volunteer, is on the right. (Courtesy of Carolyn Henderson.)

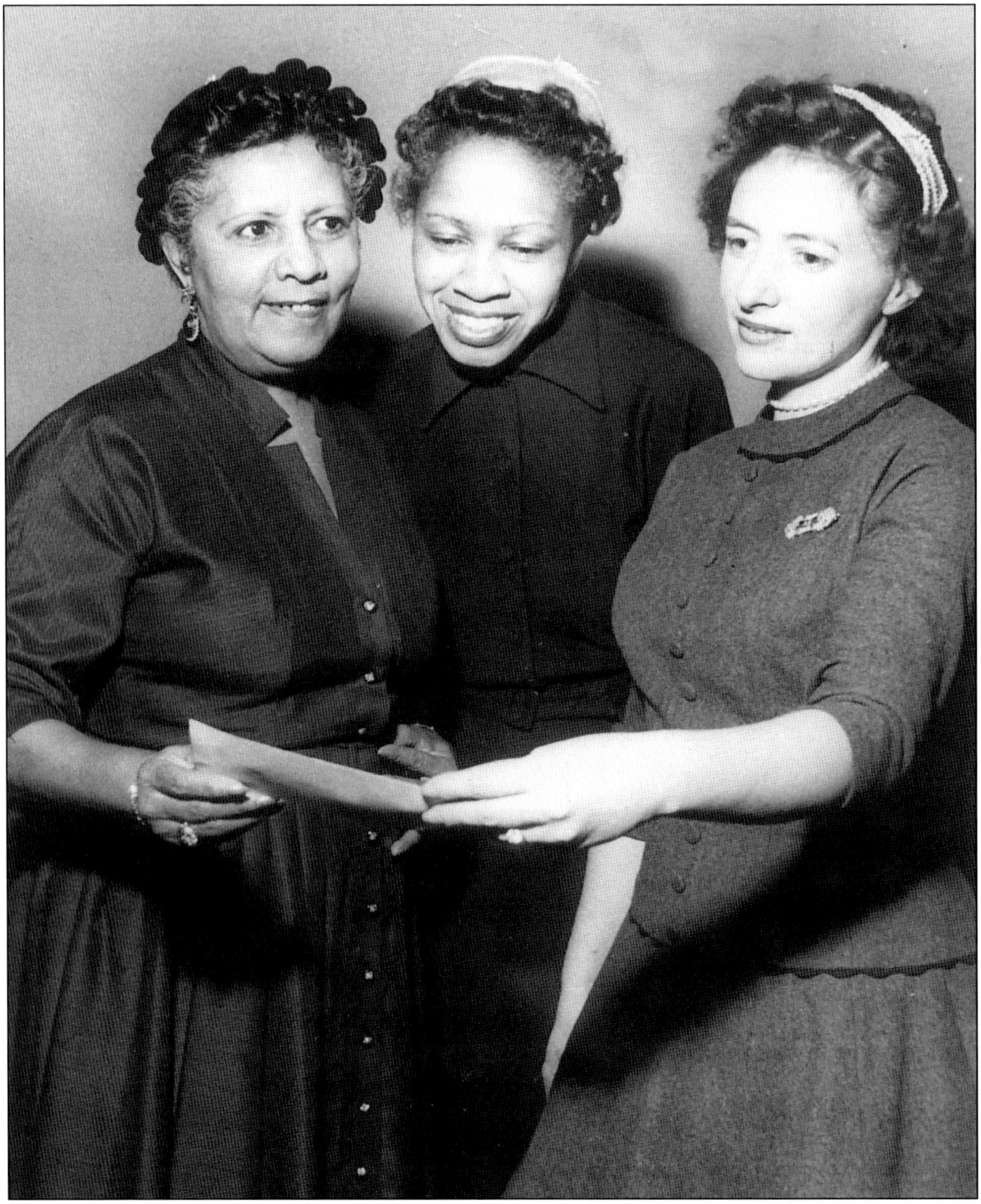

Mrs. Mary Duke Biddle Trent (Semans) joined the Lincoln Hospital Board of Trustees in 1948 to fill the seat left vacant by the death of her husband, Dr. Josiah Trent. She remained an active member of the board of trustees until the hospital closed in 1976. Every Christmas Mrs. Semans wrote to friends a letter letting them know the needs of the hospital and requesting their generosity during the gift-giving season. These funds were directed to various areas such as repainting the hospital wards and purchasing resources for the nursing school. Shown in this *c.* 1953 image, from left to right, are Mrs. Martha Donnell, Mrs. Lucille Zimmerman Williams, R.N., and Mrs. Mary D.B. Trent (Semans). (Courtesy of Margaret Kennedy Goodwin.)

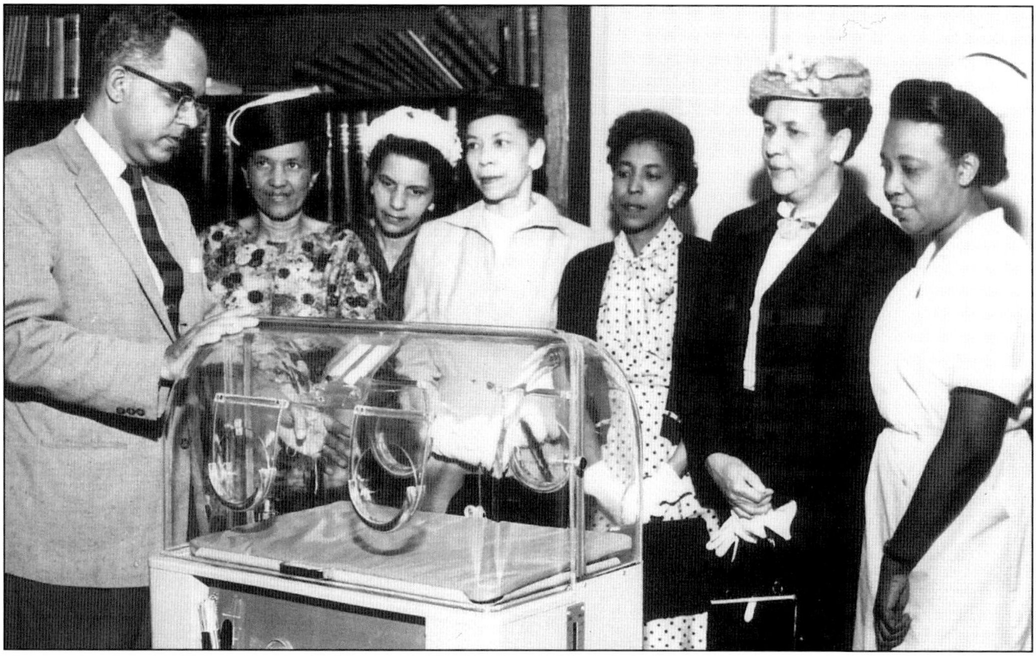

In 1955 Dr. William Cleland, Durham's first African-American pediatrician, completed a master of science with a post-graduate fellowship in neonatology at New York University. Upon his return the Women's Auxiliary raised money to purchase the first modern incubator for his use at Lincoln Hospital. Pictured here, from left to right, are Frank Scott, superintendent (1960–1968); Althea Holmes; Elizabeth Pratt; Bernadine Bailey; Thelma Bass; Josie Pittman; and Elizabeth W. Thorpe. (Courtesy of Margaret Kennedy Goodwin.)

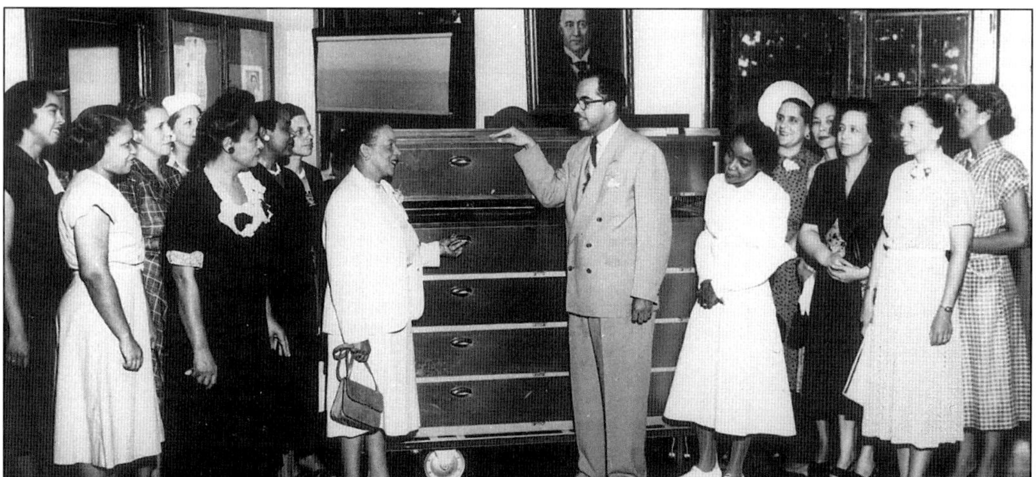

The Durham chapter of Alpha Kappa Alpha Sorority donated the first electrical food warmer to Lincoln Hospital. The food warmer was loaded in the kitchen and then rolled up to the hospital floors, allowing the meals to stay warm much longer. Pictured here are Marian Cordice, Josie Pittman, Lola Riddick, Pearl Cordice, Pauline Newton, Elizabeth Pratt, Bea Burnette, Frank Scott, Sallie Norcott, Grace C. Massey, Bernadine Bailey, Elna Spaulding, and Selena Wheeler. (Courtesy of Margaret Kennedy Goodwin.)

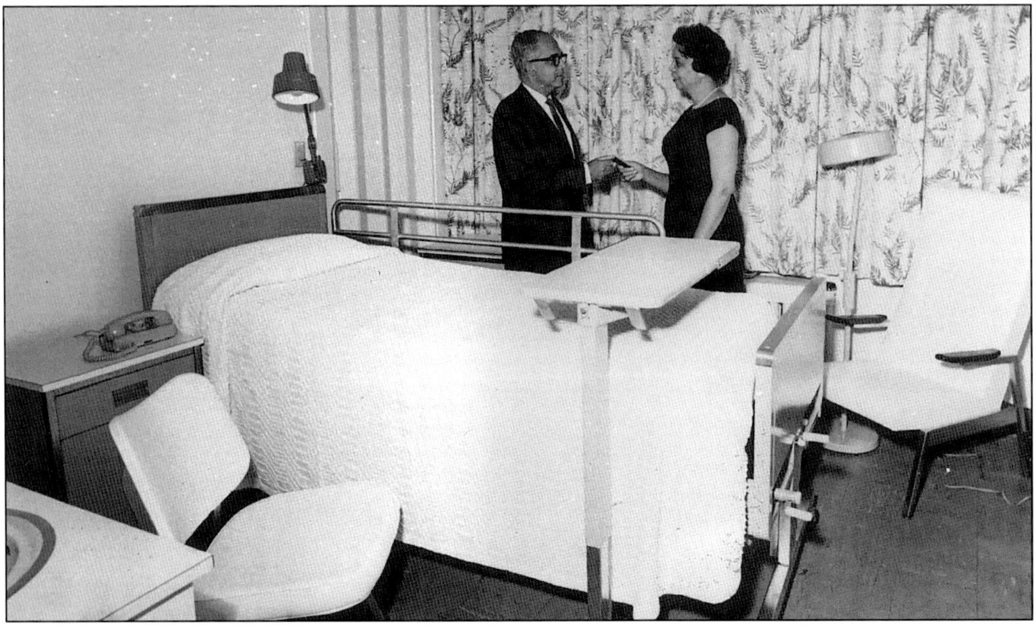

The administrators of Lincoln Hospital welcomed all types of contributions of money and volunteer service from the community. Mrs. Ruth Bolden, president of the local chapter of IOTA Phi Lambda Sorority, presents Frank Scott with the keys to room 217 that they had remodeled at a cost of $2,000, *c.* 1965. This was the only private room in Lincoln Hospital. Patients admitted to this room were of the business and social elite. (Courtesy of Margaret Kennedy Goodwin.)

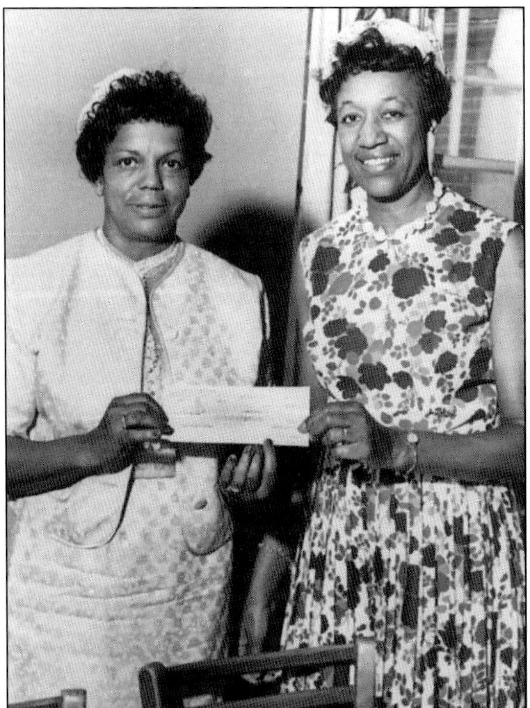

In addition to medical and hospital equipment, the Women's Auxiliary also raised money to help cover operating deficits, and distinguished alumni provided donations to the Lincoln Hospital School of Nursing. Pictured here, from left to right, are Della Rainey Jackson, R.N., Ph.D., and Lyda Ruth Flintall Betts, R.N. (Courtesy of Carolyn Henderson.)

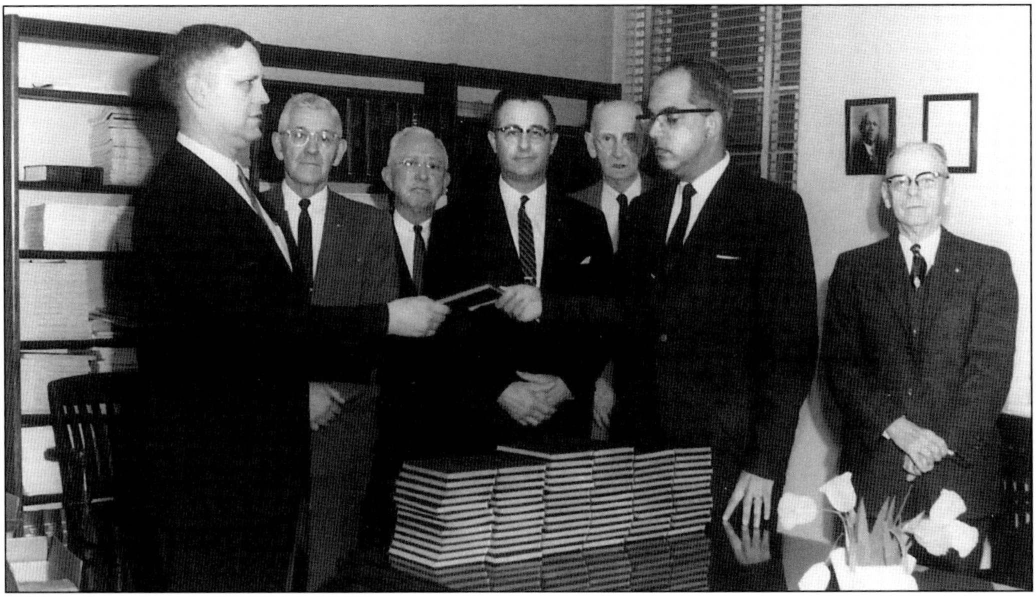

Hospitals were not hotels; nevertheless, the Gideons donated Bibles for every room in Lincoln Hospital. Pictured here is Frank Scott receiving them. (Courtesy of Margaret Kennedy Goodwin and photographer Claude Burthey.)

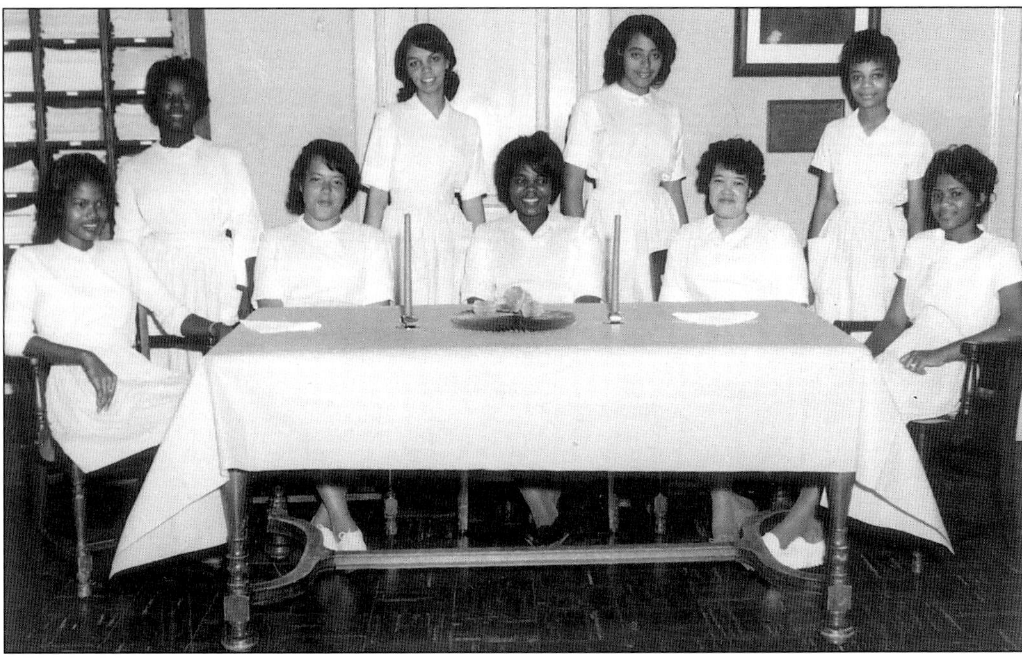

Lincoln Hospital had an active volunteer candy-striper program, shown here, *c.* 1963. Similar to hospitals throughout the country, these young volunteers helped transport patients, delivered flowers, ran errands for the administration, and assisted the Women's Auxiliary with the selling of sodas and candies. This was a way for young women to learn about careers as nurses, physicians, and medical technicians and to gain volunteer experience working with patients. (Courtesy of Carolyn Henderson.)

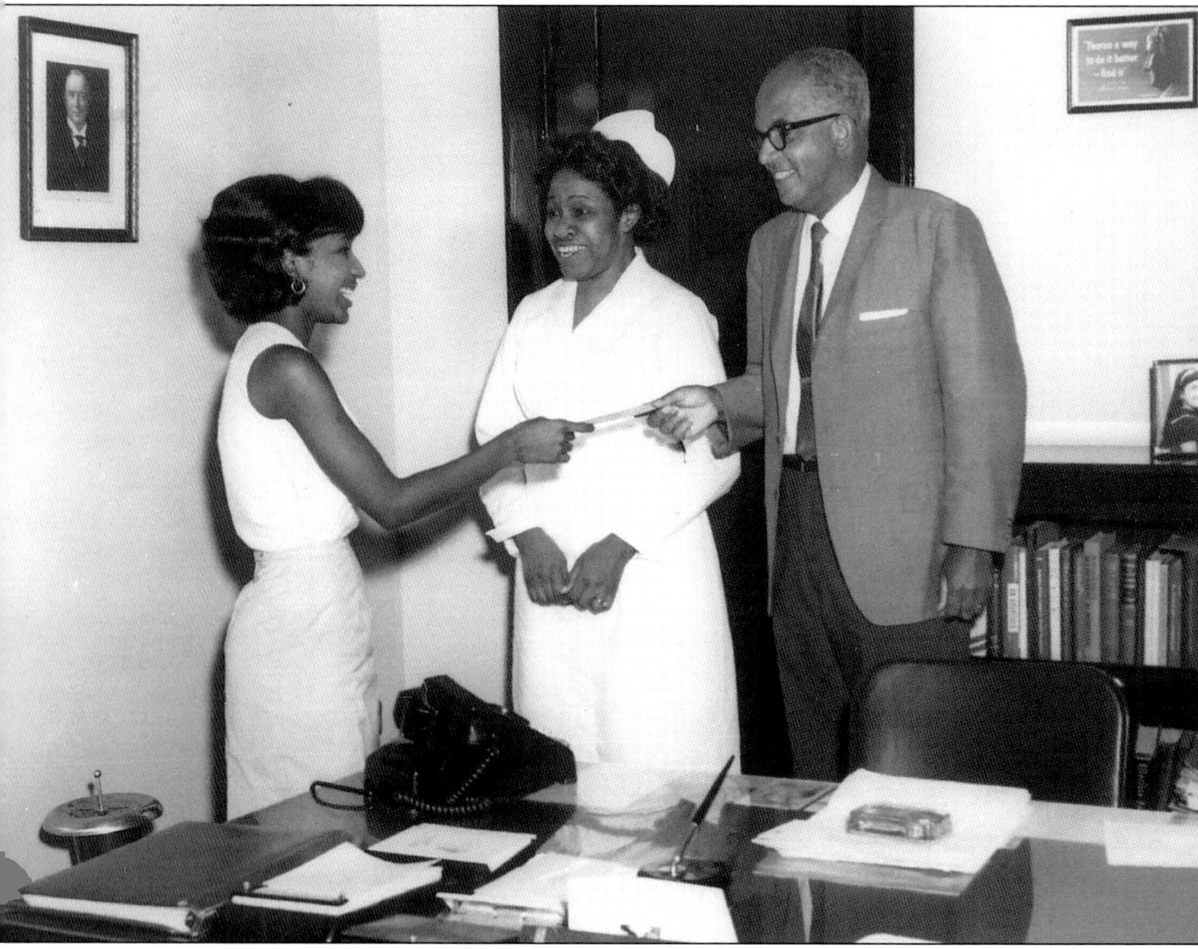

Mary Lee Mills, R.N., one of the outstanding graduates of the Lincoln Hospital School of Nursing, established a scholarship in honor of her mother, Margaret Ann Mills. The scholarship was to be awarded to a high school student from Durham because of her superior scholastic rank. Miss Carolyn Martin, a graduate of Hillside High School in June 1965, was awarded the Margaret Ann Mills scholarship that year. Pictured here, from left to right, are Carolyn Martin, Mrs. Lucille Zimmerman Williams, R.N., and Frank Scott. (Courtesy of Carolyn Henderson.)

Nine

From Civil Rights to the City of Medicine

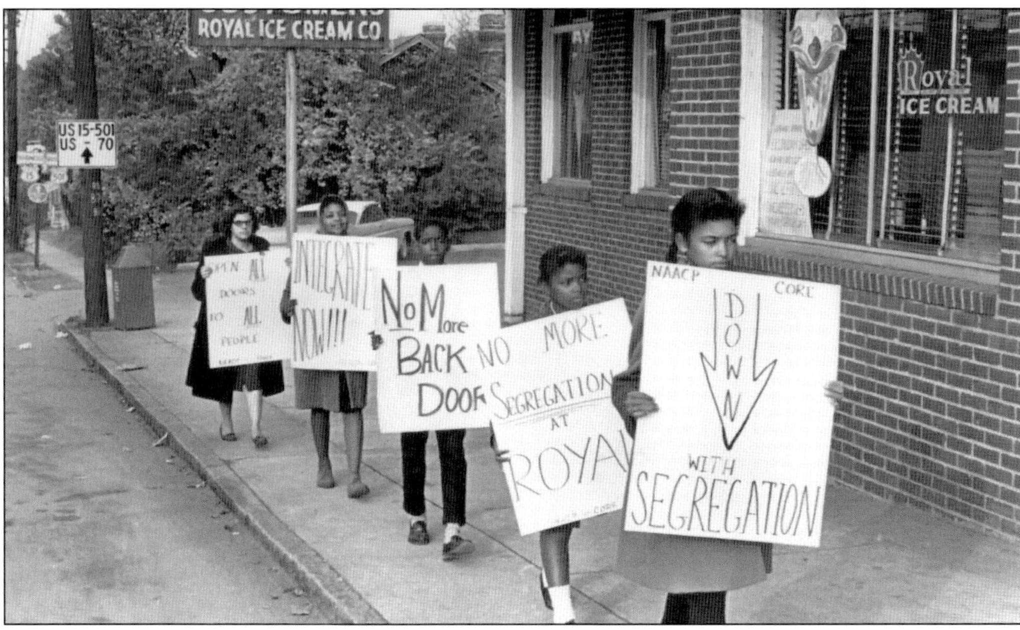

Durham felt the anger of civil rights protests that swept through Southern towns. The sit-in movement spread quickly from Shaw University in Raleigh and A&T College in Greensboro to North Carolina Central University in Durham and, in its wake, brought the boycotting of downtown businesses. By the end of 1964, negotiations among the city's leadership opened hotels, theaters, restaurants, parks, and other public and private establishments; however, the festering wound of Jim Crow hospitals was yet to be openly addressed, cleansed, and healed. (Courtesy of *Durham Herald-Sun* and photographer Herald Moore.)

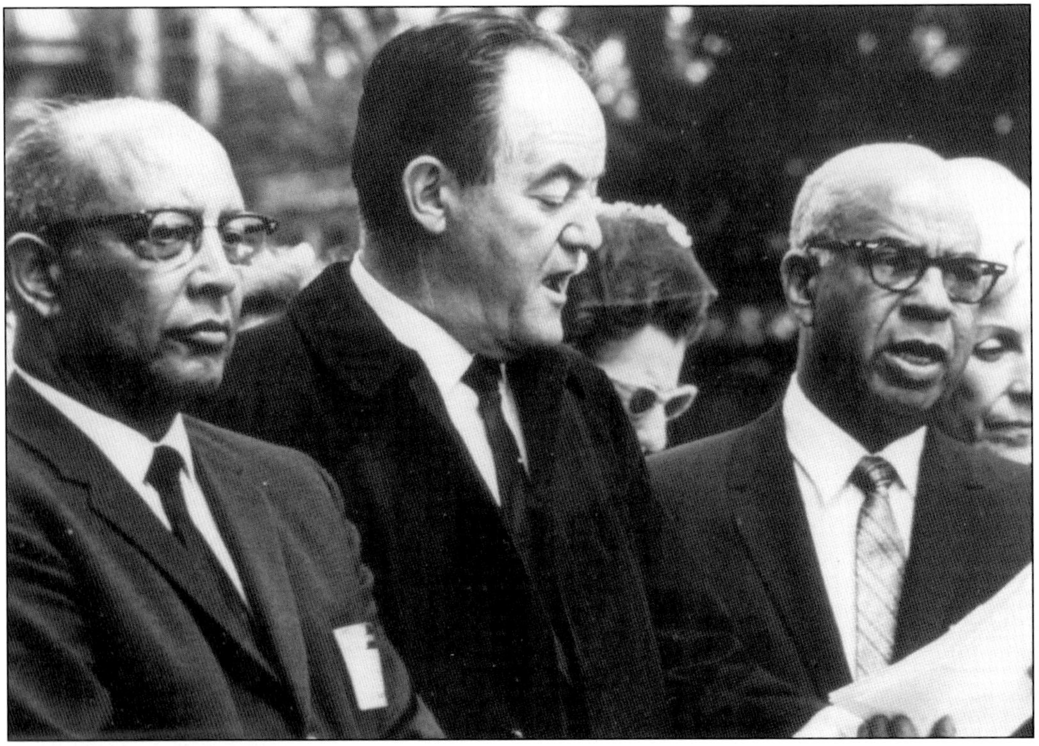

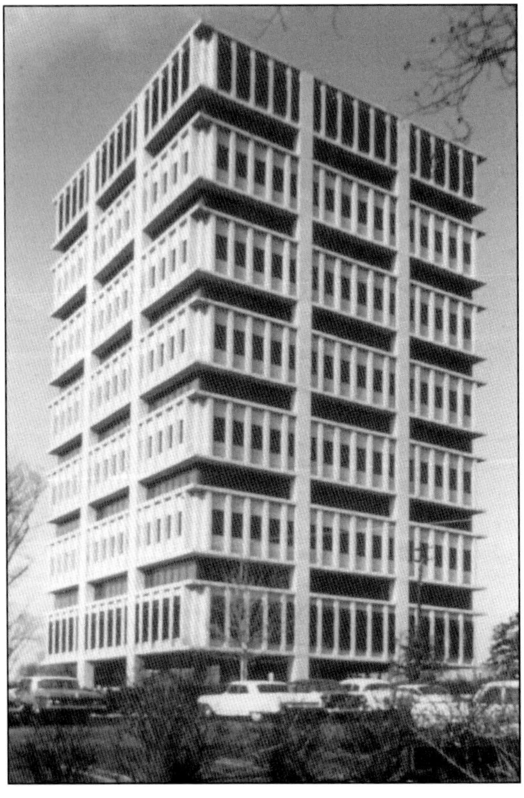

On April 2, 1966, the new home office of the North Carolina Mutual Life Insurance Company, along with the home office of Mechanics and Farmers Bank located on the first floor, were dedicated before one of the largest gatherings, including people from both the white and African-American communities, in Durham. Vice President Hubert Humphrey said in his keynote address, "History teaches us that the great revolutions aren't started by people who are utterly down and out—without hope and vision. They take place when people begin to live a little better—and when they see how much yet remains to be achieved. I say these demands and this striving will not and cannot end until all Negroes enjoy the full rights and privileges and opportunities of other American citizens, both in law and in fact." Pictured here, from left to right, are Joseph W. Goodloe, vice president; Hubert Humphrey; Mr. Asa T. Spaulding, president of the North Carolina Mutual from 1958 to 1967; and Mrs. Muriel Humphrey. (Courtesy of Charles D. Watts.)

In the wake of defeat of the 1966 Hospital Bond Issue to merge services at Watts and Lincoln Hospitals, the Lincoln Hospital trustees faced mounting operating deficits that threatened the survival of the institution. Asa T. Spaulding, Lincoln Hospital trustee, spearheaded a one-month fund-raising campaign in December 1967. Spaulding wrote letters to corporate and foundation presidents around the country. The team raised $115,000 with $40,000 coming from outside Durham, and contributions from $5 to $5,000 from local residents and businesses. The message was clear—Lincoln Hospital would remain a part of the health care system, at least in the foreseeable future. (Courtesy of Charles D. Watts.)

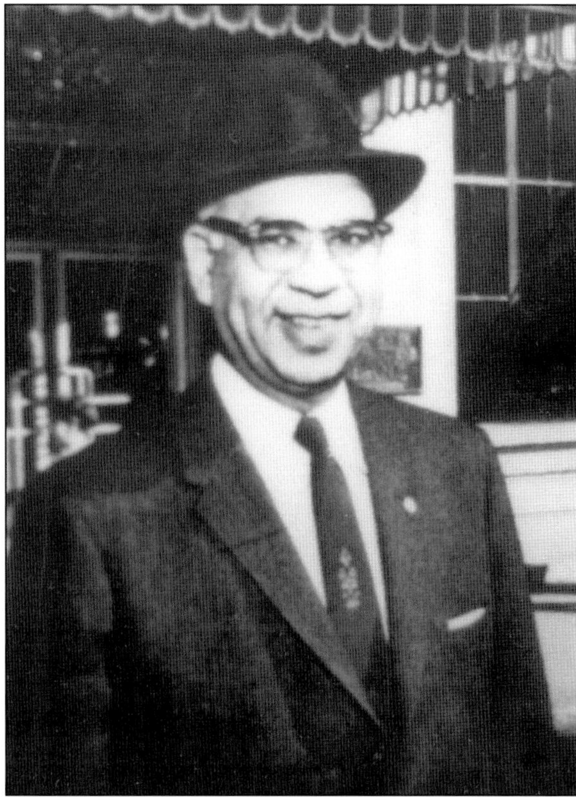

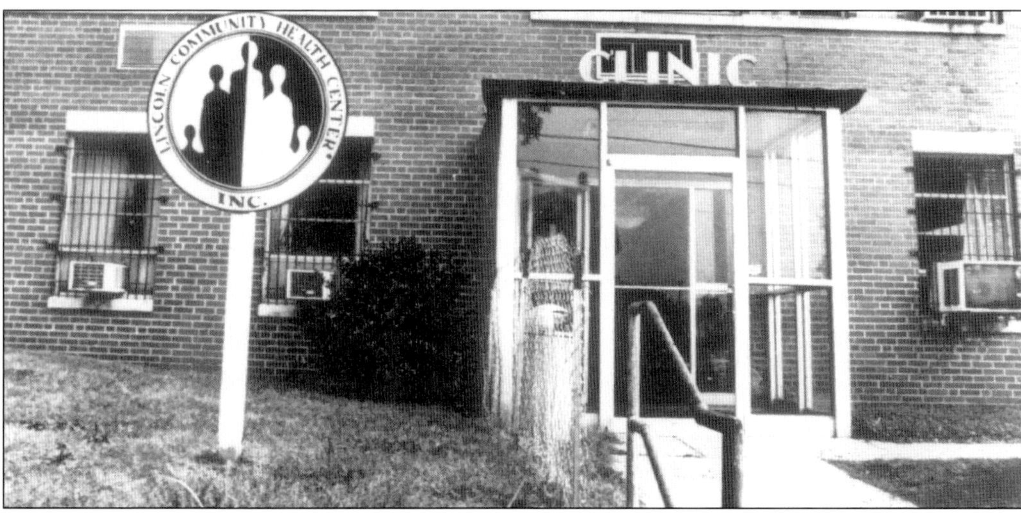

Spearheaded by Dr. Charles Watts, chair of Operation Breakthrough and medical director of North Carolina Mutual, the Lincoln Community Health Center opened in September 1971 with funding from the Office of Economic Opportunity. The LCHC was designed to provide comprehensive primary medical care to the poor in Durham County, improve access to more specialized services not offered by the LCHC, decrease the need for hospitalization among its patients, and contribute to the social and economic well-being of the population. (Courtesy of Charles D. Watts.)

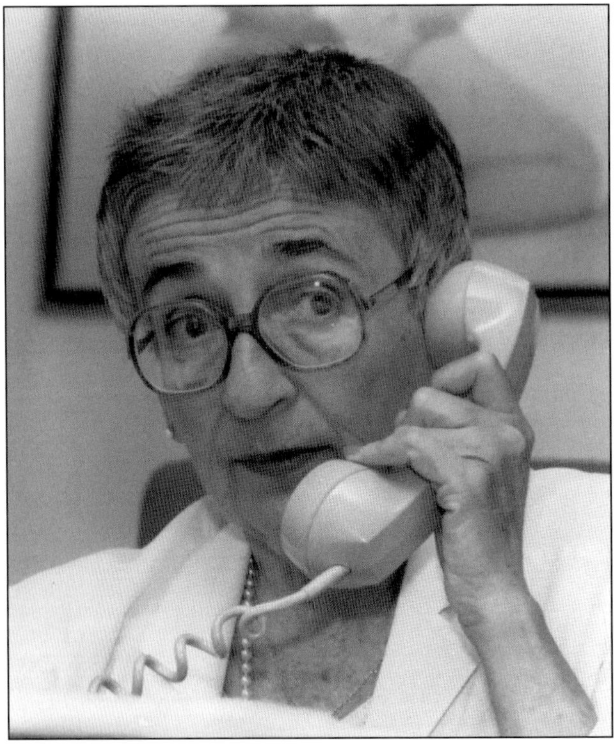

Dr. Evelyn Schmidt was the first full-time director of the LCHC, joining the staff in 1971. After graduating from Duke University with honors and its school of medicine, Dr. Schmidt obtained her residency at Babies and Children's Hospital in Cleveland and at Jefferson Medical College in Philadelphia. Before returning to Durham, Dr. Schmidt worked at Gouveneur Health Services Program as pediatrician-in-charge and then at the Comprehensive Health Program for Children and Youth as associate director. The LCHC symbolized a link to the past and a vision of the future to its staff, its board of directors, and the trustees of Lincoln Hospital who had begun negotiations to enter the Durham County Hospital Corporation. (Courtesy of Evelyn Schmidt.)

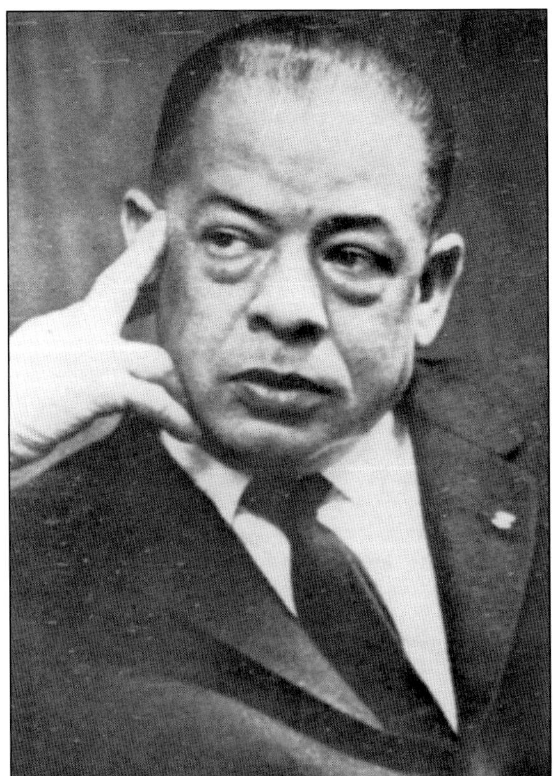

John Hervey Wheeler graduated from Morehouse College summa cum laude and later obtained a law degree from North Carolina College School of Law. He rose within the banking industry to become president of Mechanics and Farmers Bank. In two class action suits, Wheeler sued the Durham City Board of Education for discrimination in public school facilities, once in 1950 and again in 1960, and won both cases. Highly respected as a businessman and civic-political leader, John Wheeler was the most powerful person negotiating the future of Lincoln Hospital prior to and following the turbulent years of the Civil Rights Movement. As a member of the Lincoln Hospital Board of Trustees and Regional Health Planning Council, Wheeler fought to retain a center for medical care in the heart of the African-American community. (Courtesy of Atlanta University Archives.)

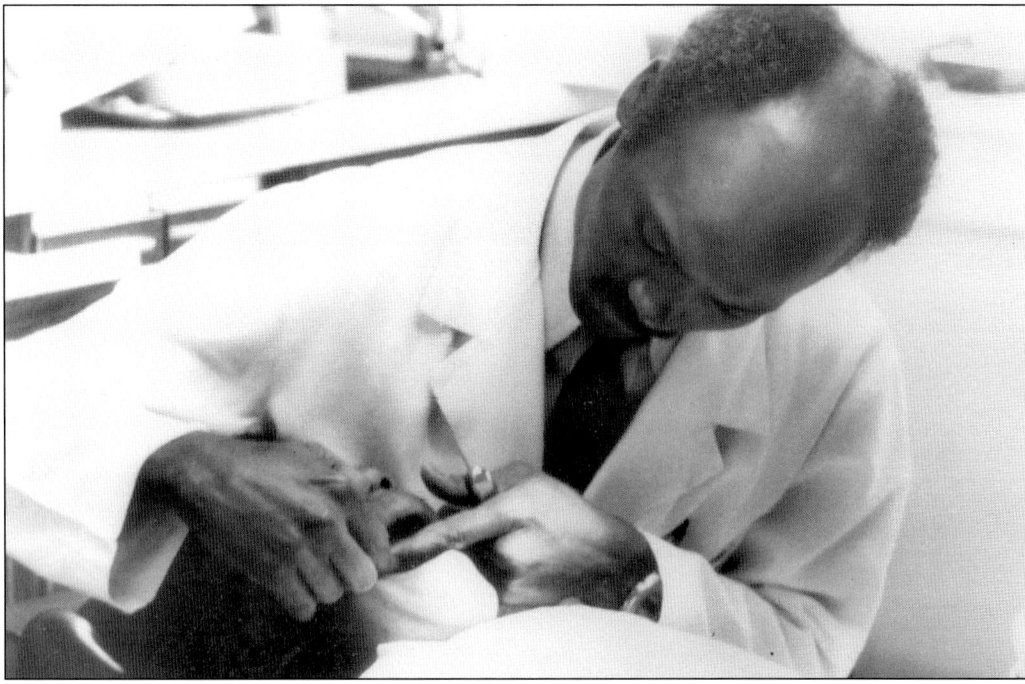

The Lincoln Community Health Center specialized in "team care with a doctor, family health care worker, and nurses." Meeting a federal requirement that the center enroll 5,000 to 8,000 patients the first year was easy. Dr. Donald Madison, a professor at the University of North Carolina–Chapel Hill and author of the LCHC grant proposal, wrote another grant to provide breakfast and complete health services to all the children attending the two schools located within walking distance of the center. When the children came for dental and health assessments, the staff urged their parents to enroll. By July 1972, over 8,400 residents were receiving health care at the LCHC. (Courtesy of Evelyn Schmidt.)

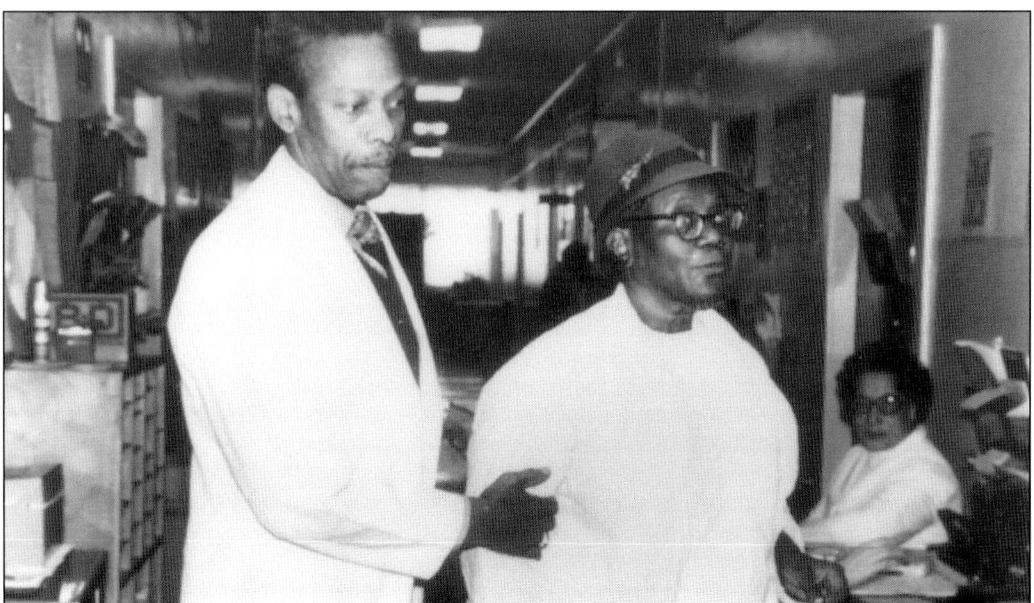

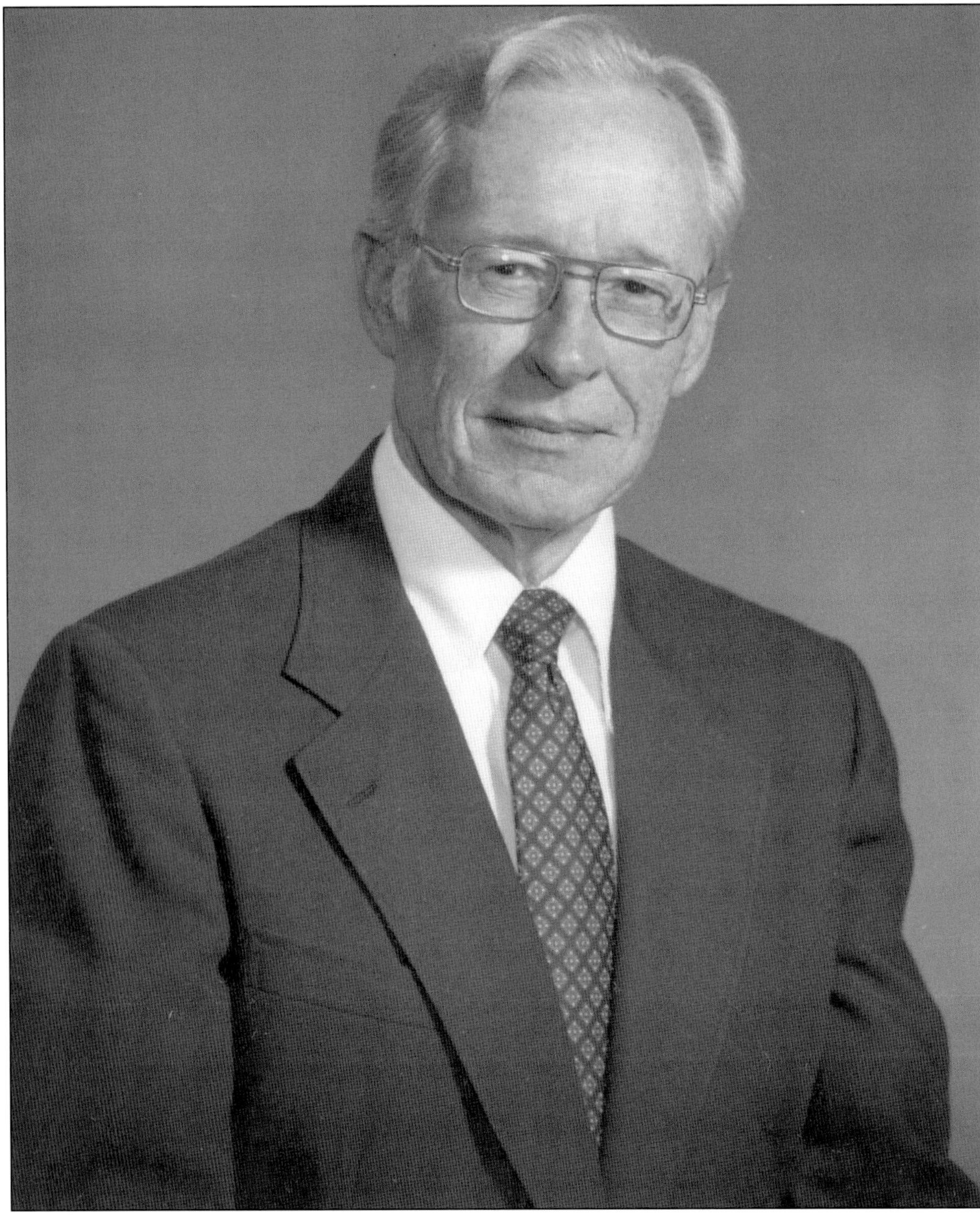

Thomas R. Howerton grew up in Durham where he attended public schools and graduated from Duke University. After service in World War II with the 231st Station Hospital, he returned to Duke to join the first class of hospital administration students. After receiving a master's degree in hospital administration, Howerton worked for the North Carolina Medical Care Commission and then as president/CEO of a hospital in Pinehurst and then one in Wilson. In 1970 he returned to Durham as executive director of the Durham County Hospital Corporation. With integrity and grace, Tom Howerton facilitated the merger of Watts and Lincoln Hospitals into the Hospital Corporation and oversaw construction of Durham County General Hospital. (Courtesy of Durham Regional Hospital.)

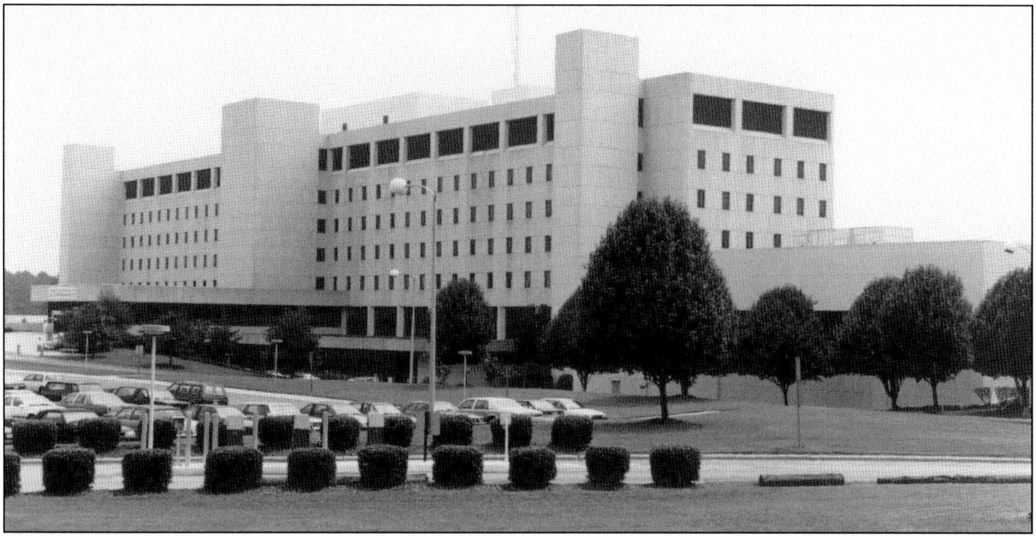

Lincoln Hospital ceased to exist as an inpatient facility on September 25, 1976, when patients were transferred to Watts Hospital. From there all patients were moved into Durham County General Hospital on October 10, 1972. Built at a cost of $20 million, the new seven-story hospital housed 326 private and 134 semi-private rooms. along with 12 operating rooms; medical, cardiac, and surgical intensive care units; and 4 delivery suites. The fifth floor was devoted exclusively to pediatrics. Under Howerton's leadership, the local hospitals were racially integrated with the creation of one board of directors; one administrative, medical, and nursing staff; and one school of nursing. (Courtesy of Durham Regional Hospital.)

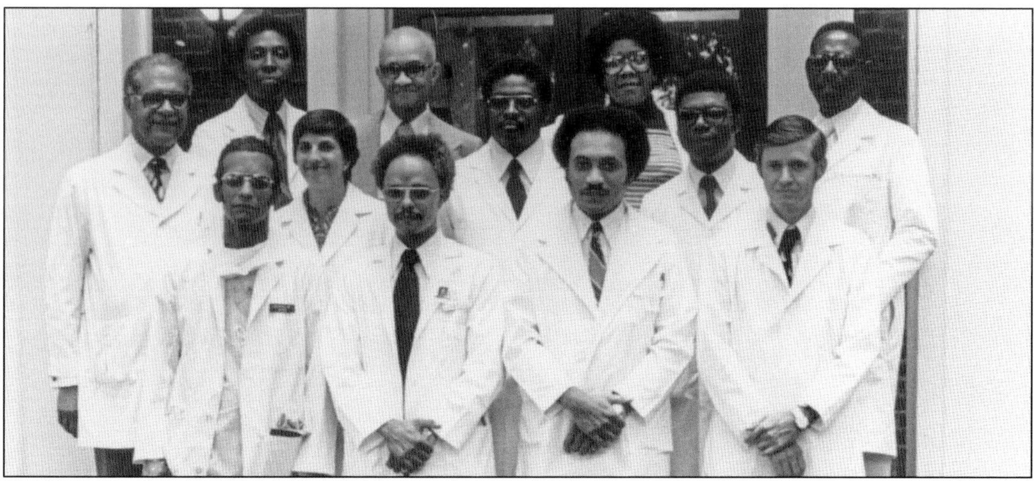

The medical and surgical staff of Lincoln Hospital changed with the racial integration of area hospitals since physicians could now admit their patients to one or two hospitals (Watts and Duke Hospitals) rather than three (Lincoln, Watts, and Duke Hospitals). The physicians on the regular staff of Lincoln Hospital when the hospital closed as an inpatient facility in 1976, are pictured above. They are, from left to right, (front row) Drs. Donald Moore, James O'Rourke, John Daniel, and George M. Paddison; (middle row) Drs. Charles Watts, Lois T. Harris, Sampson Harrell, and unidentified; (back row) Drs. Ernest White, Robert Randolph, Armayne Dunston, and Robert Dawson. (Courtesy of Charles D. Watts.)

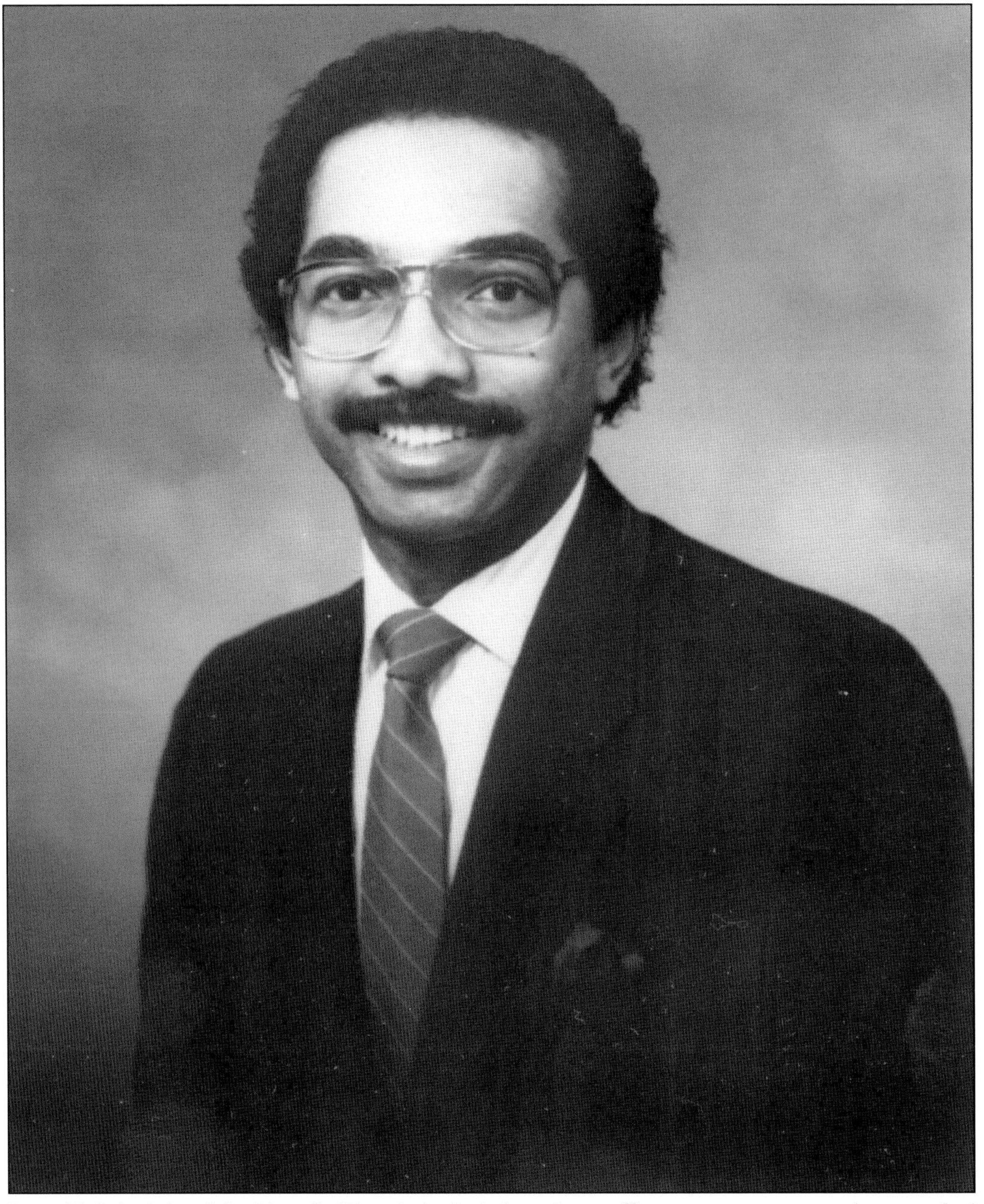

Larry T. Suitt joined the Lincoln Hospital administrative staff as an accountant and succeeded Frank Scott as superintendent of Lincoln Hospital in 1968. Working closely with Dr. Clyde Donnell, president of the board of trustees, and Tom Howerton, executive director of the Durham County Hospital Corporation, Mr. Suitt oversaw the recruitment of Lincoln Hospital physicians, nurses, and administrative personnel into Durham County General Hospital when the two hospitals merged in 1976. He retired from Durham Regional Hospital in 1999, having served as senior vice president from 1987 to 1999. His steady hand and administrative leadership helped smooth rough waters and calm unspoken fears. (Courtesy of Durham Regional Hospital.)

The Lincoln Community Health Center was housed originally in the 1925 Lincoln Hospital structure. Many realized the need for modern facilities to meet the demand for clinical services among the uninsured and underinsured residents of Durham County. The county commissioners allocated $1.5 million; however, the great majority of the money was raised from grants, foundations, and public drives. Groundbreaking for the Lincoln Community Health Center took place in July 1981. Pictured here, from left to right, are Mrs. Lyda Moore Merrick, daughter of Dr. Aaron Moore; John ("Shag") Stewart; and Dr. Evelyn Schmidt. (Courtesy of Charles D. Watts.)

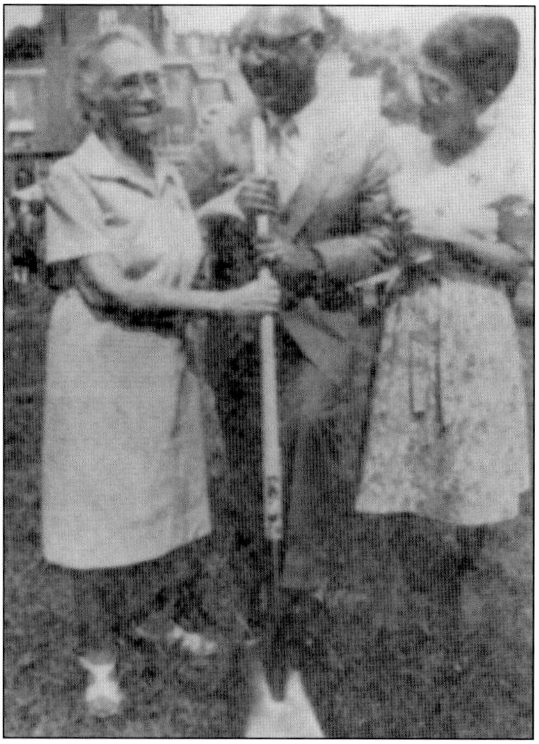

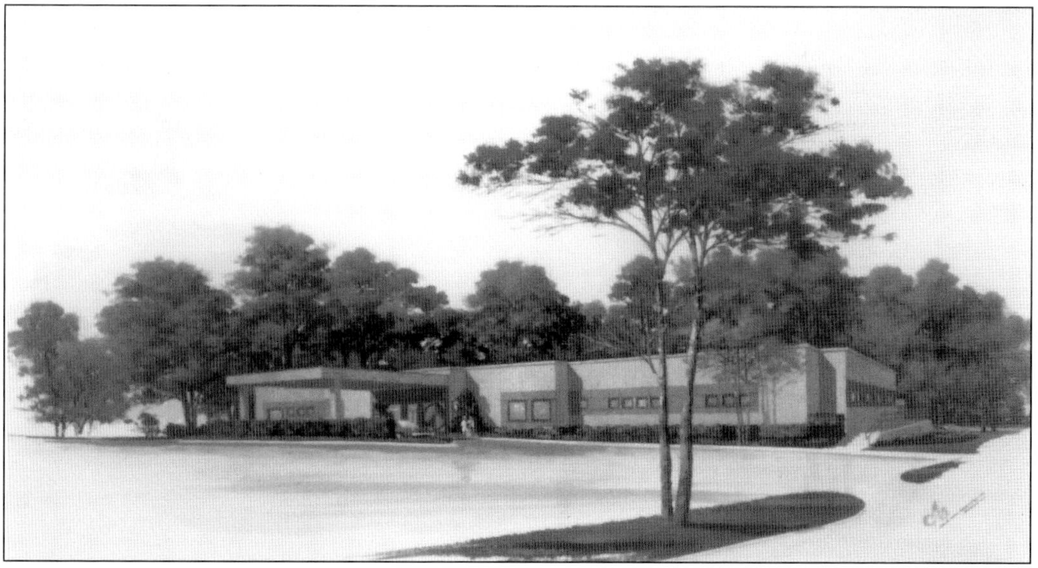

Constructed at an estimated cost of $4 million, the new Lincoln Community Health Center opened for patients in December 1982. Housed on two floors were administrative offices and conference rooms (ground floor) and clinical services (top floor). Occupying 60,000 square feet, the Lincoln Community Health Center now had modern space for pediatrics, adult medicine, prenatal and family planning, social work, mental health, dental care, and specialty clinics. In addition, it offered pharmacy, laboratory, and radiology services on site. (Courtesy of Evelyn Schmidt.)

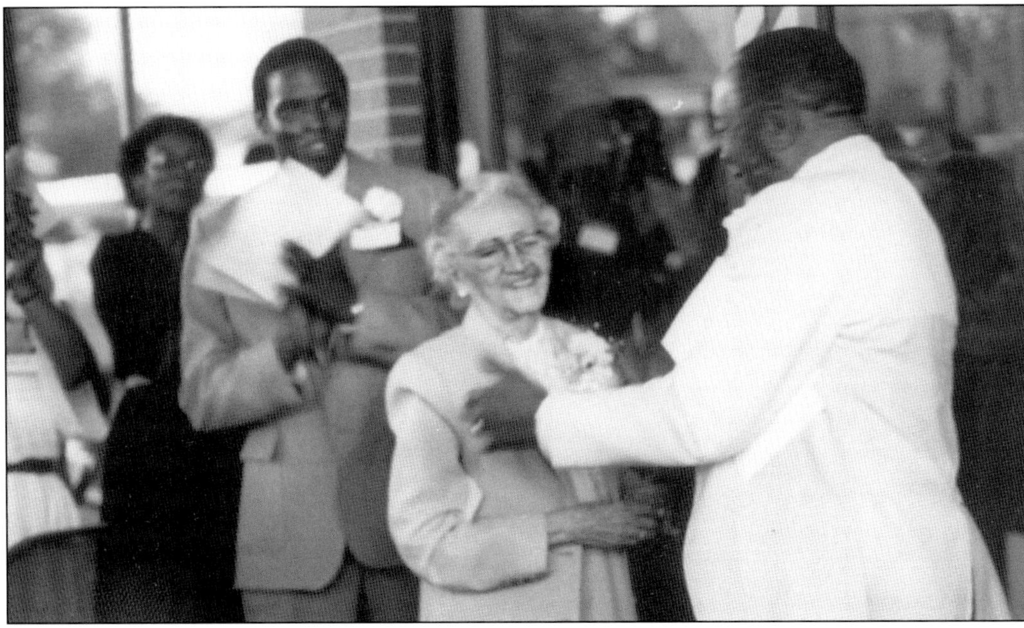

The dedication ceremony for the LCHC in August 1983 drew one of the largest crowds in Durham with both white and African-American residents celebrating the new clinical facility. Mrs. Lyda Moore Merrick, daughter of Dr. Aaron Moore and daughter-in-law of John Merrick, two of the founders of Lincoln Hospital, cut the ribbon. Here was the legacy of leadership passed down through generations of family members, each dedicated to preserving a place of health and healing in Durham. (Courtesy of Charles D. Watts.)

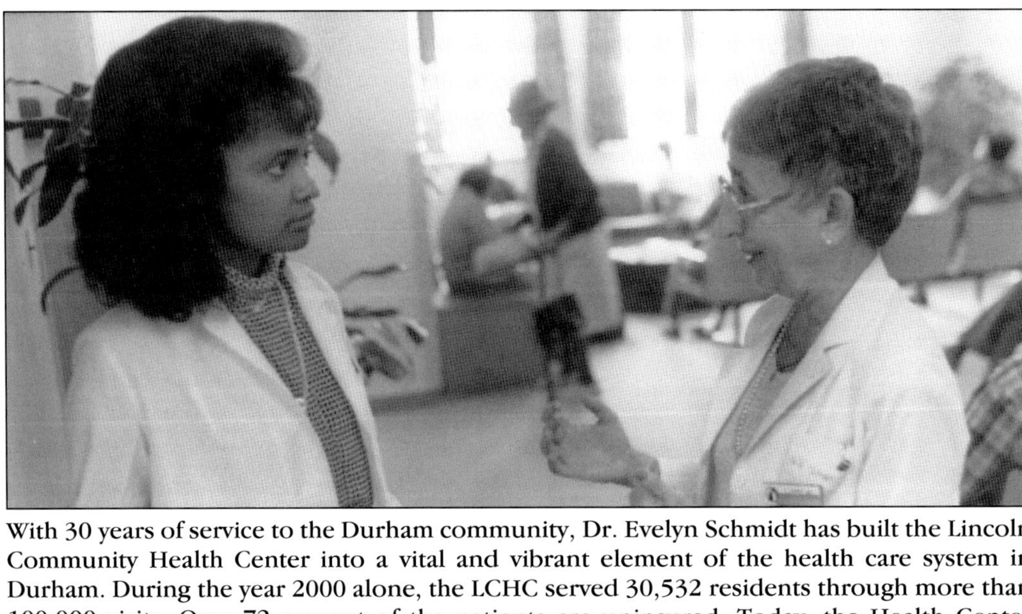

With 30 years of service to the Durham community, Dr. Evelyn Schmidt has built the Lincoln Community Health Center into a vital and vibrant element of the health care system in Durham. During the year 2000 alone, the LCHC served 30,532 residents through more than 100,000 visits. Over 72 percent of the patients are uninsured. Today, the Health Center represents the legacy of Lincoln Hospital and its dedication to provide comprehensive primary care to patients regardless of race, ethnicity, or socioeconomic conditions. (Courtesy of Evelyn Schmidt.)

Mrs. Margaret Kennedy Goodwin retired from the Lincoln Community Health Center in 1982 after 40 years of service to Lincoln Hospital and the center. The great-niece of Dr. Aaron Moore and daughter of William Jesse Kennedy Jr., Mrs. Goodwin was raised with a commitment to service. Her life was Lincoln Hospital, its patients, nursing students, physicians, and residents. Her contributions came in every form from helping with fund-raising campaigns to assembling the student yearbook to teaching dozens and dozens of allied health professionals skills as medical technicians. As she is often heard saying, "Lincoln born, Lincoln bred, and when I'm gone, Lincoln dead." Her dedication to the hospital will continue through this book of photographs since many came from her personal collection as Lincoln Hospital's amateur photographer. (Courtesy of Durham Regional Hospital.)

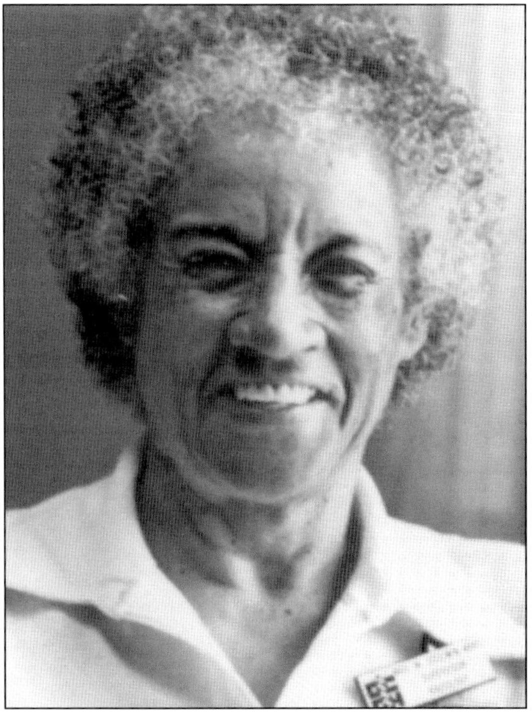

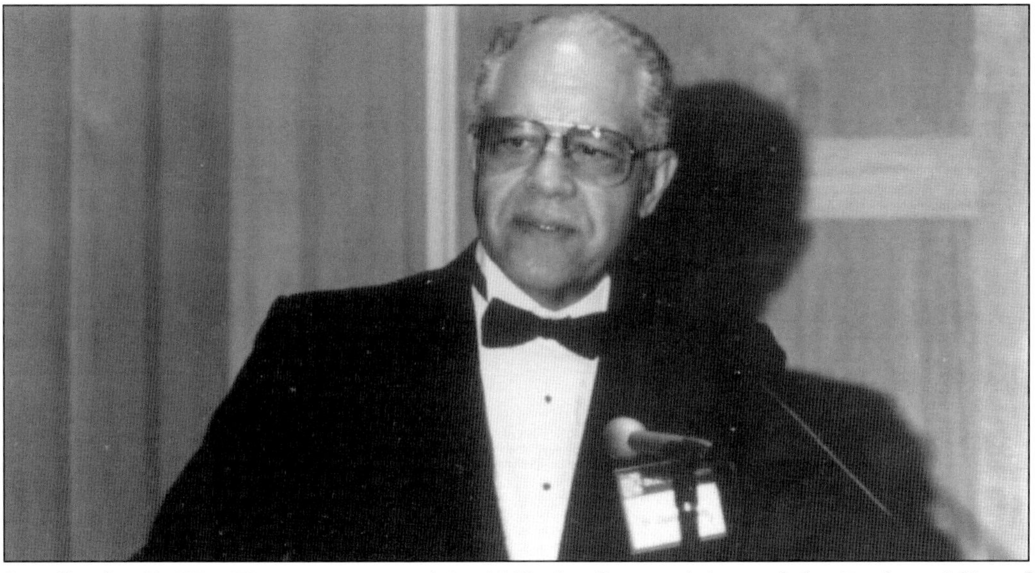

Dr. Charles DeWitt Watts was named in 1999 the first recipient of the Durham "City of Medicine" Community Service award for his leadership in founding the Lincoln Community Health Center. He served as part-time director of the center until Dr. Schmidt's recruitment and in that role oversaw training of health workers, hiring of physicians and social workers, and opening of adult and pediatric clinics. Dr. Watts's greater legacy was his relentless and tireless fight against hospital discrimination through service on state and local commissions, task forces, and regional health planning bodies. In 1975, he was elected a member of the Institute of Medicine/National Academy of Science. (Courtesy of Charles D. Watts.)

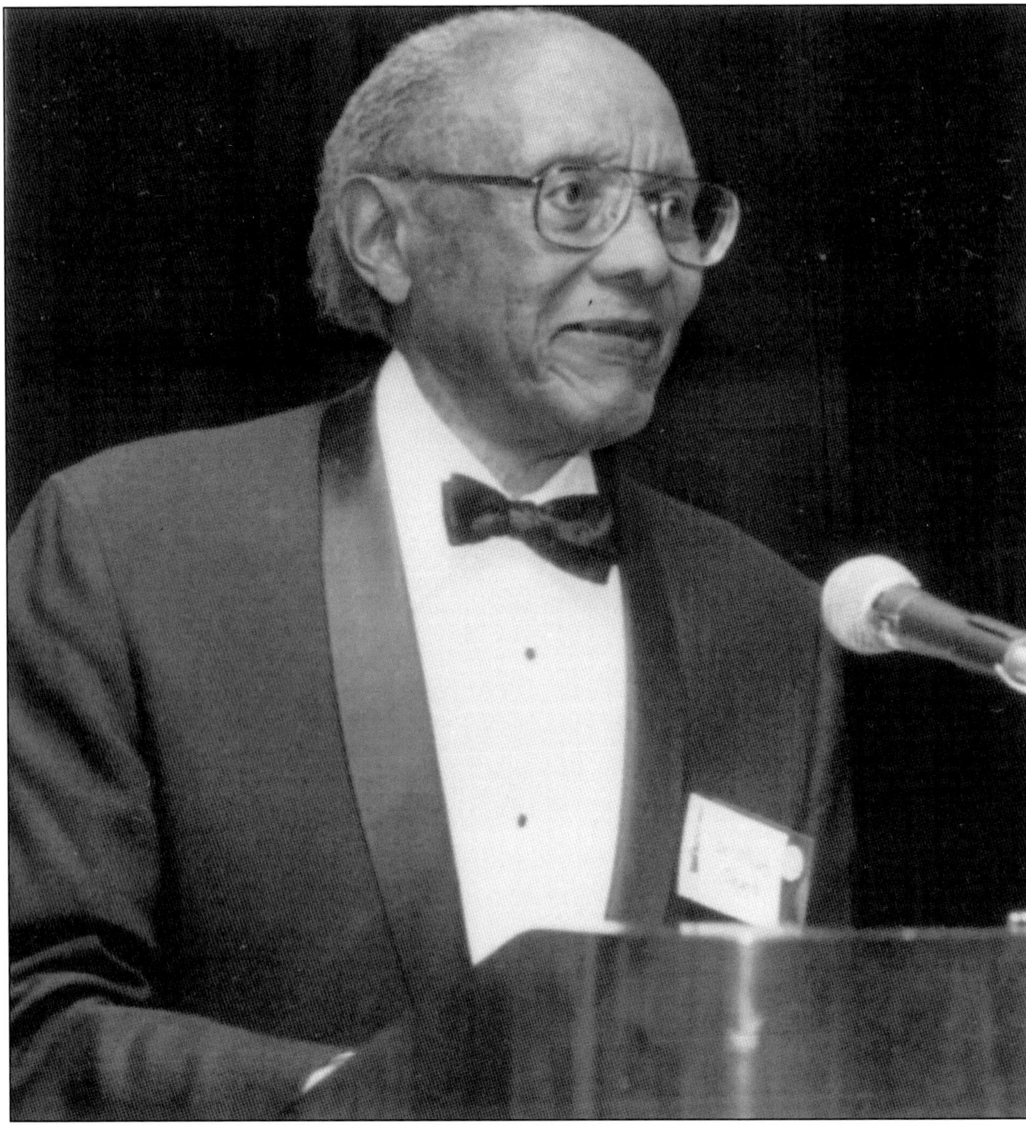

In 2000, Dr. William Alexander Cleland was named the recipient of the "City of Medicine" Community Service award for his dedication to Durham's "baby patients." His patients are now parents, grandparents, and great-grandparents. They have entered every professional line of work and carried his legacy of clinical excellence and professionalism into another generation of physicians. He was Durham's first African-American physician to be admitted to the clinical faculty of Duke University School of Medicine, bridging yet another chasm of racism in medicine. And despite all the odds (and with all the honors), he is often heard telling a joke when reflecting on a lifetime of effort working to provide the best care possible for his patients and in doing so, healing his people and strengthening his community. (Courtesy of William A. Cleland.)